Breakaway
MA

Level 3
Teacher's Resource Book

Nelson

Thomas Nelson and Sons Ltd
Nelson House Mayfield Road
Walton-on-Thames Surrey
KT12 5PL UK

Thomas Nelson Australia
102 Dodds Street
South Melbourne
Victoria 3205 Australia

Nelson Canada
1120 Birchmount Road
Scarborough Ontario
M1K 5G4 Canada

© Peter Gash 1995

First published by Thomas Nelson and Sons Ltd 1995
I(T)P Thomas Nelson is an International Thomson Publishing Company
I(T)P is used under licence

ISBN 0-17-421726-9
NPN 9 8 7 6 5 4 3 2 1

All rights reserved. No paragraph of this publication may be reproduced, copied or transmitted save with written permission or in accordance with the provisions of the Copyright, Design and Patents Act 1988, or under the terms of any licence permitting limited copying issued by the Copyright Licensing Agency, 90 Tottenham Court Road, London W1P 9HE.

The publisher grants permission for copies of pages 22–33 to be made without fee as follows:
Private purchasers may make copies for their own use or for use by their own students; school purchasers may make copies for use within and by the staff and students of the institution only. This permission to copy does not extend to additional institutions or branches of an institution, who should purchase a separate master copy of the book for their own use.

For copying in any other circumstances prior permission must be obtained in writing from Thomas Nelson and Sons Ltd.

The author and publishers would like to thank the following for their valuable contributions when advising on the draft versions of Breakaway Maths:

Elizabeth Byrne, *Senior Area Learning Support Teacher, South Gloucestershire*

Alison Fairley, *Beech Lawn School, Hillsborough, Northern Ireland*

David Holdstock and Anne Twells, *Walsall Learning Support Service*

Gerald Morris, *The Castle School, Castleford, West Yorkshire*

John Wright, *Field Lane Primary School, Brighouse, West Yorkshire*

Thanks are also due to the illustrator Louise Hill, who helped to devise the four main characters.

Printed by Ebenezer Baylis & Son Ltd, Worcester

Contents

Preface	4
The structure of *Breakaway Maths*	5
The *Breakaway Maths* materials	6
Classroom organisation	8
Breakaway Maths and the National Curriculum	10
Breakaway Maths and the 5–14 Guidelines	14
Breakaway Maths and the Northern Ireland Curriculum	18
Pathways through the materials / record sheets	22
Level 3:1 An activity weekend	34
Level 3:2 Water sports	48
Level 3:3 The museum	62
Level 3:4 Saturday night	76
Level 3:5 Climbing and shooting	90
Level 3:6 Going home	104
Answers	118
Key vocabulary	143

Preface

It is common to find that people who claim to have been 'hopeless' at mathematics in school use it very skilfully and thoughtfully in everyday life. They have devised their own methods of solving problems, and developed skills appropriate to their work or situation. Whilst problem solving in everyday life may be motivating, there are difficulties in bringing this type of motivation into the classroom through maths textbooks.

Mainstream mathematics schemes assume a steady learning progression, from simple numbers and facts to larger numbers and more complex ideas. For most children, the schemes can be tailored to suit their natural pace and development. However, any child may become 'stuck' on a particular aspect of mathematics or arithmetic. This may be because of illness, absence or a learning difficulty. Other children will consistently make slower progress than their peers.

Breakaway Maths is designed to provide a resource for children who are having problems with remembering facts and acquiring mathematical skills. These problems can arise at any time, but are most likely to be identified, and cause concern, between Years 2 and 3. For example, a child of 7 years old may still be counting inaccurately, forming numbers poorly, or unable to distinguish between addition and subtraction.

These children need time, confidence building and a sense of achievement in order to overcome their difficulties. *Breakaway Maths* allows children to revisit any area of mathematics with which they are having problems. This does not mean that they will be simply repeating work. The mathematics is presented in a variety of contexts, through textbooks, workbooks and copymasters.

Wherever possible, the mathematics has been related to everyday life, or situations with which children can identify. The characters' environments and interests reflect children's own. Every effort has been made to make the characters, illustrations and examples neutral in terms of age, so that children do not see the work as 'babyish'. The stories take them to places they would like to go to. The scheme avoids the stereotyping of characters and concentrates on their strengths, constantly highlighting what they can do rather than what they cannot.

An important consideration in writing *Breakaway Maths* has been that whilst children may be working at a relatively low level of mathematics, they are maturing in other ways. Many will be developing wide interests and practical skills. The scheme recognises this and aims to exploit it through model-making activities, games, investigations and problem solving.

Practical work should be at the heart of any mathematics programme, particularly one designed to help children with difficulties. The use of counters, cubes and base-ten materials is essential to help children to model numbers and operations such as addition and subtraction. These materials should never be seen as being 'babyish', or associated with failure. Practical activities are perhaps more important than paper and pencil exercises in providing sound learning experiences in measuring, handling data and making patterns. The *Breakaway Maths* books should in no way replace these practical classroom activities; in fact, this Teacher's Resource Book suggests many more.

Above all, *Breakaway Maths* shows that mathematics can be an exciting and rewarding activity rather than a daunting, theoretical study. *Breakaway Maths* equips real children for real life.

The structure of Breakaway Maths

Breakaway Maths is led by the textbooks. Each book tells a story, and each page contains one main mathematical theme. However, everyday life can involve the use of all sorts of mathematical skills and present lots of information to decode, and so do the textbook pages.

If children have any problems with an aspect of the mathematics, or need to try it again to develop their confidence, they can go straight to the appropriate workbook. There are two workbooks corresponding to each textbook. The first one contains all the supporting number work such as sorting, counting, addition and subtraction. The second contains work on shape and space, measurement and handling data, although number work will be encountered here as well.

Children may require yet more practice, and this can be found in the copymaster book. This also contains materials for games, models and pattern making, and sheets to help children record their answers to questions on the textbook pages.

The diagram on the right shows how the components could fit together.

The idea is to give, to those children who need them, plenty of experiences of each mathematical theme, before moving them on to the next page in the textbook. However, it is not necessary to use every single page or component, as this can be just as frustrating as moving on too quickly. As always, the teacher's judgement is crucial.

The charts on pages 22 to 33 give a detailed description of the mathematical content of each textbook, and its links with the other materials.

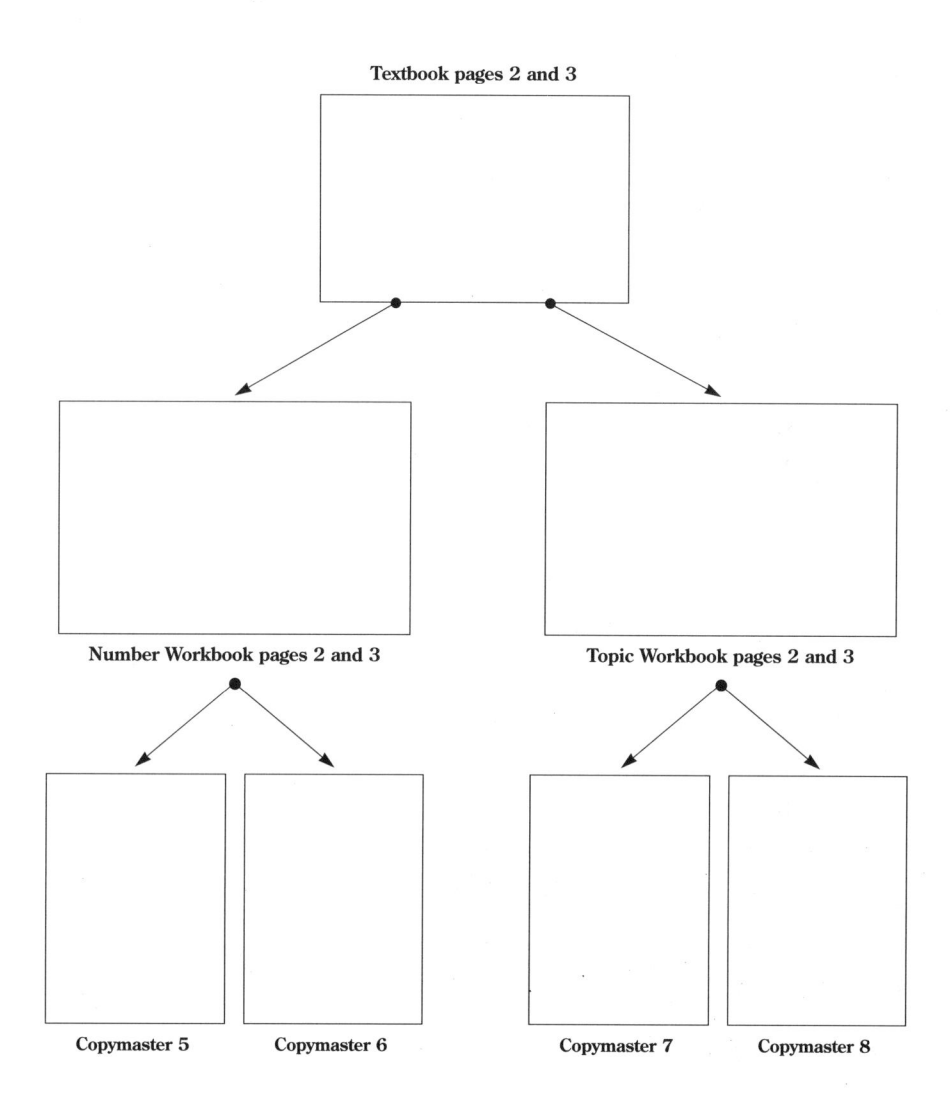

The Breakaway Maths materials

To provide the breadth and quantity of material to support children with special needs in mathematics, *Breakaway Maths* has four main components:

1 THE TEACHER'S RESOURCE BOOK

This book is intended to provide a guide to the materials, suggestions about their organisation, and links with the statutory curricula. It places mathematics in the context of everyday life, and gives ideas for practical work and activities. It also provides an answer key for the materials.

On pages 8 and 9, ways of organising are outlined, and links with the statutory curricula (for England and Wales, Scotland and Northern Ireland) are presented on pages 10 to 21.

Pages 22 to 33 show how the content of each textbook links to all the other materials. These pages may be photocopied and used as record sheets.

On pages 34 to 117, each double-page spread from the textbooks is taken in turn; there is a synopsis of the story, and the links between the textbook pages, the workbook pages and the copymasters are explained. There are suggestions for discussions, and some examples of the mathematics to look for in the school. Games and activities are also suggested. These either use readily available classroom equipment, or can be made from the copymasters. They can be used before or after the printed materials.

The answer key for all the pupil materials begins on page 118. This can be used either by teachers or by children who can check their own work.

At the back of the book, lists of key vocabulary show the restricted general vocabulary used in the textbooks, and the specialised language of mathematics which is systematically introduced.

2 THE TEXTBOOKS

There are six textbooks at Level 3. They should be read in sequence.

The textbooks feature the characters, Rupa, Lisa, David and Nicky, from Levels 1 and 2. They describe the situations in which they find themselves, and invite children to help them solve problems.

The context for Level 3 is an activity weekend. Each textbook offers a self-contained story about a different activity.

In Book 1, the characters pay for the trip, pack, and travel to the Warren Study Centre by minibus. Book 2 covers Saturday morning, when they have breakfast and then participate in water sports. After lunch, they visit the local museum (Book 3), and then spend Saturday night negotiating an orienteering course/treasure hunt and playing board games and pool (Book 4). In Book 5, the characters go target shooting on Sunday morning, followed by archery and an assault course. In Book 6 they pack up and travel home, making a detour in the village near the Warren Study Centre for shopping, and another at a service station for lunch.

The text has been kept to a minimum with picture clues, plenty of repetition and very simple sentence structures. (See page 144 for vocabulary lists.)

At the foot of each page there are references to the other materials (workbooks and copymasters) which relate to the mathematical content of that page. This is to make the provision of extra practice as straightforward as possible.

The mathematical skills featured in the work on that page are also listed here. It is suggested that children move from a textbook page to those workbook pages which support it. If further work, for practice or enrichment, is needed, there are extra copymaster worksheets.

The Breakaway Maths materials

3 THE WORKBOOKS

For each textbook there are two workbooks, a Number Workbook and a Topic Workbook.

The Number Workbook provides more opportunities to develop and practise number skills.

The Topic Workbook contains further experiences of algebra, shape and space and handling data.

Each double-page spread in the workbooks corresponds to a single textbook page. The workbook pages present the same mathematical concepts as the associated textbook pages. Wherever possible, they also use some of the characters, or an aspect of the story, from the textbook. This can help children to recognise that they are already familiar with the kinds of problem being presented.

The workbooks provide an opportunity to revisit a mathematical theme and they allow teachers to show children some more applications of mathematics in everyday life. For example, children may identify, sort and name a wide range of 2D shapes, look for them in the real world, draw them and use them to make patterns.

On page 16 of each workbook there is a simple review of some of its contents. It is entitled 'I can ...', to give parents and children an indication of what has been covered. It can be signed by the teacher, the child, or both. It is not intended to be a formal assessment.

The note at the foot of every workbook page summarises the mathematical skills which have been practised. There are also references to the textbook pages and the associated copymasters.

4 THE COPYMASTERS

Copymasters may be used before, after or alongside the textbooks and workbooks.

Most of the worksheets provide more materials for the purpose of revisiting particular mathematical themes.

The pro-forma worksheets provide skeleton formats of activities which will be familiar to children who have already used the workbooks and copymaster worksheets. These sheets can be 'customised' to provide further practice.

The answer sheets provide formats for children to record their answers to questions in the textbook.

Some worksheets provide templates for making games and models and for pattern making. They offer children the opportunity to cut, paste and choose colours, and achieve a satisfying result.

Certificates to mark the completion of each textbook are also included. These are intended to give children a sense of achievement and a record of their progress.

An advantage of photocopying is that sheets can be modified to meet particular needs. After making a copy, correction fluid or 'post it' notes can be used to mask areas to leave space for teachers to write their own numbers, questions or instructions. It is always worth keeping a clean copy of any modified worksheet, to avoid having to repeat the task. Enlarging the photocopies can also help children, by giving them more space or making the images clearer. Some of the sheets can be turned into board games in this way.

The Breakaway Maths materials

Classroom organisation

Classroom organisation

The most common ways in which children are organised to work on mathematics are individually, in pairs or in groups.

WORKING INDIVIDUALLY

A child is given a textbook, workbook or worksheet and asked to solve a series of problems. *Breakaway Maths* provides all these components at different levels, so that if the children are organised to work individually, those with difficulties can be using materials which look the same as those being used by the rest of the class. In this way they can avoid being perceived as doing special work.

In this situation, some children may have difficulty in reading the instructions in some texts. Long, involved instructions do not feature in *Breakaway Maths*, so that teachers, or other children, can quickly explain what the task is. The repetition of phrases and the picture clues will give the child the opportunity to work with a degree of independence.

WORKING IN PAIRS

Children with similar problems can be encouraged to work together on a particular set of problems, or a topic such as 2D shapes. The great advantage of this kind of classroom organisation is that it gives children the opportunity to discuss their difficulties and suggest solutions to each other. They can share the ownership of the work, which may help to build their confidence.

The investigations, problems and practical activities in *Breakaway Maths* are ideal vehicles for working in this way. The teacher's notes also suggest several games which are ideally played in pairs. Once these have been learned, children can play them repeatedly, and modify them by altering the range of cards or numbers used. In this way, they do not need to learn a new game in order to extend their use of mathematics.

WORKING IN GROUPS

All sorts of problems, particularly mathematical ones, can be very daunting if they have to be solved alone. Using teamwork is now an accepted way of addressing problems in an ever more complex world.

Similar ability groups

This is where a group of four to six children work together because they have similar abilities or problem areas, and it is more economical to introduce a body of work to them all. An example might be a group of children who do not understand the process of subtraction.

The teacher introduces the topic, showing how to use cubes to model subtraction problems. The children are then left to work on some examples together. In this way, they have all seen and heard what to do, and can help each other with any misunderstandings or difficulties. They can also be encouraged to check each other's work.

A session with such a group can be finished off with a simple game which uses the skill they have been developing. Alternatively, they can report back on what they have done.

Mixed ability groups

Pupils experiencing difficulties with aspects of mathematics need not be deprived of the chance to work with more able pupils. There are many practical problem-solving situations where children of different abilities can contribute to the solution.

The work in *Breakaway Maths* on building the housing estate and the castle is a good example of work suitable for a group of children with different abilities. These problems are open-ended in that there is no right answer, but rather a range of good, satisfactory or bad results. All the children can contribute by suggesting different approaches. The great advantage is that they will talk about what they are doing, and gain many incidental mathematical experiences.

Withdrawal groups

In some situations, children will be withdrawn from the classroom for a short period. This is more common for language work than mathematics. *Breakaway Maths* provides all the materials and structure needed to plan a programme for such groups.

The textbooks each provide a storyline which can be the stimulus for a session – 'I wonder what the children will do next time?' The workbooks and copymasters give plenty of scope for written work and recording. The games in the Teacher's Resource Book can be learned in withdrawal groups, for use back in the classroom.

Alternatively, teachers may wish to focus on one aspect of mathematics – such as naming, sorting and drawing 2D shapes – in this situation. In this case, they can use the problems on a particular textbook page to introduce the work. Children can then use the related pages in the Topic Workbook to continue the work. There will also be related copymasters, and ideas for further practical work in the Teacher's Resource Book.

HOW TO USE THE MATERIALS

The simplest way to use *Breakaway Maths* is for each child to begin with the textbook.

If the children are not using exercise books, each child will need to keep his/her own answer sheets. These will need to be photocopied in advance.

The textbooks provide a starting point. A highly structured approach is not essential, as any pages children can do easily will give them confidence. However, the textbooks are designed so that they can also be used in a structured way.

If children succeed on a page, they can simply continue through the textbook. The content increases in difficulty very gradually. However, to build confidence and a sense of achievement, they can revisit the mathematics on the appropriate workbook pages. References to these are at the foot of each textbook page. Workbooks are very useful, particularly if children experience difficulty with any of the material in the textbook. Workbooks hold the children's interest in work which they are beginning to understand. The copymasters also provide appropriate games and activities which reflect the content of the textbooks.

When children and teachers are confident to move on, they can turn to the next textbook page and all its associated materials. However, the textbooks regularly revisit topics so that children can build steadily on their success.

This is only one model for using the materials. Teachers may wish to concentrate on all the workbook pages about a particular subject, such as counting to 10, and then follow up with the copymasters. *Breakaway Maths* is a flexible resource which can support individual ways of organising the materials.

Breakaway Maths and the National Curriculum

ENGLAND AND WALES — Mathematics in the National Curriculum (1995)

The National Curriculum Programme of Study for Key Stage 2 has informed the textbooks, workbooks and copymasters for Level 3. The skills described in 'Using and applying mathematics' underpin all the materials, and references to these are not included in this chart.

Textbook 1

Page		NUMBER	SHAPE, SPACE AND MEASURES	HANDLING DATA
2	Counting to 30 Addition to 30	2ac		
3	Subtraction of two-digit numbers from 40 (money)	3d		
4	Making a table Making a block chart			2abd
5	Identifying 3D shapes		2b, 3a	
6	Multiplication tables (2×)	3ce		
7	Half of a set (division)	3eg		
8	Addition problems using decimal notation (money)	4a		
9	Distance in miles Analogue time		4ab	
10	Co-ordinates		3b	
11	Identifying 2D shapes Drawing 2D shapes		2ab	
12	Groups of four	3ce		
13	Reading a chart			2ad
14	Addition to 20 Subtraction from 20	2ac		
15	Addition facts to 20	2ac		

Textbook 2

Page		NUMBER	SHAPE, SPACE AND MEASURES	HANDLING DATA
2	Addition to 20 Subtraction from 20	2ac		
3	3D shapes – growing cubes and cuboids		2b, 3a	
4	Collecting information and making a chart			2abd
5	Multiplication tables (2×)	3ce		
6	Co-ordinates and compass points		3b	
7	Ordering numbers to 70 Addition to 130	3d		
8	Ordering numbers to 70 Subtraction from 70	2a 3d		
9	Growing a number pattern of threes	3ce		
10	Dividing by 2 Multiplying by 2 and 4	3ce		
11	Distance in metres	4a	4ab	
12	Identifying 2D shapes Drawing 2D shapes		2ab	
13	Tens and ones	2a, 3d		
14	Hundreds, tens and ones	2a, 3d		
15	Reading a pictogram			2bd

Textbook 3			NUMBER	SHAPE, SPACE AND MEASURES	HANDLING DATA
Page	2	Identifying 2D shapes Making a table		2ab	2bd
	3	Co-ordinates and compass points		3b	
	4	Addition of two-digit numbers to 70	3d		
	5	Pentominoes	3c		
	6	Time lines (number lines)	4a		2d
	7	Time lines (number lines)	3ce		
	8	Roman numerals	3a		
	9	Multiplication tables (4×)	3ce		
	10	Addition facts to 20	2ac		
	11	Place value, addition of three-digit numbers to 500	2a, 3d		
	12	Place value, subtraction of three-digit numbers from 300	2a, 3d		
	13	Making a table Making a block chart			2abd
	14	Multiplication tables (3×)	3ce		
	15	Litres and millilitres Kilograms and grams		4ab	

Textbook 4			NUMBER	SHAPE, SPACE AND MEASURES	HANDLING DATA
Page	2	Identifying 2D shapes		2b, 3ac	
	3	Dividing by 5 Finding one fifth	2c, 3eg		
	4	Addition of two-digit numbers to 130 Subtraction of two-digit numbers from 70	3d		
	5	Co-ordinates and compass points		3b	
	6	Distance in metres		4ab	
	7	Time in 5-minute intervals		4ab	
	8	Reading a bar chart			2bd
	9	Making a bar chart			2bd
	10	Addition facts to 20	2ac		
	11	Adding lists of numbers	2ac, 4bc		
	12	Hundreds, tens and ones	2a, 3d		
	13	Thousands, hundreds, tens and ones	2a, 3d		
	14	Multiplying by 2 Dividing by 2	3d		
	15	Litres and millilitres		4ab	

Breakaway Maths and the National Curriculum

Textbook 5		NUMBER	SHAPE, SPACE AND MEASURES	HANDLING DATA
Page 2	Identifying 3D shapes		2b, 3a	
3	Kilograms and grams	2a, 3d	4ab	
4	Adding lists of numbers	2ac, 4bc		
5	Hundreds, tens and ones	2a, 3d		
6	Multiplication tables (3×)	3ce		
7	Making a tally chart Making a bar chart			2abd
8	Reading a bar chart	2ac		2bd
9	Multiplying by 2 Multiplying by 3	3ac		
10	Identifying 2D shapes		2b, 3ac	
11	Co-ordinates		3b	
12	Time in 5-second intervals		4a	
13	Subtraction of three-digit numbers from 300	2a		
14	Addition of two-digit numbers to 70	2a, 3d		
15	Thousands, hundreds, tens and ones (millilitres)	2a, 3d	4a	

Textbook 6		NUMBER	SHAPE, SPACE AND MEASURES	HANDLING DATA
Page 2	Making a tally chart Making a bar chart			2abd
3	Half of a set (division)	2c, 3eg		
4	Area		4c	
5	Distance in miles		4ab	
6	Subtraction of four-digit numbers from 2000	2a		
7	Identifying 2D shapes		2ab, 3a	
8	Change from £5.50	2a, 4abc		
9	Change from £5.50	2a, 4abc		
10	Multiplication tables (2×, 3×, 4×, 5×)	3c		
11	Reading instruments		4b	
12	Rounding to the nearest £1	2a, 4abc		
13	Change from £10	2a, 4abc		
14	Thousands, hundreds and tens	2a		
15	Numbers and shapes in the environment			

Breakaway Maths and the National Curriculum

Many pages in *Breakaway Maths* cover more than one area of mathematics, as defined by the National Curriculum Programmes of Study. This chart is to help teachers who wish to find pages in the textbooks with an emphasis on a particular area of mathematics. 'Opportunities' described in 'Number 1' and 'Shape, space and measures 1' pervade the whole scheme, and are especially emphasised in this book.

		Textbook 1 pages	*Textbook 2 pages*	*Textbook 3 pages*	*Textbook 4 pages*	*Textbook 5 pages*	*Textbook 6 pages*
NUMBER							
2	Developing an understanding of place value and extending the number system	2, 14, 15	2, 8, 13, 14	10, 11, 12	3, 4, 5, 8, 13, 14, 15	3, 10, 11, 12, 13	3, 6, 8, 9, 12, 13, 14
3	Understanding relationships between numbers and developing methods of computation	3, 6, 7, 12	5, 7, 8, 9, 10, 13, 14	4, 5, 7, 8, 9, 11, 12, 14	3, 5, 6, 9, 14, 15	3, 4, 12, 13, 14	
4	Solving numerical problems	8	11	6	4	11	
SHAPE, SPACE AND MEASURES							
2	Understanding and using properties of shape	5, 11	3, 12	2	2, 10	2	7
3	Understanding and using properties of position and movement	5, 10	3, 6	3	2, 10, 11	5	7
4	Understanding and using measures	9	11	15	3, 12, 15	6, 7, 15	4, 5, 11
HANDLING DATA							
2	Collecting, representing and interpreting data	4, 13	4, 15	2, 6, 13	7, 8	8, 9	2

Breakaway Maths and the National Curriculum

Breakaway Maths and the 5–14 Guidelines

SCOTLAND The Scottish Office Education Department: Mathematics 5–14 Guidelines

The strands of the Scottish 5–14 Guidelines have informed the textbooks, workbooks and copymasters. The 'Handling information' strands Collect A and Interpret A underpin all the work, as children can gain all the necessary information from the pictures and diagrams in *Breakaway Maths*. These are not included in this chart.

Textbook 1 Page	HANDLING INFORMATION	NUMBER, MONEY AND MEASUREMENT	SHAPE, POSITION AND MOVEMENT
2 Counting to 20 Addition to 30		Range and type of numbers B Add and subtract B	
3 Subtraction of two-digit numbers from 40 (money)		Add and subtract B	
4 Making a table Making a block chart		Organise B Interpret B/C Display B Collect B	
5 Identifying 3D shapes			Range of shapes B
6 Multiplication tables (2×)		Multiply and divide B Patterns and sequences B	
7 Half of a set (division)		Fractions, percentages and ratios B	
8 Addition problems using decimal notation (money)		Money B Add and subtract D	
9 Distance in miles Analogue time		Measure and estimate B/C Time B	
10 Co-ordinates			Position and movement B
11 Identifying 2D shapes Drawing 2D shapes			Range of shapes B
12 Groups of four		Multiply and divide B	
13 Reading a chart	Interpret B/C		
14 Addition to 20 Subtraction from 20		Add and subtract B	
15 Addition facts to 20		Add and subtract B	

Textbook 2 Page	HANDLING INFORMATION	NUMBER, MONEY AND MEASUREMENT	SHAPE, POSITION AND MOVEMENT
2 Addition to 20 Subtraction from 20		Add and subtract B	
3 3D shapes – growing cubes and cuboids			Range of shapes B
4 Collecting information and making a chart	Collect B Organise B Display B		
5 Multiplication tables (2×)		Multiply and divide B Patterns and sequences B	
6 Co-ordinates and compass points			Position and movement B
7 Ordering numbers to 70 Addition to 130		Range and type of numbers B Add and subtract B	
8 Ordering numbers to 70 Subtraction from 70		Range and type of numbers B Add and subtract B	
9 Growing a number pattern of threes		Multiply and divide B Patterns and sequences B	
10 Dividing by 2 Multiplying by 2 and 4		Multiply and divide B	
11 Distance in metres		Measure and estimate B/C	
12 Identifying 2D shapes Drawing 2D shapes			Range of shapes B
13 Tens and ones		Range and type of numbers B	
14 Hundreds, tens and ones		Range and type of numbers B	
15 Reading a pictogram	Interpret C		

14 Breakaway Maths and the 5–14 Guidelines

Textbook 3

Page		HANDLING INFORMATION	NUMBER, MONEY AND MEASUREMENT	SHAPE, POSITION AND MOVEMENT
2	Identifying 2D shapes Making a table	Collect B Display B Organise B Interpret B		Range and type of numbers B
3	Co-ordinates and compass points			Position and movement B
4	Addition of two-digit numbers to 70		Add and subtract B	
5	Pentominoes		Multiply and divide B Patterns and sequences B	Symmetry B
6	Time lines (number lines)		Add and subtract B	
7	Time lines (number lines)		Add and subtract B Multiply and divide B	
8	Roman numerals		Patterns and sequences B	
9	Multiplication tables (4×)		Multiply and divide B Patterns and sequences B	
10	Addition facts to 20		Add and subtract B	
11	Place value Addition of three-digit numbers to 500		Range and type of numbers B	
12	Place value Subtraction of three-digit numbers from 300		Add and subtract B/C	
13	Making a table Making a block chart	Collect B Interpret B Organise B Display B		
14	Multiplication tables (3×)		Multiply and divide B Patterns and sequences B	
15	Litres and millilitres Kilograms and grams		Measure and estimate B	

Textbook 4

Page		HANDLING INFORMATION	NUMBER, MONEY AND MEASUREMENT	SHAPE, POSITION AND MOVEMENT
2	Identifying 2D shapes			Range of shapes B Symmetry B Position and movement B
3	Dividing by 5 Finding one fifth		Fractions, percentages and ratios B	
4	Addition of two-digit numbers to 130 Subtraction of two-digit numbers from 70		Add and subtract B	
5	Co-ordinates and compass points			Position and movement B
6	Distance in metres		Measure and estimate B	
7	Time in 5-minute intervals		Time B	
8	Reading a bar chart	Interpret C		
9	Making a bar chart	Organise B Display C		
10	Addition facts to 20		Add and subtract B	
11	Adding lists of numbers		Add and subtract B	
12	Hundreds, tens and ones		Range and type B of numbers	
13	Thousands, hundreds, tens and ones		Range and type of numbers B	
14	Multiplying by 2 Dividing by 2		Multiply and divide B	
15	Litres and millilitres		Measure and estimate B	

Breakaway Maths and the 5–14 Guidelines   15

Textbook 5 Page	HANDLING INFORMATION	NUMBER, MONEY AND MEASUREMENT	SHAPE, POSITION AND MOVEMENT
2 Identifying 3D shapes			Range of shapes B
3 Kilograms and grams		Measure and estimate B Range and type of numbers B	
4 Adding lists of numbers		Add and subtract B	
5 Hundreds, tens and ones		Range and type of numbers B Add and subtract B	
6 Multiplication tables (3×)		Multiply and divide B Patterns and sequences B	
7 Making a tally chart Making a bar chart	Collect B Interpret C Organise B Display C		
8 Reading a bar chart	Interpret C	Add and subtract B	
9 Multiplying by 2 Multiplying by 3		Multiply and divide B Patterns and sequences B	
10 Identifying 2D shapes			Range of shapes B Symmetry B
11 Co-ordinates			Position and movement B
12 Time in 5-second intervals		Time D	
13 Subtraction of three-digit numbers from 300		Add and subtract B	
14 Addition of two-digit numbers to 70		Add and subtract B	
15 Thousands, hundreds, tens and ones (millilitres)		Measure and estimate B Range and type of numbers B	

Textbook 6 Page	HANDLING INFORMATION	NUMBER, MONEY AND MEASUREMENT	SHAPE, POSITION AND MOVEMENT
2 Making a tally chart Making a bar chart	Collect B Display C Organise B Interpret C		
3 Half of a set (division)		Fractions, percentages and ratios B Multiply and divide B	
4 Area		Measure and estimate C	
5 Distance in miles		Measure and estimate B	
6 Subtraction of four-digit numbers from 2000		Add and subtract B	
7 Identifying 2D shapes			Range and type of numbers B Position and movement B Symmetry B
8 Change from £5.50		Money B Add and subtract B	
9 Change from £5.50		Money B Add and subtract B	
10 Multiplication tables (2×, 3×, 4×, 5×)		Multiply and divide B	
11 Reading instruments		Measure and estimate B	
12 Rounding to the nearest £1		Round numbers B/D Money B	
13 Change from £10		Money B	
14 Thousands, hundreds and tens		Range and type of numbers B Add and subtract B	
15 Numbers and shapes in the environment			

16 Breakaway Maths and the 5–14 Guidelines

Many pages in *Breakaway Maths* cover more than one area of mathematics as defined by the 5–14 Guidelines.
This chart is to help teachers who wish to find pages in the textbooks with an emphasis on a particular strand.

	Textbook 1 pages	*Textbook 2 pages*	*Textbook 3 pages*	*Textbook 4 pages*	*Textbook 5 pages*	*Textbook 6 pages*
HANDLING INFORMATION *Strands*						
Collect	4	4	2, 13		7	2
Organise	4	4	2, 13	9	7	2
Display	4	4	2, 13	9	7	2
Interpret	4, 13	15	2, 13	8	7, 8	2
NUMBER, MONEY AND MEASUREMENT *Strands*						
Range and type of numbers	2	7, 13, 14	11	12, 13	3, 5, 15	14
Money	8					8, 9, 12, 13
Addition and subtraction	2, 3, 8, 14, 15	2, 7	4, 6, 7, 10, 12	4, 10, 11	4, 5, 8, 13, 14	6, 8, 9, 14
Multiplication and division	6, 12	5, 9, 10	5, 7, 9, 14	14, 15	6, 9	3, 10
Round numbers						12
Fractions, percentages and ratios	7			3		3
Patterns and sequences	6	5, 9	5, 8		6, 9	
Measurement and estimation	9	11	15	6	3, 15	4, 5, 11
Time	9			7	12	
SHAPE, POSITION AND MOVEMENT *Strands*						
Range of shapes	5, 11	3, 12	2	2	2, 10	7
Position and movement	10	5	2	2	10	7
Symmetry			5	2	10	7

Breakaway Maths and the 5–14 Guidelines 17

Breakaway Maths and the Northern Ireland Curriculum

NORTHERN IRELAND **Department of Education for Northern Ireland:**
Mathematics Programmes of Study and Attainment Targets

The Northern Ireland National Curriculum Attainment Targets have informed the textbooks, workbooks and copymasters. The use of materials and talking about work, as described in 'Processes in mathematics (P1)', underpin all the work in *Breakaway Maths*, and references to these are not included in this chart.

	NUMBER	ALGEBRA	MEASURES	SHAPE AND SPACE	HANDLING DATA
Textbook 1 *Page*					
2 Counting to 30 / Addition to 30	N/3ad				
3 Subtraction of two-digit numbers from 40 (money)	N/3e				
4 Making a table / Making a block chart					D/3a
5 Identifying 3D shapes				S/3a	
6 Multiplication tables (2×)	N/3f	A/3ac			
7 Half of a set (division)	N/3cf	A/3ac			
8 Addition problems using decimal notation (money)	N/3beg				
9 Distance in miles / Analogue time			M/3b		
10 Co-ordinates				S/4d	
11 Identifying 2D shapes / Drawing 2D shapes				S/3abc	
12 Groups of four	N/3f				
13 Reading a chart					D/3b
14 Addition to 20 / Subtraction from 20	N/3d				
15 Addition facts to 20	N/3d				

	NUMBER	ALGEBRA	MEASURES	SHAPE AND SPACE	HANDLING DATA
Textbook 2 *Page*					
2 Addition to 20 / Subtraction from 20	N/3d				
3 3D shapes – growing cubes and cuboids		A/3a			
4 Collecting information and making a chart					D/3ab
5 Multiplication tables (2×)	N/3f	A/3ac			
6 Co-ordinates and compass points				S/4cd	
7 Ordering numbers to 70 / Addition to 130	N/3e				
8 Ordering numbers to 70 / Subtraction from 70	N/3ae				
9 Growing a number pattern of threes	N/3f	A/3a			
10 Dividing by 2 / Multiplying by 2 and 4	N/3fj				
11 Distance in metres			M/3abc		
12 Identifying 2D shapes / Drawing 2D shapes				S/3abc	
13 Tens and ones	N/3a	A/3b			
14 Hundreds, tens and ones	N/3a	A/3b			
15 Reading a pictogram					D/3d

Textbook 3	NUMBER	ALGEBRA	MEASURES	SHAPE AND SPACE	HANDLING DATA
Page					
2 Identifying 2D shapes Making a table				S/3abc	D/3a
3 Co-ordinates and compass points				S/4d	
4 Addition of two-digit numbers to 70	N/3e				
5 Pentominoes	N/3f	A/3ac			
6 Time lines (number lines)	N/3af				
7 Time lines (number lines)	N/3a				
8 Roman numerals		A/3a			
9 Multiplication tables (×4)	N/3f	A/3ac			
10 Addition facts to 20	N/3d				
11 Place value Addition of three-digit numbers to 500	N/3ag				
12 Place value Subtraction of three-digit numbers from 300	N/3g				
13 Making a table Making a block chart					D/3a
14 Multiplication tables (3×)	N/3f	A/3a			
15 Litres and millilitres Kilograms and grams			M/3abc		

Textbook 4	NUMBER	ALGEBRA	MEASURES	SHAPE AND SPACE	HANDLING DATA
Page					
2 Identifying 2D shapes				S/3abc	
3 Dividing by 5 Finding one fifth	N/3c	A/3ac			
4 Addition of two-digit numbers to 130 Subtraction of two-digit numbers from 70	N/3e				
5 Co-ordinates and compass points				S/4cd	
6 Distance in metres			M/3abc		
7 Time in 5-minute intervals			M/3b		
8 Reading a bar chart					D/3c
9 Making a bar chart					D/3c
10 Addition facts to 20	N/3d				
11 Adding lists of numbers	N/3d				
12 Hundreds, tens and ones	N/3a				
13 Thousands, hundreds, tens and ones	N/3a				
14 Multiplying by 2 Dividing by 2	N/3g				
15 Litres and millilitres			M/3abc		

Breakaway Maths and the Northern Ireland Curriculum

Textbook 5 Page	NUMBER	ALGEBRA	MEASURES	SHAPE AND SPACE	HANDLING DATA
2 Identifying 3D shapes				S/3a	
3 Kilograms and grams	N/3a				
4 Adding lists of numbers	N/3d				
5 Hundreds, tens and ones	N/3a				
6 Multiplication tables (3×)	N/3f	A/3a			
7 Making a tally chart / Making a bar chart					D/3ac
8 Reading a bar chart	N/3a				
9 Multiplying by 2 / Multiplying by 3	N/3fg	A/3acd			
10 Identifying 2D shapes				S/3abc	
11 Co-ordinates				S/4d	
12 Time in 5-second intervals			M/3b		
13 Subtraction of three-digit numbers from 300	N/3e				
14 Addition of two-digit numbers to 70	N/3e				
15 Thousands, hundreds, tens and ones	N/3a		M/3abc		

Textbook 6 Page	NUMBER	ALGEBRA	MEASURES	SHAPE AND SPACE	HANDLING DATA
2 Making a tally chart / Making a bar chart					D/3ac
3 Half of a set (division)	N/3c				
4 Area			M/3b		
5 Distance in miles			M/3b		
6 Subtraction of four-digit numbers from 2000	N/3e				
7 Identifying 2D shapes				S/3abc	
8 Change from £5.50	N/3be				
9 Change from £5.50	N/3be				
10 Multiplication tables (2×, 3×, 4×, 5×)		A/3ac			
11 Reading instruments			M/3bc		
12 Rounding to the nearest £1	N/3beh				
13 Change from £10	N/3beh				
14 Thousands, hundreds and tens	N/3a				
15 Numbers and shapes in the environment				S/3a	

20 Breakaway Maths and the Northern Ireland Curriculum

Many pages in *Breakaway Maths* cover more than one area of mathematics as defined by the National Curriculum.
This chart is to help teachers who wish to find pages in the textbooks with an emphasis on a particular area of mathematics.

	Textbook 1 pages	*Textbook 2 pages*	*Textbook 3 pages*	*Textbook 4 pages*	*Textbook 5 pages*	*Textbook 6 pages*
NUMBER (N/3)	2, 3, 6, 7, 8, 12, 14, 15	2, 5, 7, 8, 9, 10, 13, 14	4, 5, 6, 7, 9, 10, 11, 12, 14	3, 4, 10, 11, 12, 13, 14	3, 4, 5, 6, 8, 9, 13, 14, 15	3, 6, 8, 9, 12, 13, 14
ALGEBRA (A/3)	6, 7	3, 5, 9, 13, 14	5, 8, 9, 14	3	6, 9	10
MEASURES (M/3)	9	11	15	6, 7, 15	12, 15	5, 6, 11
SHAPE AND SPACE (S/3)	5, 10, 11	6, 12	2, 3	2, 5	2, 10, 11	7, 15
HANDLING DATA (D/3)	4, 13	4, 15	2, 13	8, 9	7	2

Breakaway Maths and the Northern Ireland Curriculum

Pathways through the materials/record sheets

Textbook 1 – An activity weekend

✓ Pages 22–33 may be photocopied and used as individual record sheets.

TEXTBOOK 1 PAGES	
2 Counting to 30, addition to 30	☐
3 Subtraction of two-digit numbers from 40 (money)	☐
4 Making a table, making a block chart	☐
5 Identifying 3D shapes	☐
6 Multiplication tables (2×)	☐
7 Half of a set (division)	☐
8 Addition problems using decimal notation (money)	☐
9 Distance in miles, analogue time	☐
10 Co-ordinates	☐
11 Identifying 2D shapes, drawing 2D shapes	☐
12 Groups of four	☐
13 Reading a chart	☐
14 Addition to 20, subtraction from 20	☐
15 Addition facts to 20	☐

COPYMASTERS (ANSWER SHEETS)

1 Textbook 1 An activity weekend pages 2 to 5

2 Textbook 1 An activity weekend pages 6 to 9

3 Textbook 1 An activity weekend pages 10 to 12

4 Textbook 1 An activity weekend pages 13 to 15

NUMBER WORKBOOK 1 PAGES

- 2 Addition to 20
- 3 Subtraction from 20

- 4 Addition of two-digit numbers to 50 (money)
- 5 Subtraction of two-digit numbers from 50 (money)

- 6 Multiplication tables (2×)
- 7 Multiplication tables (2×)

- 8 Finding half of a shape
- 9 Finding half of a number

- 10 Decimal notation (money)
- 11 Addition using decimal notation (money)

- 12 Subtraction from 20
- 13 Addition to 20

- 14 Addition facts to make 11, 12, 13 and 14
- 15 Subtraction facts to make 11, 12, 13 and 14

TOPIC WORKBOOK 1 PAGES

- 2 Making a tally chart
- 3 Making a block chart

- 4 Identifying 3D shapes
- 5 Identifying 3D shapes

- 6 Adding distances in miles
- 7 Adding time in hours and minutes

- 8 Reading co-ordinates
- 9 Using co-ordinates for drawing

- 10 Identifying 2D shapes
- 11 Drawing 2D shapes

- 12 Patterns of four
- 13 Counting in fours

- 14 Reading a chart
- 15 Making a chart

COPYMASTERS

- 5 Counting to 20, addition to 20
- 6 Subtraction from 20

- 7 Addition of two-digit numbers to 60 (money)
- 8 Subtraction of two-digit numbers from 40 (money)

- 16 Multiplication tables (2×)

- 17 Finding half of a shape
- 18 Finding half of a number

- 19 Decimal notation (money)
- 20 Decimal notation (money)

- 31 Adding 8, subtracting 8
- 32 Adding 9, subtracting 9

COPYMASTERS

- 9 Making a tally chart
- 10 Making a block chart
- 11 Blank tally chart, blank block chart

- 12 Net of a square-based pyramid, net of a tetrahedron
- 13 Net of a triangular prism
- 14 Net of a cuboid
- 15 Net of a cube

- 21 Showing analogue time – adding 1 hour
- 22 Showing analogue time – adding half an hour

- 23 Co-ordinates
- 24 Co-ordinates
- 25 Blank grid with co-ordinates (5 × 5)

- 26 Drawing 2D shapes

- 27 Counting in fours
- 28 Multiplication tables (4×)

- 29 Reading a chart
- 30 Making a chart

Pathways through the materials/record sheets 23

Textbook 2 – Water sports

TEXTBOOK 2 PAGES

2	Addition to 20, subtraction from 20	☐
3	3D shapes – growing cubes and cuboids	☐
4	Collecting information and making a chart	☐
5	Multiplication tables (2×)	☐
6	Co-ordinates and compass points	☐
7	Ordering numbers to 70, addition to 130	☐
8	Ordering numbers to 70, subtraction from 70	☐
9	Growing a number pattern of threes	☐
10	Dividing by 2, multiplying by 2 and 4	☐
11	Distance in metres	☐
12	Identifying 2D shapes, drawing 2D shapes	☐
13	Tens and ones	☐
14	Hundreds, tens and ones	☐
15	Reading a pictogram	☐

COPYMASTERS (ANSWER SHEETS)

33	Textbook 2 Water sports pages 2 to 4
34	Textbook 2 Water sports pages 5 to 8
35	Textbook 2 Water sports pages 9 to 12
36	Textbook 2 Water sports pages 13 to 15

Pathways through the materials/record sheets

NUMBER WORKBOOK 2 PAGES

- **2** Addition to 20
- **3** Subtraction from 20

- **4** Multiplication tables (2×)
- **5** Multiplication tables (2×)

- **6** Addition to 90 using base-ten apparatus
- **7** Ordering numbers to 70, addition to 120

- **8** Subtraction from 60 using base-ten apparatus
- **9** Ordering numbers to 70, subtraction from 70

- **10** Multiplying by 2
- **11** Dividing by 2

- **12** Tens and ones
- **13** Hundreds, tens and ones

- **14** Hundreds, tens and ones
- **15** Hundreds, tens and ones

COPYMASTERS

- **37** Addition facts to 20
- **38** Subtraction facts from 20

- **43** Multiplication tables (2×)
- **44** Multiplication tables (2×)

- **47** Addition to 90 using base-ten apparatus
- **48** Addition to 110 using base-ten apparatus

- **49** Subtraction from 50 using base-ten apparatus
- **50** Subtraction from 70 using base-ten apparatus

- **53** Multiplying by 2
- **54** Dividing by 2

- **59** Tens and ones
- **60** Tens and ones

- **61** Hundreds, tens and ones
- **62** Hundreds, tens and ones

TOPIC WORKBOOK 2 PAGES

- **2** 3D shapes – growing cubes
- **3** 3D shapes – growing cuboids

- **4** Identifying 2D shapes, reading a chart
- **5** Identifying 2D shapes, making a chart

- **6** Co-ordinates and compass points
- **7** Co-ordinates

- **8** Growing a number pattern of threes
- **9** Multiplication tables (3×)

- **10** Distance in metres
- **11** Measuring in centimetres

- **12** Identifying 2D shapes
- **13** Drawing 2D shapes

- **14** Reading a pictogram
- **15** Making a pictogram

COPYMASTERS

- **39** 3D shapes – growing cuboids
- **40** 3D shapes – growing cuboids

- **41** Reading a chart
- **42** Making a chart

- **45** Co-ordinates
- **46** Compass points

- **51** Multiplication tables (3×)
- **52** Multiplication tables (3×)

- **55** Distance in metres
- **56** Measuring in centimetres

- **57** Identifying 2D shapes
- **58** Drawing quadrilaterals

- **63** Reading a pictogram
- **64** Making a pictogram

Pathways through the materials/record sheets

Textbook 3 – The museum

TEXTBOOK 3 PAGES

2	Identifying 2D shapes, making a table	☐
3	Co-ordinates and compass points	☐
4	Addition of two-digit numbers to 70	☐
5	Pentominoes	☐
6	Time lines (number lines)	☐
7	Time lines (number lines)	☐
8	Roman numerals	☐
9	Multiplication tables (4×)	☐
10	Addition facts to 20	☐
11	Place value, addition of three-digit numbers to 500	☐
12	Place value, subtraction of three-digit numbers from 400	☐
13	Making a table, making a block chart	☐
14	Multiplication tables (3×)	☐
15	Litres and millilitres, kilograms and grams	☐

COPYMASTERS (ANSWER SHEETS)

65	Textbook 3 The museum pages 2 to 4
66	Textbook 3 The museum pages 5 to 8
67	Textbook 3 The museum pages 9 to 11
68	Textbook 3 The museum pages 12 to 15

Pathways through the materials/record sheets

NUMBER WORKBOOK 3 PAGES

- **2** Addition to 100 using base-ten apparatus
- **3** Subtraction from 70 using base-ten apparatus
- **4** Time lines (number lines)
- **5** Time lines (number lines)
- **6** Counting on and counting back (using number lines)
- **7** Counting on in twos (using number lines)
- **8** Multiplication tables (4×)
- **9** Multiplication tables (4×)
- **10** Addition facts to 20
- **11** Subtraction facts from 20
- **12** Tens and ones
- **13** Addition to 70 using base-ten apparatus
- **14** Tens and ones
- **15** Subtraction from 60 using base-ten apparatus

TOPIC WORKBOOK 3 PAGES

- **2** Drawing 2D shapes, symmetry
- **3** Identifying 2D shapes, making a table, making a block chart
- **4** Co-ordinates
- **5** Compass points
- **6** Multiplication tables (5×)
- **7** Multiplication tables (5×)
- **8** Roman numerals
- **9** Roman numerals
- **10** Making a table, making a block chart
- **11** Reading a block chart
- **12** Multiplication tables (2×, 3×, 4×, 5×)
- **13** Multiplication tables (2×, 3×, 4×, 5×)
- **14** Litres, half-litres and millilitres
- **15** Kilograms, half-kilograms and grams

COPYMASTERS

- **73** Addition to 90 using base-ten apparatus
- **74** Subtraction from 60 using base-ten apparatus
- **77** Counting on (using number lines)
- **78** Counting back (using number lines)
- **79** Multiplication tables (2×, 3×, 4×, 5×) on number lines
- **80** Blank number lines
- **83** Multiplication tables (4×)
- **84** Multiplication tables (4×)
- **85** Addition facts to 20
- **86** Subtraction facts from 20
- **87** Hundreds, tens and ones
- **88** Addition to 100 using base-ten apparatus
- **89** Hundreds, tens and ones
- **90** Subtraction from 100 using base-ten apparatus

COPYMASTERS

- **69** Drawing 2D shapes, symmetry
- **70** Drawing 2D shapes, symmetry
- **71** Drawing 2D shapes, reading a block chart
- **72** Co-ordinates
- **75** Multiplication tables (5×)
- **76** Multiplication tables (5×)
- **81** Roman numerals
- **82** Mayan numerals
- **91** Making a table, making a block chart
- **92** Reading a block chart
- **93** Multiplication tables (2×, 3×, 4×, 5×)
- **94** Multiplication tables (2×, 3×, 4×, 5×)
- **95** Litres and half-litres
- **96** Litres and half-litres (blank measuring cylinders)
- **97** Kilograms and half-kilograms
- **98** Kilograms and half-kilograms (blank scales)

Pathways through the materials/record sheets

Textbook 4 – Saturday night

TEXTBOOK 4 PAGES

2	Identifying 2D shapes	☐
3	Dividing by 5, finding one fifth	☐
4	Addition of two-digit numbers to 130, subtraction of two-digit numbers from 70	☐
5	Co-ordinates and compass points	☐
6	Distance in metres	☐
7	Time in 5-minute intervals	☐
8	Reading a bar chart	☐
9	Making a bar chart	☐
10	Addition facts to 20	☐
11	Adding lists of numbers	☐
12	Hundreds, tens and ones	☐
13	Thousands, hundreds, tens and ones	☐
14	Multiplying by 2, dividing by 2	☐
15	Litres and millilitres	☐

COPYMASTERS (ANSWER SHEETS)

99	Textbook 4 Saturday night pages 2 to 5
100	Textbook 4 Saturday night pages 6 to 8
101	Textbook 4 Saturday night pages 9 to 11
102	Textbook 4 Saturday night pages 12 to 15

Pathways through the materials/record sheets

NUMBER WORKBOOK 4 PAGES

2	Finding one fifth	☐
3	Finding one fifth	☐
4	Addition of two-digit numbers to 90	☐
5	Subtraction of two-digit numbers from 60	☐
6	Addition facts to 20	☐
7	Subtraction facts from 20	☐
8	Adding lists of numbers, finding tens	☐
9	Adding lists of numbers, finding tens	☐
10	Hundreds, tens and ones	☐
11	Hundreds, tens and ones	☐
12	Thousands, hundreds, tens and ones	☐
13	Thousands, hundreds, tens and ones	☐
14	Multiplying by 2	☐
15	Dividing by 2	☐

COPYMASTERS

105	Finding one fifth	☐
106	Finding one fifth	☐
107	Addition of two-digit numbers to 70	☐
108	Subtraction of two-digit numbers from 60	☐
121	Addition facts to 20, subtraction facts from 20	☐
122	Adding lists of numbers, finding tens	☐
123	Hundreds, tens and ones	☐
124	Hundreds, tens and ones	☐
125	Thousands, hundreds, tens and ones	☐
126	Thousands, hundreds, tens and ones	☐
127	Multiplying by 2	☐
128	Dividing by 2	☐

TOPIC WORKBOOK 4 PAGES

2	Identifying 2D shapes	☐
3	Identifying 2D shapes	☐
4	Compass points	☐
5	Co-ordinates	☐
6	Measuring in centimetres	☐
7	Measuring in centimetres	☐
8	Digital time in 5-minute intervals	☐
9	Analogue time in 5-minute intervals	☐
10	Reading a bar chart	☐
11	Making a bar chart	☐
12	Reading a tally chart, making a bar chart	☐
13	Making a tally chart	☐
14	Litres and millilitres	☐
15	Litres and millilitres	☐

COPYMASTERS

103	Continuing patterns	☐
104	Drawing 2D shapes	☐
109	Blank grid with co-ordinates (6 × 6)	☐
110	Co-ordinates and compass points	☐
111	Measuring in centimetres	☐
112	Measuring in centimetres	☐
113	Digital time in 5-minute intervals (blank clocks)	☐
114	Digital time in 5-minute intervals	☐
115	Analogue time in 5-minute intervals (blank clocks)	☐
116	Analogue time in 5-minute intervals	☐
117	Blank bar chart	☐
118	Reading a bar chart	☐
119	Reading a tally chart, making a bar chart	☐
120	Making a tally chart	☐
129	Litres and half-litres	☐
130	Litres and millilitres	☐

Pathways through the materials/record sheets

Textbook 5 – Climbing and shooting

TEXTBOOK 5 PAGES

2	Identifying 3D shapes	☐
3	Kilograms and grams	☐
4	Adding lists of numbers	☐
5	Hundreds, tens and ones	☐
6	Multiplication tables (3×)	☐
7	Making a tally chart, making a bar chart	☐
8	Reading a bar chart	☐
9	Multiplying by 2, multiplying by 3	☐
10	Identifying 2D shapes	☐
11	Co-ordinates	☐
12	Time in 5-second intervals	☐
13	Subtraction of three-digit numbers from 300	☐
14	Addition of two-digit numbers to 70	☐
15	Thousands, hundreds, tens and ones (millilitres)	☐

COPYMASTERS (ANSWER SHEETS)

131	Textbook 5 Climbing and shooting pages 2 to 5
132	Textbook 5 Climbing and shooting pages 6 to 8
133	Textbook 5 Climbing and shooting pages 9 to 11
134	Textbook 5 Climbing and shooting pages 12 to 15

NUMBER WORKBOOK 5 PAGES

- 2 Adding lists of numbers
- 3 Adding lists of numbers
- 4 Hundreds, tens and ones
- 5 Hundreds, tens and ones
- 6 Multiplication tables (3×)
- 7 Multiplication tables (3×)
- 8 Multiplying by 2, 3 and 4
- 9 Multiplying by 2, 3 and 5
- 10 Subtraction of three-digit numbers from 700
- 11 Addition of three-digit numbers to 800
- 12 Addition of two-digit numbers to 90
- 13 Addition of three-digit numbers to 800
- 14 Thousands, hundreds, tens and ones
- 15 Thousands, hundreds, tens and ones

TOPIC WORKBOOK 5 PAGES

- 2 Identifying 3D shapes
- 3 Identifying 3D shapes
- 4 Kilograms and grams
- 5 Kilograms and grams
- 6 Making a tally chart
- 7 Making a bar chart
- 8 Reading a bar chart
- 9 Making a bar chart
- 10 Making patterns with 2D shapes
- 11 Drawing 2D shapes
- 12 Co-ordinates
- 13 Co-ordinates
- 14 Analogue time in 5-second intervals
- 15 Digital time in 5-second intervals

COPYMASTERS

- 139 Adding lists of numbers (target)
- 140 Adding lists of numbers (blank targets)
- 141 Adding lists of numbers
- 142 Adding lists of numbers
- 143 Hundreds, tens and ones
- 144 Hundreds, tens and ones
- 145 Hundreds, tens and ones (blank grid for drawing base-ten blocks)
- 146 Multiplication tables (blank tables to 5×)
- 147 Multiplication tables (blank puzzle sheet)
- 150 Multiplying by 2, multiplying by 3
- 151 Multiplying by 2, multiplying by 4
- 161 Subtraction of three-digit numbers from 700
- 162 Addition of three-digit numbers to 800
- 163 Addition of two-digit numbers to 100
- 164 Addition of three-digit numbers to 1000
- 165 Thousands, hundreds, tens and ones
- 166 Thousands, hundreds, tens and ones

COPYMASTERS

- 135 Identifying 3D shapes
- 136 Identifying 3D shapes
- 137 Kilograms and grams (blank scales)
- 138 Kilograms and grams
- 148 Making a tally chart
- 149 Reading a bar chart
- 152 Drawing 2D shapes – symmetry
- 153 Co-ordinates
- 154 Co-ordinates, identifying 2D shapes
- 155 Co-ordinates, drawing 2D shapes
- 156 Analogue time in 5-second intervals
- 157 Analogue time in 5-second intervals (blank stopwatches)
- 158 Digital time in 5-second intervals
- 159 Digital time in 5-second intervals (blank stopwatches)
- 160 Analogue time (blank clocks)

Pathways through the materials/record sheets

Textbook 6 – Going home

TEXTBOOK 6 PAGES

2	Making a tally chart, making a bar chart	☐
3	Half of a set (division)	☐
4	Area	☐
5	Distance in miles	☐
6	Subtraction of four-digit numbers from 2000	☐
7	Identifying 2D shapes	☐
8	Change from £5.50	☐
9	Change from £5.50	☐
10	Multiplication tables (2×, 3×, 4×, 5×)	☐
11	Reading instruments	☐
12	Rounding to the nearest £1	☐
13	Change from £10	☐
14	Thousands, hundreds and tens	☐
15	Numbers and shapes in the environment	☐

COPYMASTERS (ANSWER SHEETS)

167	Textbook 6 Going home pages 2 to 5
168	Textbook 6 Going home pages 6 to 9
169	Textbook 6 Going home pages 10 to 11
170	Textbook 6 Going home pages 12 to 15

Pathways through the materials/record sheets

NUMBER WORKBOOK 6 PAGES

- **2** Addition facts to 20, subtraction facts from 20
- **3** Addition of two-digit numbers to 90, subtraction of two-digit numbers from 70
- **4** Decimal notation (money)
- **5** Coin combinations
- **6** Addition using decimal notation
- **7** Change from £2.50
- **8** Multiplication tables (2×, 3×)
- **9** Multiplication tables (4×, 5×)
- **10** Rounding to the nearest £1
- **11** Rounding to the nearest £1, approximating
- **12** Change from £10
- **13** Change from £10
- **14** Thousands, hundreds and tens
- **15** Thousands, hundreds, tens and ones

COPYMASTERS

- **178** Addition facts to 20, subtraction facts from 20
- **179** Addition of two-digit numbers to 100, subtraction of two-digit numbers from 70
- **182** Decimal notation (money)
- **183** Coin combinations
- **184** Change from £5
- **185** Rounding to the nearest £1
- **186** Rounding to the nearest £1, approximating
- **187** Change from £10
- **188** Thousands, hundreds, tens and ones

TOPIC WORKBOOK 6 PAGES

- **2** Making a tally chart
- **3** Making a bar chart
- **4** Finding half by partitioning
- **5** Finding quarters by partitioning
- **6** Area
- **7** Area in centimetres
- **8** Thousands, hundreds, tens and ones
- **9** Subtraction of four-digit numbers from 2000
- **10** Identifying 2D shapes
- **11** Drawing 2D shapes
- **12** Reading instruments
- **13** Reading instruments
- **14** Numbers in the environment
- **15** Continuing patterns

COPYMASTERS

- **171** Finding half by partitioning
- **172** Finding quarters by partitioning
- **173** Finding thirds by partitioning
- **174** Finding fifths by partitioning
- **175** Finding tenths by partitioning
- **176** Area
- **177** Area in centimetres
- **180** Thousands, hundreds, tens and ones
- **181** Thousands, hundreds, tens and ones

Pathways through the materials/record sheets

L3:1 An activity weekend

PAGES 2 AND 3

At school

SKILLS, CONCEPTS AND KNOWLEDGE

- Counting to 30
- Addition to 30
- Subtraction of two-digit numbers from 40 (money)

PRE-ASSESSMENT

Can the child:

- count up to 30 accurately?
- write the numerals 1–30?
- add two numbers which make a total of less than 30?
- subtract a two-digit number from a number less than 40?
- use the £ sign?

The story

The classroom scene on page 2 reintroduces the characters Lisa, Rupa, Nicky and David. Twenty of the children are going on a trip, and the teacher is asking them to bring in the last payment on the following day. Page 3 shows them producing the money.

The pages may be used as a basis for comparing the classroom in the illustrations with children's own classrooms, and for discussing the sports and activities in which the characters are likely to participate. Children may want to discuss their own favourite sports and pastimes.

Copymaster 1 provides a format for children to record their answers to questions in the textbook.

Maths content and resources

The classroom scene on page 2 shows counting and addition in a real-life situation.

Pages 2 and 3 of Number Workbook 1 give children more experience of addition and subtraction. They remind children of the symbols +, – and =, and give pictorial clues to the processes. Addition and subtraction to 20 are frequently and regularly revisited throughout Level 3 to encourage the development of quick recall of the addition and subtraction facts.

Copymasters 5 and 6 provide more addition and subtraction work. These sheets may be modified with correction fluid if yet more practice is needed.

Page 3 of the textbook extends subtraction to two-digit numbers in the context of money. The emphasis is on arranging the subtraction vertically, using drawings of £10 notes and £1 coins as a starting point. The work is developed on pages 4 and 5 of Number Workbook 1 and on Copymasters 7 and 8.

Two-digit numbers

Use base-ten apparatus and numeral cards 0–9.

Children with difficulties need to revise place value regularly. Base–ten apparatus is ideal for this, and can be supported by cards which show how the position of a numeral shows its value. For example, 23 can be shown as 2 tens and 3 ones with base-ten apparatus, and as 20 and 3 with numeral cards.

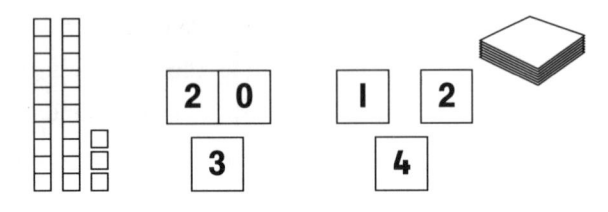

The cards can also help with addition and subtraction. For example, 23 + 12 can be shown as 20 + 10 and 3 + 2.

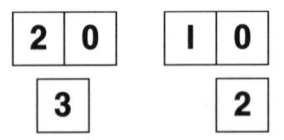

The materials

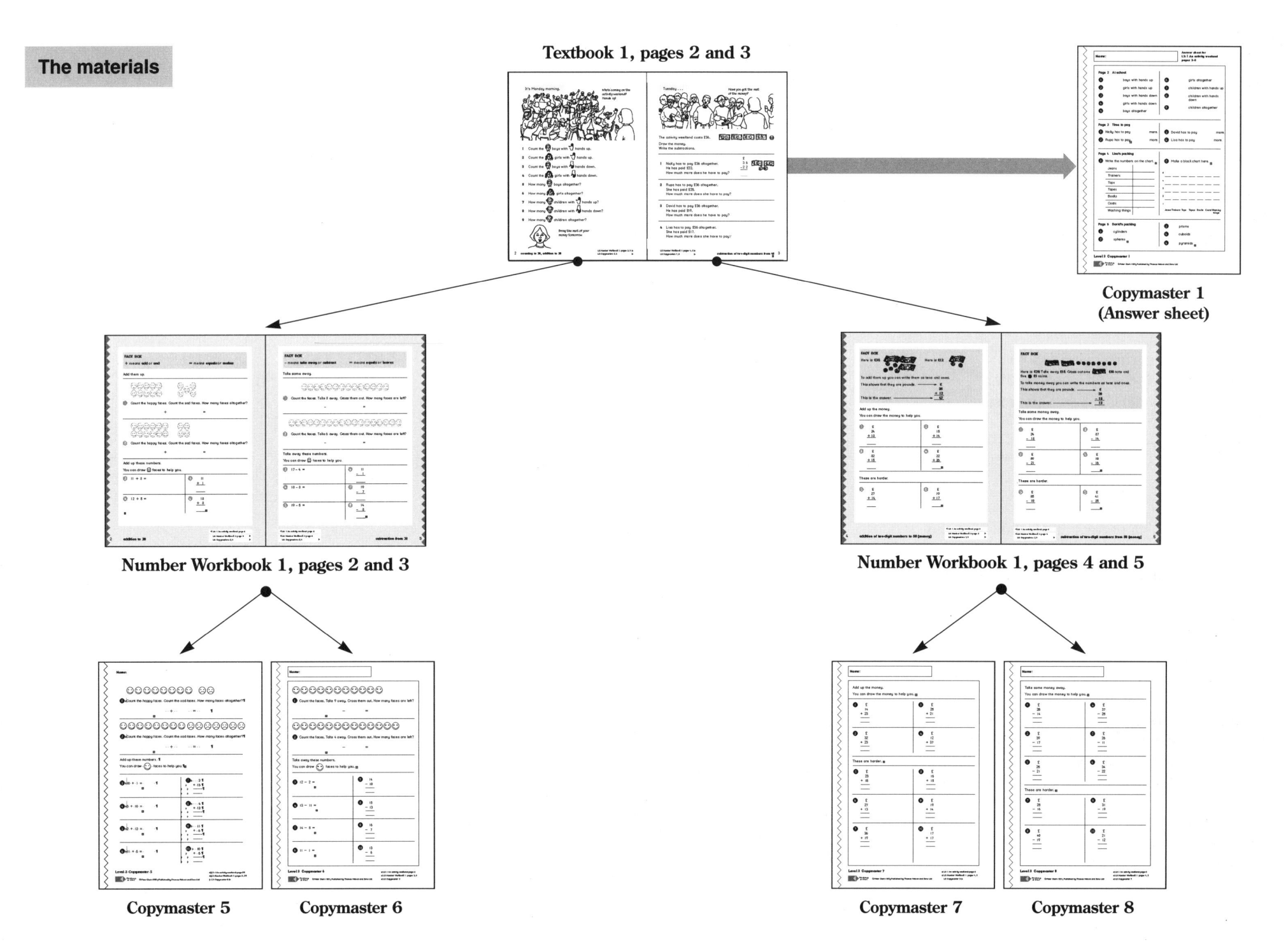

Textbook 1, pages 2 and 3

Copymaster 1 (Answer sheet)

Number Workbook 1, pages 2 and 3

Number Workbook 1, pages 4 and 5

Copymaster 5

Copymaster 6

Copymaster 7

Copymaster 8

L3:1 An activity weekend

PAGES 4 AND 5

Packing for the weekend

SKILLS, CONCEPTS AND KNOWLEDGE

- Making a table
- Making a block chart
- Identifying 3D shapes

PRE-ASSESSMENT

Can the child:
- make a table when collecting data?
- make a block chart to show results?
- identify cylinders, spheres, prisms, cuboids and pyramids?

The story

The illustrations on pages 4 and 5 show Lisa and David packing for the activity weekend. Discuss with children which clothes they would take on such a weekend, bearing in mind that they would be out in all kinds of weather, doing water sports as well as dry activities.

Lisa is fairly disorganised, and is trying to sort out her clothes. David is more concerned with the food supplies he is taking. As well as looking at the shapes of the containers, ask children to list 5 sweets which they would need to survive a weekend away.

Copymaster 1 provides a format for children to record their answers to questions in the textbook.

Maths content and resources

Page 4 of the textbook asks children to sort Lisa's clothes and make a table of the results. This is followed up by making a block chart to show the information, building on work covered at Level 2. There are formats for a larger table and a larger block chart on Copymaster 11. This can be used for a variety of data collection and presentation activities.

Pages 2 and 3 of Topic Workbook 1 provide a parallel exercise using the same context. Page 2 also introduces the convention of tallying in fives.

Copymasters 9 and 10 give children practice in tallying and translating a tally into a block chart.

Page 5 of the textbook looks at 3D shapes commonly used for packaging: cylinders, spheres, prisms, cuboids and pyramids. These, and cones and cubes, are revisited on pages 4 and 5 of Topic Workbook 1.

Copymasters 12 to 15 provide nets of a square-based pyramid, a tetrahedron, a triangular prism, a cuboid and a cube. They are designed to fit together to make structures when they are made up.

All the work on 3D shape should be introduced and reinforced by handling, rolling and stacking real shapes. Packaging is a rich resource for this.

Making nets into shapes

Copymasters 12 to 15 provide nets of 3D shapes. They do not have flaps because children can find it frustrating to try to glue a flap inside a shape, and the results can be disappointing. It is recommended that they use masking tape to join the edges after cutting and folding. This allows some leeway for repositioning. The nets should be photocopied on to stiff paper or thin card for the best results. They can be enlarged to A3-size to make bigger shapes.

Children can use the 3D shapes they make for projects such as:
- Designing packaging for sweets and cosmetics
- Making structures which use a combination of shapes
- Sorting into sets of shapes with different numbers of faces, edges and corners (vertices)

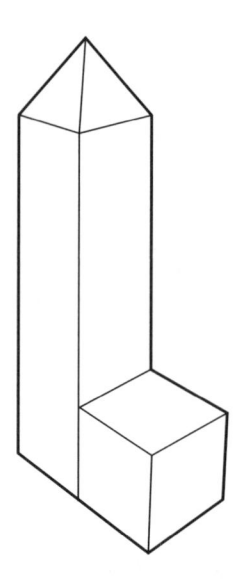

L3:1 An activity weekend

The materials

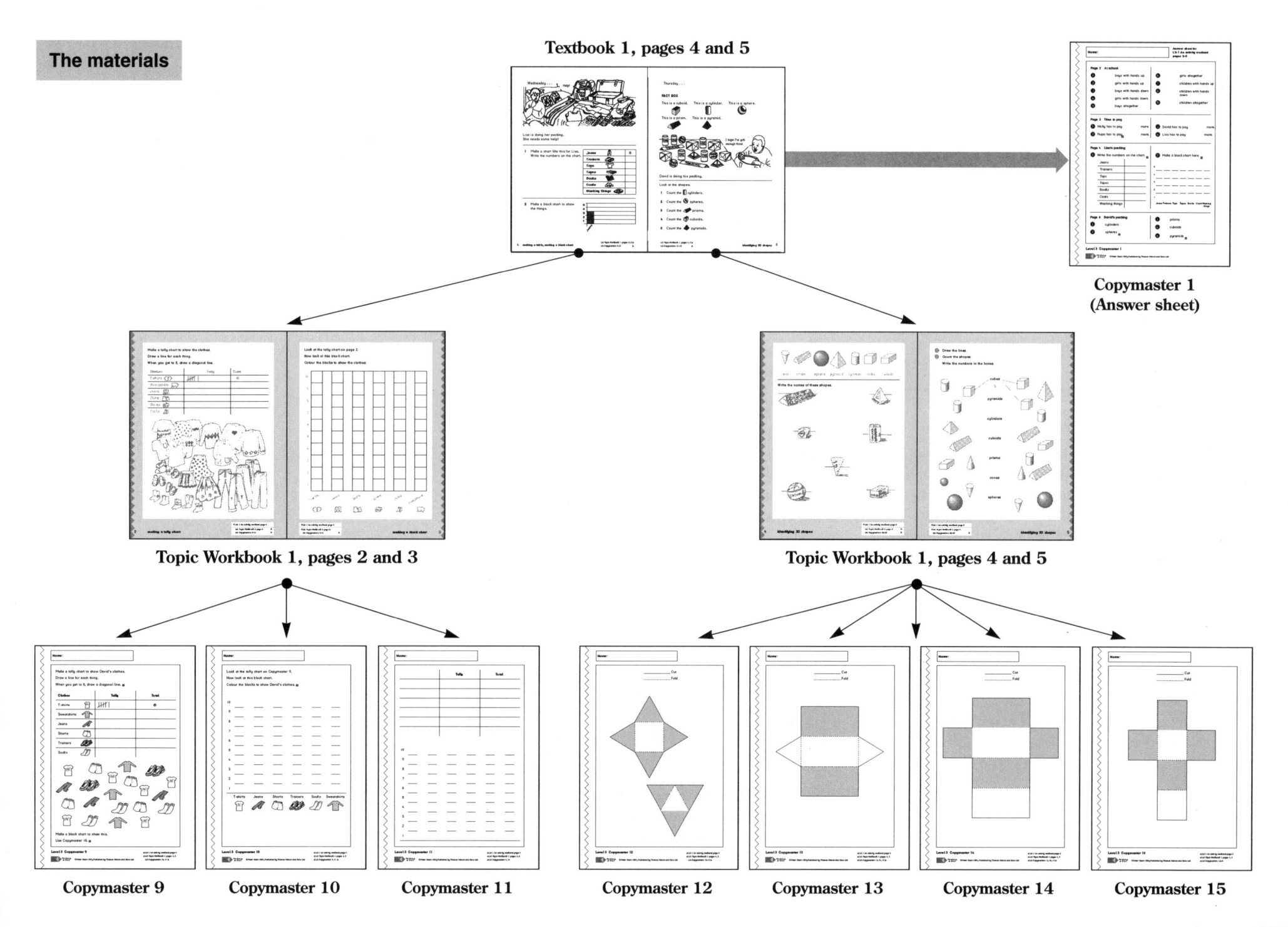

Textbook 1, pages 4 and 5

Copymaster 1 (Answer sheet)

Topic Workbook 1, pages 2 and 3

Topic Workbook 1, pages 4 and 5

Copymaster 9

Copymaster 10

Copymaster 11

Copymaster 12

Copymaster 13

Copymaster 14

Copymaster 15

L3:1 An activity weekend

PAGES 6 AND 7
Setting off

SKILLS, CONCEPTS AND KNOWLEDGE

▶ Multiplication tables (2×)
▶ Half of a set (division)

PRE-ASSESSMENT

Can the child:
▶ count in twos?
▶ continue a pattern of twos?
▶ find half of a set?

The story

These pages reflect the preparation all school parties experience immediately before a trip. Discuss why the children line up in twos, and why the minibuses should be loaded equally. Children could investigate queues in school, and look at how things are shared out in the classroom.

Copymaster 2 provides a format for children to record their answers to questions in the textbook.

Maths content and resources

Page 6 of the textbook takes the context of organising people and things into pairs for looking at the development of a pattern of twos and the two-times table. This work is revisited throughout Level 3. Pages 6 and 7 of Number Workbook 1 reinforce the work and show the pattern of twos in an array of numbers.

Copymaster 16 gives children another chance to develop the sequence of numbers in the two-times table, with visual clues.

Page 7 of the textbook complements the work on pairs and the two-times table by looking at dividing by 2 and halves. Children should have access to apparatus such as counters to demonstrate the process in a practical way. This is followed up on page 8 of Number Workbook 1 which asks children to divide 2D shapes in half. There are more shapes to divide in half on Copymaster 17. These can be cut out and cut in half with scissors.

On page 9 of Number Workbook 1, children draw lines to partition sets into halves. This is supported by a worksheet on Copymaster 18.

Patterns of 2

Use squared paper.
Children can make their own square and rectangular arrays of numbers on squared paper. 2-centimetre squares are best.

1	2	3
4	5	6
7	8	9

1	2	3	4	5	6	7
8	9	10	11	12	13	14
15	16	17	18	19	20	21

They then colour the appropriate squares to show the two-times table. Encourage them to look at the resulting patterns and try to explain why they look different.

Half, odd, even

Use small cubes.

Two children play. They choose whether to be 'even' or 'odd'. They take turns to take a handful of cubes and set them out in front of them. Encourage them to estimate the number of cubes. Co-operatively, they then divide the cubes in half either by partitioning or by sharing.

If there is one cube left over the number is odd and 'odd' wins. If there is no remainder, 'even' wins.

The materials

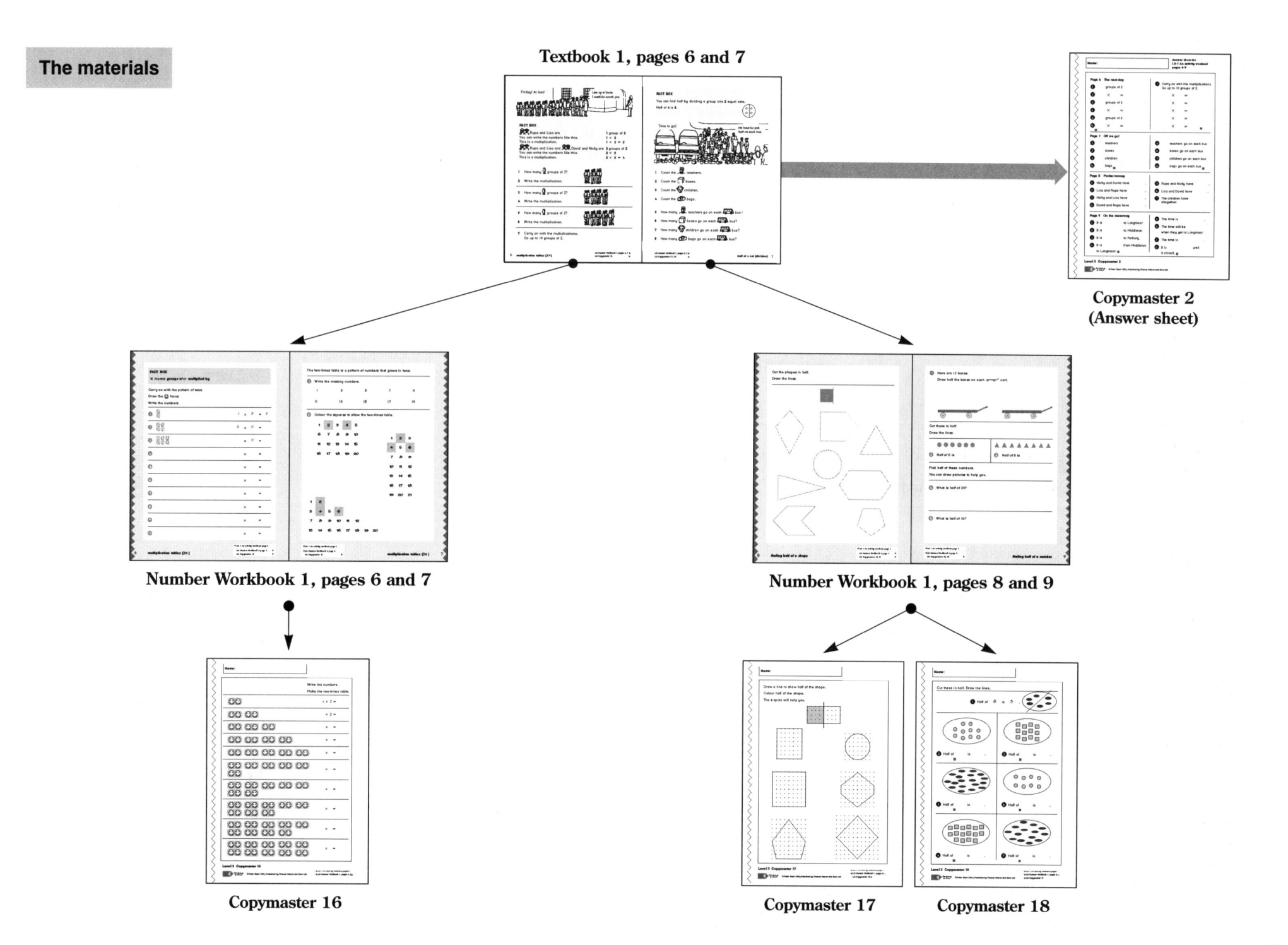

Textbook 1, pages 6 and 7

Copymaster 2
(Answer sheet)

Number Workbook 1, pages 6 and 7

Number Workbook 1, pages 8 and 9

Copymaster 16

Copymaster 17

Copymaster 18

L3:1 An activity weekend

PAGES 8 AND 9
On the way

SKILLS, CONCEPTS AND KNOWLEDGE

- Addition problems using decimal notation (money)
- Distance in miles
- Analogue time

PRE-ASSESSMENT

Can the child:
- identify amounts of money?
- write money in decimal form?
- add amounts of money to make a total of less than £20?
- read distance in miles from a road sign?
- calculate 'time to go' in hours and quarter hours?

The story

On the minibus, the characters discuss how much pocket money they have. They then interrogate the teacher about where they are going, how much longer the journey will be and what time they will arrive.

Discuss the issue of pocket money with the children: how much do they think they should be given, and what do they like to spend it on?

If possible, go out of school to look at signs which indicate distances, or, alternatively, ask children to write down what they see on signs when they are out of school. Discuss any regular journeys they make, and find out whether they know how long these journeys take.

Copymaster 2 provides a format for children to record their answers to questions in the textbook.

Maths content and resources

The pocket money problems on page 8 of the textbook should be supported by the use of real or plastic coins to show the amounts involved.

Page 10 of Number Workbook 1 and Copymaster 19 give children more experience of writing amounts of money in decimal notation. Page 11 provides additions (money) and asks children to draw coins to represent amounts of money. Copymaster 20 follows this up.

Page 9 of the textbook looks at distance in miles, and time in hours and quarter hours. Children are asked to add and subtract amounts of time. Page 6 of Topic Workbook 1 is also about distance, and page 7 has more time problems. There are two more time worksheets on Copymasters 21 and 22.

Decimal riches

Use a paper baseboard for each player, and two or three sets of numeral cards 0 to 9.

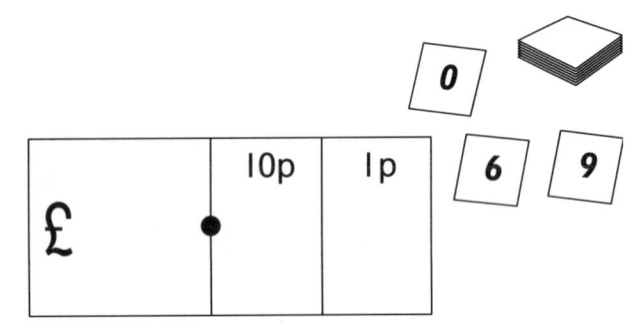

The cards are shuffled and placed face down in a pile. The players try to make the largest amount of money. They take turns to pick up a card and place it in the **£**, **10p**, or **1p** column on the baseboard. Once a card has been placed it cannot be moved. When all three spaces are filled on all the baseboards, the players decide who has the largest amount of money. That person wins. Encourage them to use plastic coins to show the amounts of money the cards represent.

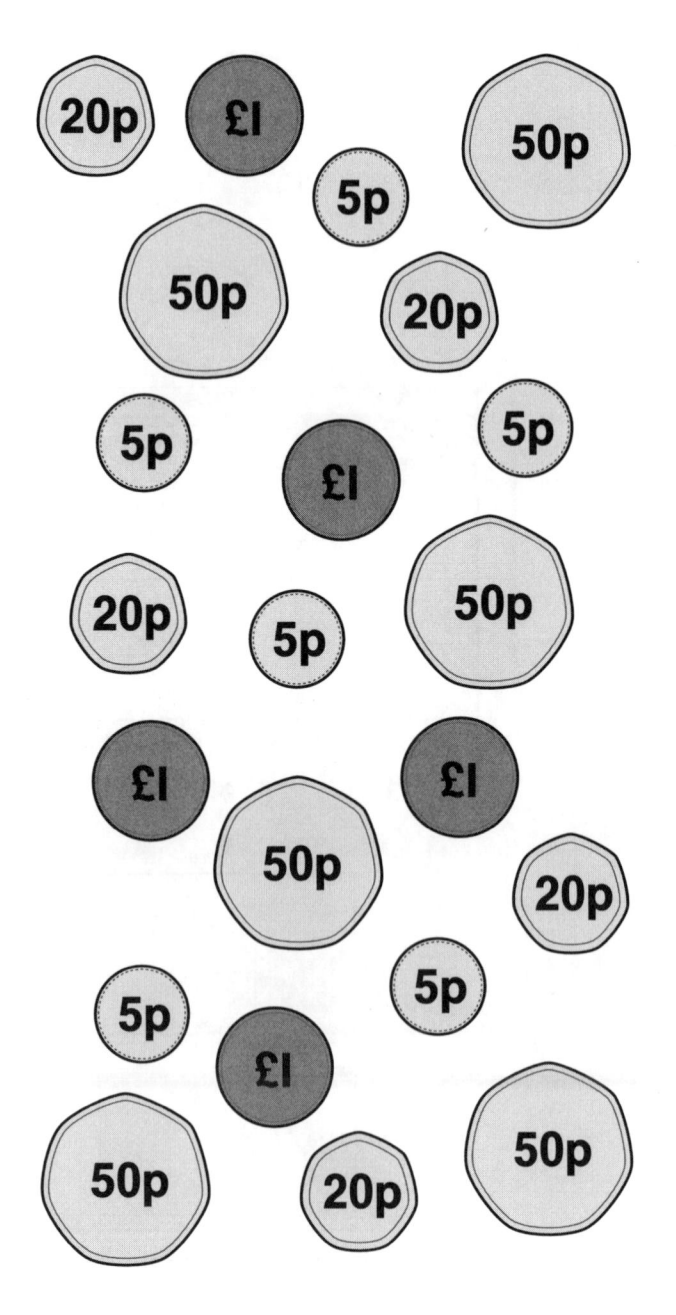

40 L3:1 An activity weekend

The materials

Textbook 1, pages 8 and 9

Copymaster 2 (Answer sheet)

Number Workbook 1, pages 10 and 11

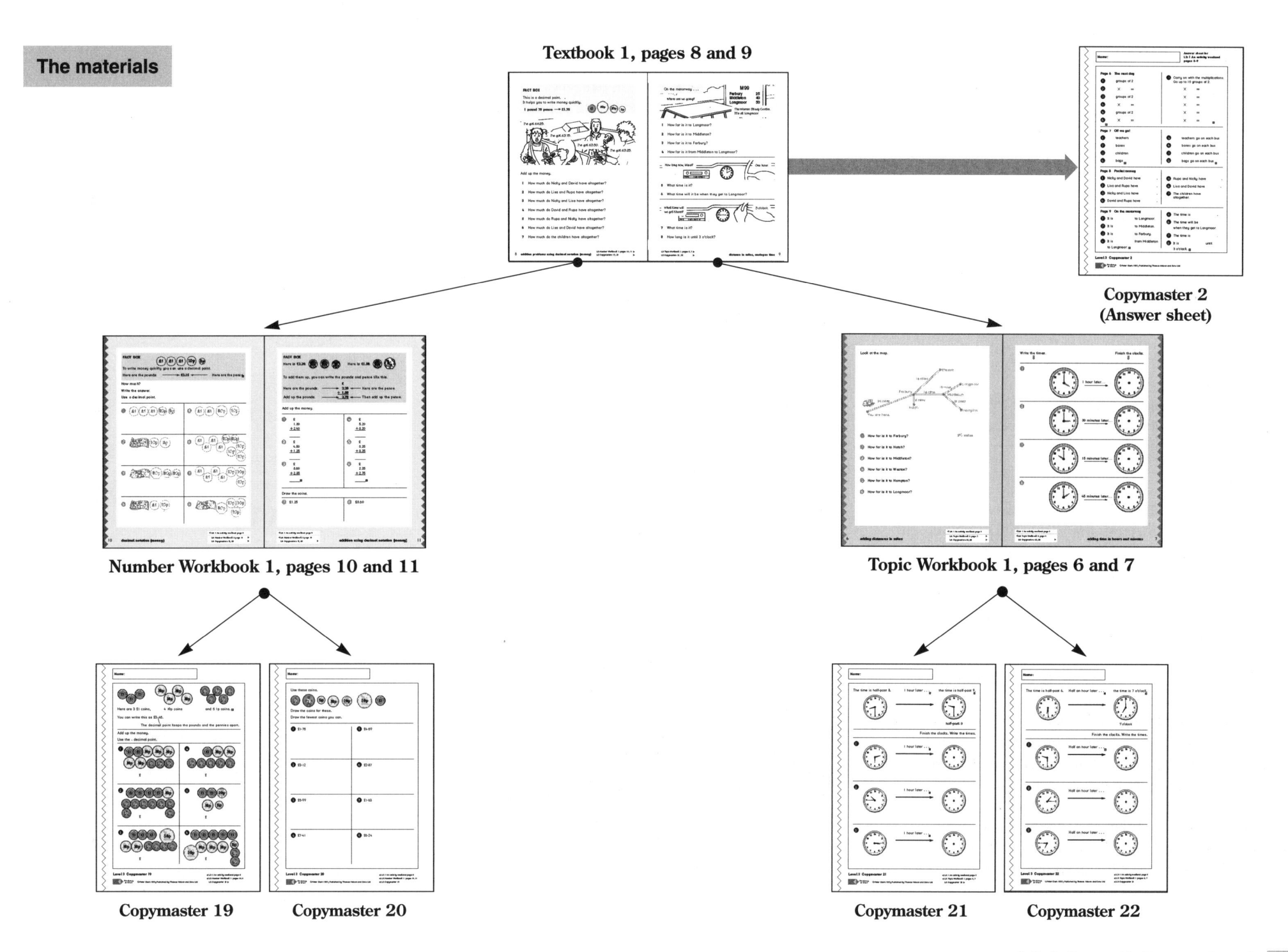

Topic Workbook 1, pages 6 and 7

Copymaster 19 **Copymaster 20**

Copymaster 21 **Copymaster 22**

L3:1 An activity weekend   41

PAGES 10 AND 11
The Warren Study Centre

SKILLS, CONCEPTS AND KNOWLEDGE

- Co-ordinates
- Identifying 2D shapes
- Drawing 2D shapes

PRE-ASSESSMENT

Can the child:
- use letter and number co-ordinates to describe position?
- identify squares, rectangles and triangles?
- draw squares, rectangles and triangles?

The story

Before arriving at the Warren Study Centre the characters pass through the village of Longmoor and look at a local map. The work on co-ordinates can be made more immediate by looking at a real local map overlaid with a grid of squares to help find places quickly. Children can look for the square containing their road, park or school. This may develop into an interest in the local area.

The front of the Warren Study Centre shows the most commonly occurring 2D shapes – squares, rectangles and triangles. Look for these in the school building. This may be a good opportunity to identify any 5-sided shape as a pentagon, and any 6-sided shape as a hexagon. It is for teachers to decide whether it is appropriate to introduce the terms 'regular' and 'irregular' to describe these shapes.

Copymaster 3 provides a format for children to record their answers to questions in the Textbook.

Maths content and resources

Page 10 of the textbook introduces a simple grid with co-ordinates as a means of identifying approximate position. The convention of using the **x** co-ordinate first and the **y** co-ordinate second should be encouraged by always using the letter first (for example, **A1**, **D4**).

Pages 8 and 9 of Topic Workbook 1 give some more work, including drawing shapes in positions specified by co-ordinates.

There are two more worksheets on co-ordinates on Copymasters 23 and 24. Copymaster 25 provides a blank grid with co-ordinates, so that children can make their own patterns and drawings and write down the co-ordinates for others to interpret. This work is developed and revisited throughout Level 3.

The work on 2D shapes on page 11 of the textbook involves identifying and drawing common 2D shapes.

This is extended to pentagons and hexagons on pages 10 and 11 of Topic Workbook 1.

Copymaster 26 introduces the heptagon.

Capture the cubes

Use Copymaster 25 and some small cubes.

Copymaster 25 has only 25 squares, which is ideal for short games involving co-ordinates. Encourage the children to suggest ideas for games.

This game is for two players. Each player has a copy of Copymaster 25 and 4 cubes. They place a screen (such as a large book) between them. They put their 4 cubes in any 4 different squares on the copymaster and then take turns to guess where the other player's cubes are. When a player gusses correctly, (s)he captures the other player's cube and puts it on his/her own sheet. The first player to capture all 8 cubes wins. Alternatively, the player with the most cubes after 5 minutes wins.

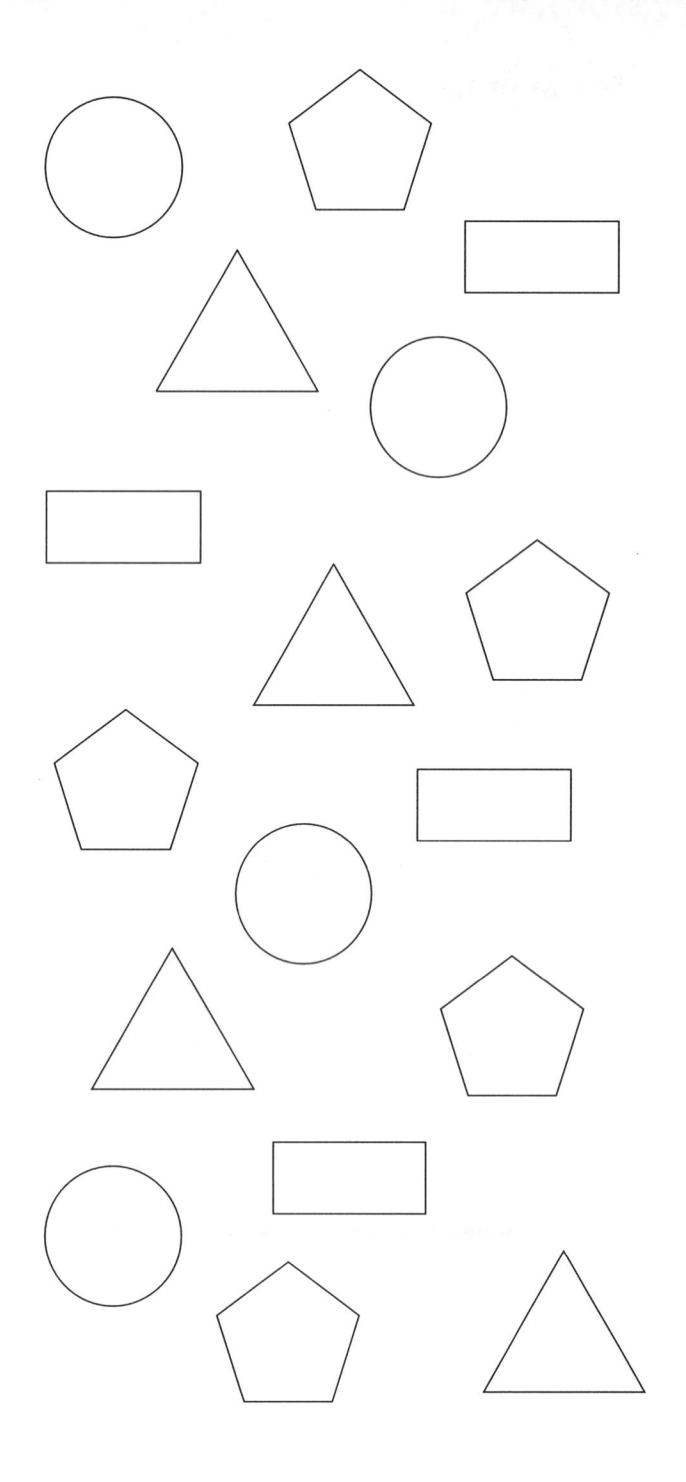

L3:1 An activity weekend

The materials

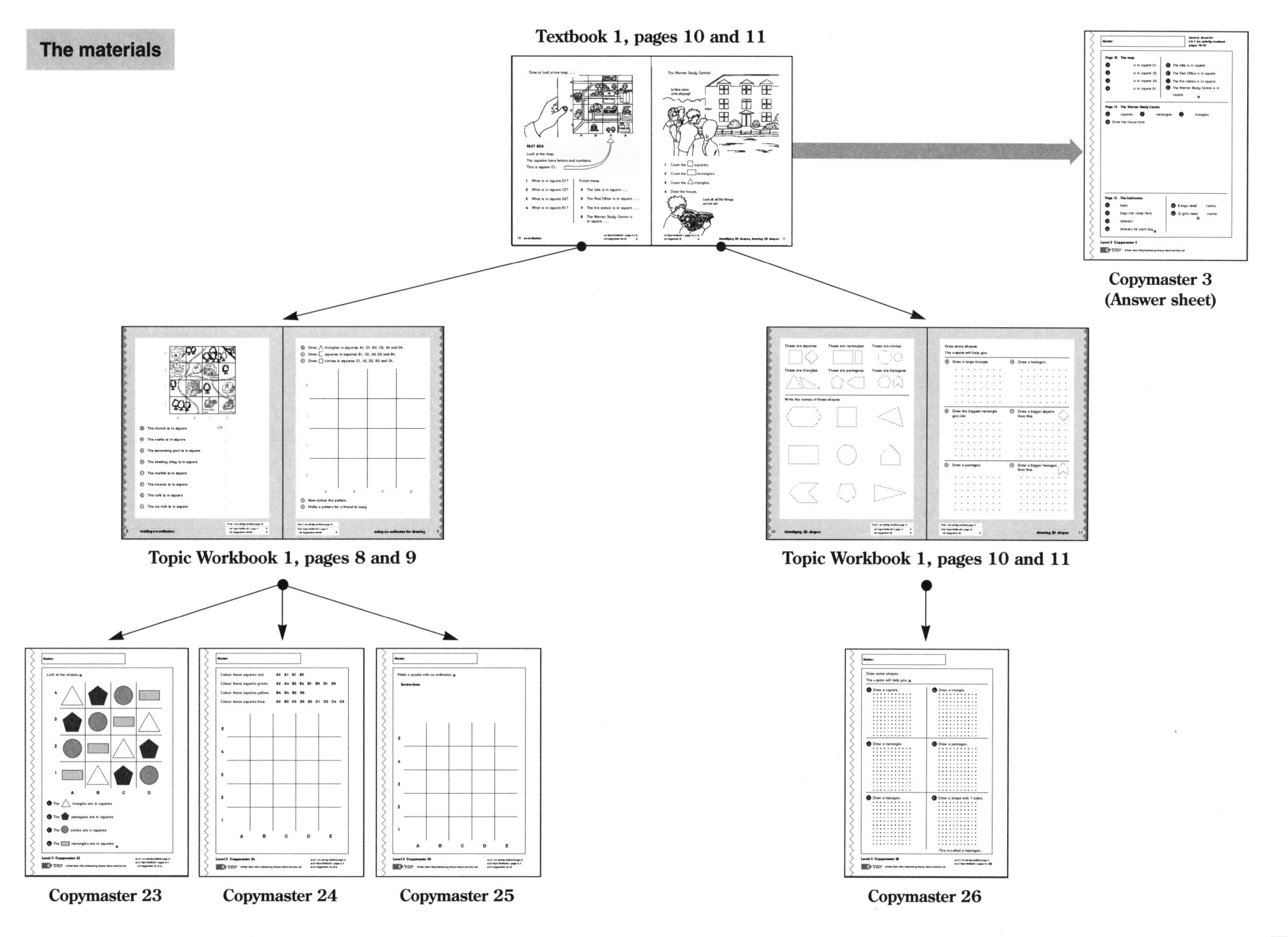

Textbook 1, pages 10 and 11

Copymaster 3 (Answer sheet)

Topic Workbook 1, pages 8 and 9

Topic Workbook 1, pages 10 and 11

Copymaster 23

Copymaster 24

Copymaster 25

Copymaster 26

L3:1 An activity weekend

43

PAGES 12 AND 13
Settling in

SKILLS, CONCEPTS AND KNOWLEDGE
▶ Groups of four
▶ Reading a chart

PRE-ASSESSMENT
Can the child:
▶ identify groups of four?
▶ continue a pattern of fours?
▶ interpret a simple chart (database)?

The story

Inside the Warren Study Centre, the characters look at their rooms. Then they find a chart showing a list of domestic jobs which they will have to do during the weekend. This is rather a surprise. These pages can be related to children's own home lives by discussing whether they have to share a room, whether they have bunk beds and how the living space is allocated in their homes. Find out which jobs they do at home. It may be possible to make a chart to show which days children do the jobs. This can also lead on to looking at school timetables.

Copymasters 3 and 4 provide formats for children to record their answers to questions in the textbook.

Maths content and resources

Page 12 of the textbook looks at groups of four in the context of four people sharing a room.

The ideas are reinforced and developed in Topic Workbook 1. Page 12 asks children to find different shapes which can be made from four squares or four equilateral triangles. Investigating all the possible shapes will lead on to a consideration of rotation.

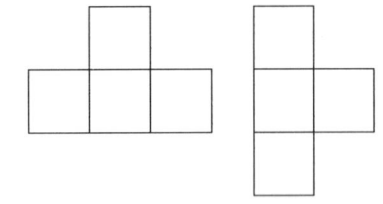

These shapes are the same (rotated).

These shapes are the same (rotated).

Page 13 develops the four-times table in the context of sides of a square.

Copymasters 27 and 28 develop this work on the four-times table. The work on multiplication is extensively developed and revisited throughout Level 3, and teachers may wish to return to these worksheets.

Page 13 of the textbook features a Carroll diagram which represents a timetable of jobs to be done.

There is further work on the same theme on pages 14 and 15 of Topic Workbook 1, where children are asked to interpret a chart, and then to make one of their own.

This method of sorting and organising is developed on Copymasters 29 and 30. These ask children to extract information from a chart showing shapes and colours and then make a chart of their own to show the properties. This work can be extended to include any kind of sorting activity where more than one criterion is involved.

A shape sort

Use a large sheet of paper, coloured shapes such as logic blocks in a bag or a box, and felt pens.

A group of children can develop their own sorting chart. They may need the chart to be started for them:

	Red	Blue
Circle		
Square		

They take turns to pick up a shape and place it in the correct box on the chart. If they pick up a shape which has not been allowed for on the chart, they will need to add a column and/or a row.

L3:1 An activity weekend

The materials

Textbook 1, pages 12 and 13

Copymaster 3 (Answer sheet)

Copymaster 4 (Answer sheet)

Topic Workbook 1, pages 12 and 13

Topic Workbook 1, pages 14 and 15

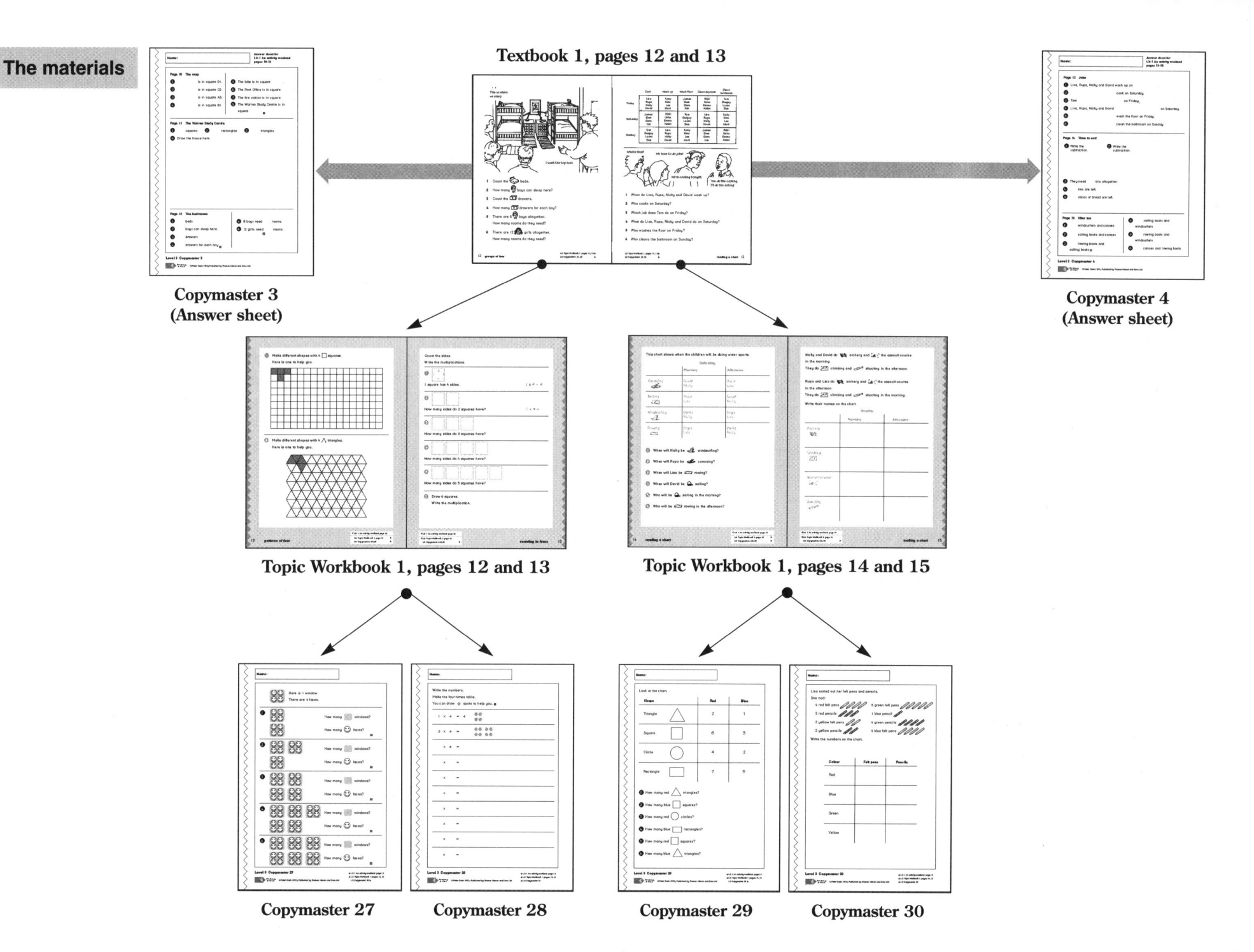

Copymaster 27

Copymaster 28

Copymaster 29

Copymaster 30

L3:1 An activity weekend

PAGES 14 AND 15
Friday evening

SKILLS, CONCEPTS AND KNOWLEDGE
▶ Addition to 20
▶ Subtraction from 20
▶ Addition facts to 20

PRE-ASSESSMENT
Can the child:
▶ add two numbers to make a total of less than 20?
▶ subtract a number from another number less than 20?
▶ recall any number facts to 20?

The story
This textbook ends with the characters making their tea and having a look outside in anticipation of the activities they will be doing over the weekend. The pages can be used as a basis for discussing whether children help to prepare meals at home and which outside interests or hobbies they enjoy.

An interesting problem-solving activity is to try to work out how much bread, butter, beans etc. a group of children would need to take away for a weekend. Use questions like *'How many slices of bread would each child need?'* and *'How many children could share a tin of baked beans?'* This work is especially relevant if children are actually going away on a trip.

Copymaster 4 provides a format for children to record their answers to questions in the textbook.

Maths content and resources
Pages 14 and 15 of the textbook revisit addition to 20 and subtraction from 20, in the contexts of preparing a meal and looking at water-sports equipment on the lake.

Pages 12 and 13 of Number Workbook 1 give more additions and subtractions. Page 14 looks at patterns of numbers in the addition facts which make 11, 12, 13 and 14, and Page 15 looks at patterns in the subtraction facts for the same numbers.

This work could easily be extended to include all the numbers between 0 and 20. To assist with preparation for such an investigation, Copymasters 31 and 32 cover the numbers 8 and 9. These worksheets could be modified to include the other numbers.

The work on addition and subtraction facts is revisited many times throughout Level 3, and teachers may wish to pace the introduction of these worksheets accordingly.

An addition facts game
Use a sheet of paper to keep score and two pots with ten counters or cubes in each.

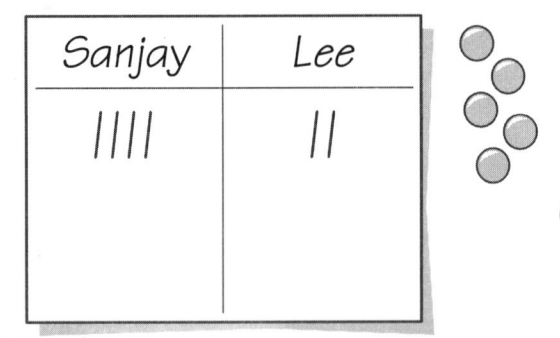

Sanjay	Lee
||||	||

Two children play. Each player has a pot. Without the other player seeing, each player selects some cubes from his/her pot. On the count of 3 they both put the cubes down on the table in front of them. The first person to say how many cubes there are altogether wins a point, and this is recorded on the scoring sheet. The first person to gain 10 points is the winner.

Each child will know the number he or she selected. The challenge is to identify the opponent's number and add it on. Initially, children may do this by counting on, but after a few games they should begin to remember some of the number facts.

The same game can be played with numeral cards (1 to 9) or playing cards (ace to 9 or 10). The number ranges of cards or cubes can be modified to limit the range of answers.

L3:1 An activity weekend

The materials

Textbook 1, pages 14 and 15

Copymaster 4
(Answer sheet)

Number Workbook 1, pages 12 and 13

Number Workbook 1, pages 14 and 15

Copymaster 31

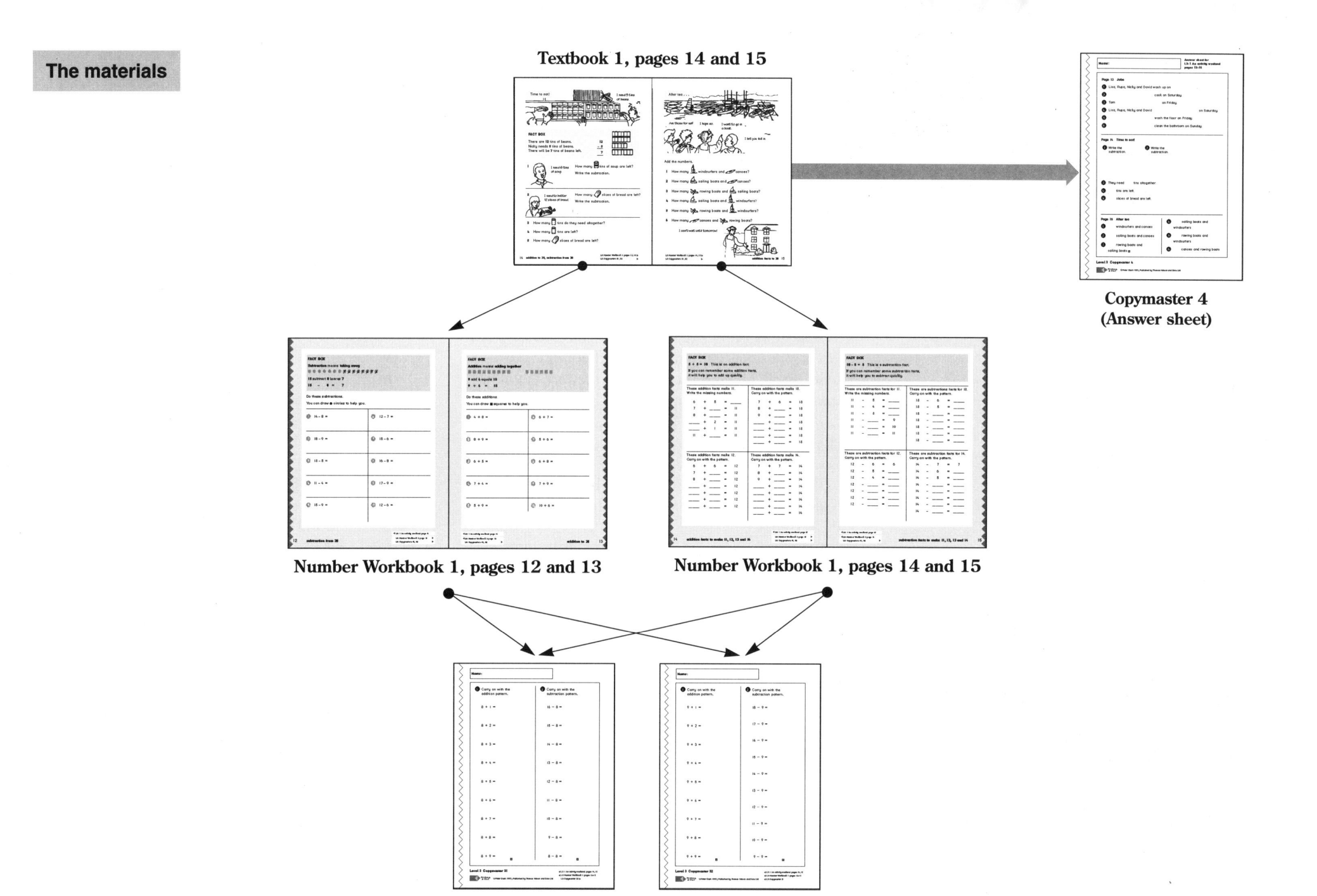

Copymaster 32

L3:1 An activity weekend

L3:2 Water sports

PAGES 2 AND 3
Saturday morning

SKILLS, CONCEPTS AND KNOWLEDGE
▶ Addition to 20
▶ Subtraction from 20
▶ 3D shapes – growing cubes and cuboids

PRE-ASSESSMENT
Can the child:
▶ recall any number facts to 20?
▶ identify cubes and cuboids?
▶ make cubes and cuboids from small cubes?

The story
The characters have breakfast at the Warren Study Centre. Discuss with the children what they and their family have for breakfast and how much washing up there is to do!

After breakfast, Lisa and Rupa sit outside on a small brick pillar waiting to start the day's events. Ask the children to guess what they will do first from the information in the picture. The canoes in the background are a clue!

Copymaster 33 provides a format for children to record their answers to questions in the textbook.

Maths content and resources
Page 2 of the textbook revisits addition and subtraction facts to 20 in the context of plates, cups and saucers.

There are more examples on pages 2 and 3 of Number Workbook 2, including additions and subtractions presented vertically.

Copymasters 37 and 38 provide additions and subtractions with the instruction *'Write the answers as fast as you can.'* This encourages children to use quick recall of those number facts they are beginning to remember.

Page 3 of the textbook concentrates on making cubes and cuboids from small cubes. Children will need access to real cubes to model the process.

Pages 2 and 3 of Topic Workbook 2 ask children to make more cubes and cuboids and to record their dimensions.

Copymasters 39 and 40 also ask children to make cuboids, and are organised so that they may be used as the start of an investigation into how cuboids grow and the number patterns generated by them.

Teachers may wish to extend this work on volume by putting cubes into boxes to see how many it takes to fill them.

Finish the facts
Use a sheet of paper and numeral cards 1 to 20.

Two children each make a list of numbers. Initially these should be between 1 and 10. Encourage them not to list the numbers in order. Each player takes a numeral card, and uses the other player's list to make the number on the card. They can use additions or subtractions. The number facts are completed on the sheet of paper.

```
6 + 1 = 7
4 + 3 = 7
2 + 5 = 7
9 − 2 = 7
1 +
8
7
```

[7]

This can be done co-operatively, or as a contest where the first to finish wins. Encourage the children to check and mark each other's lists.

The range of answers can be controlled by restricting the number range on the numeral cards. For example, use numeral cards between 5 and 10.

The materials

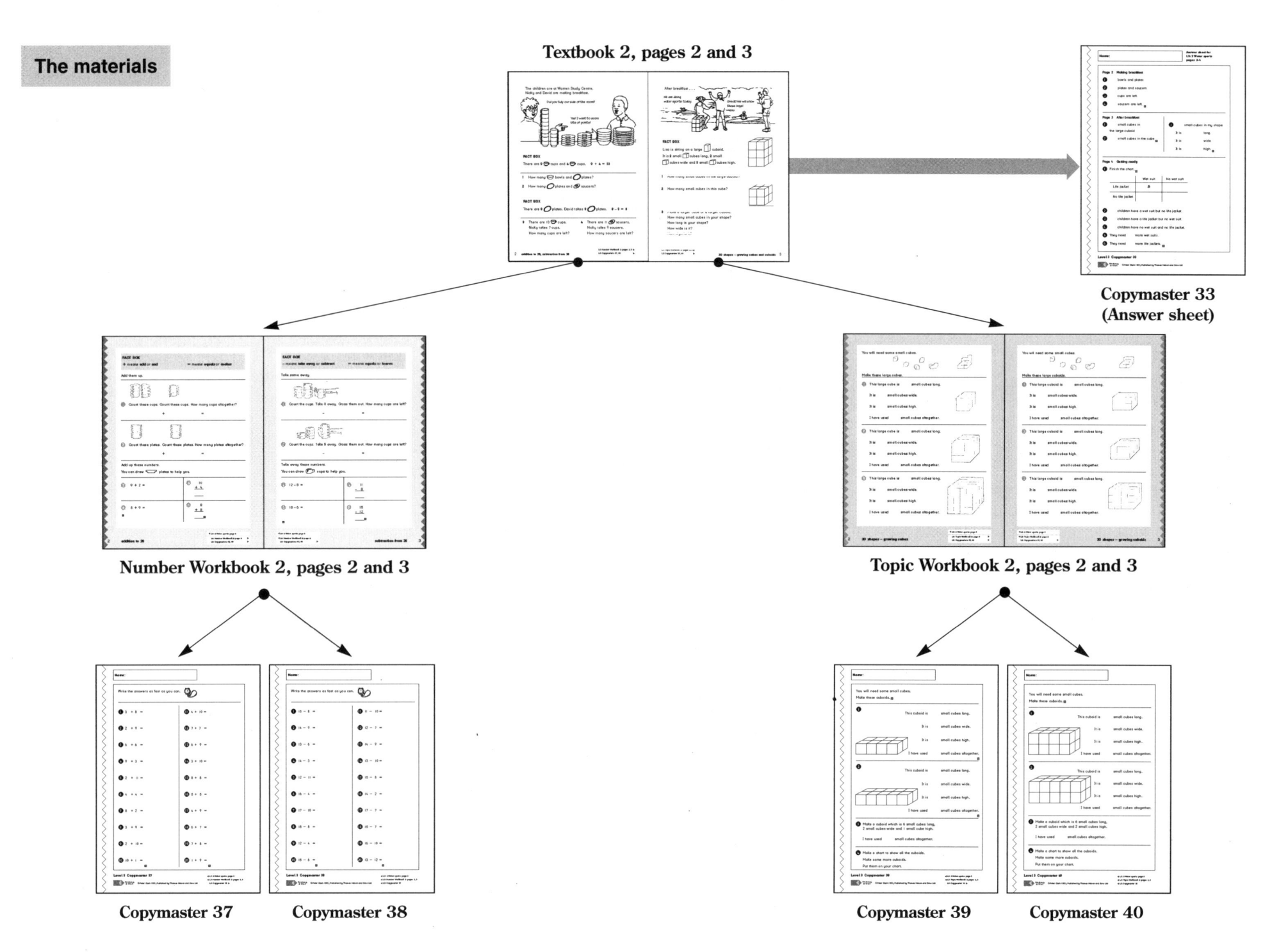

Textbook 2, pages 2 and 3

Copymaster 33 (Answer sheet)

Number Workbook 2, pages 2 and 3

Topic Workbook 2, pages 2 and 3

Copymaster 37   **Copymaster 38**

Copymaster 39   **Copymaster 40**

L3:2 Water sports 49

PAGES 4 AND 5
Canoeing

SKILLS, CONCEPTS AND KNOWLEDGE
▶ Collecting information and making a chart
▶ Multiplication tables (2×)

PRE-ASSESSMENT
Can the child:
▶ collect information in a chart?
▶ continue a pattern of twos?
▶ remember any of the two-times table?

The story

The characters get ready to go on the lake. Some are wearing wet suits and some are wearing life jackets. Ask the children what they think wet suits and life jackets are for. Discuss with them the importance of having the right safety equipment for all activities.

Once they are in their canoes the characters begin to explore the lake. Discuss the fact that there are 2 people in each canoe and each person has a paddle with 2 blades.

Copymasters 33 and 34 provide formats for children to record their answers to questions in the textbook.

Maths content and resources

Page 4 of the textbook focuses on sorting to two criteria using a Carroll diagram. Children will have some experience of this from Levels 1 and 2, but it is still a good idea for them to sort real materials on to Carroll diagrams drawn on large sheets of paper.

Pages 4 and 5 of Topic Workbook 2 give examples of how this might be done using coloured shapes such as logic blocks.

Copymasters 41 and 42 ask children to interpret and then to make a Carroll diagram.

Page 5 of the textbook looks again at the two-times table, in the context of pairs of children in canoes.

Page 4 of Number Workbook 2 sets out the two-times table in order, and page 5 emphasises the sequence of numbers generated and introduces the element of quick recall.

For children who need more practice in developing patterns of two there is another worksheet on Copymaster 43. For children who are beginning to develop quick recall there is a 'speed test' on Copymaster 44. If the twenty questions on this are too much for some children, it may be split down the middle.

Tables on a calculator

Most calculators have the capacity to store a function, for example, ×2. To set up the function to generate the two-times table, press **2**, **+**, **+**. This will have the effect of adding 2 each time **=** is pressed. The display can be reset to **0** by pressing **0**. The ×2 function can be used alongside squared paper or coloured rods to show how the two-times table develops numerically and as a staircase of rods.

To multiply any number by 2 repeatedly, press **2**, **×**, **×**. Put a number, for example **12**, into the display and press **=**. The calculator will multiply it by 2 to show **24**. This in turn will be doubled to **48**, and so on. Encourage the children to experiment with other numbers.

Suggest that children press **2**, **−**, **−**, and try to explain what is happening to the numbers.

The calculator can be reset to normal use by pressing **AC**, or by switching it off.

L3:2 Water sports

The materials

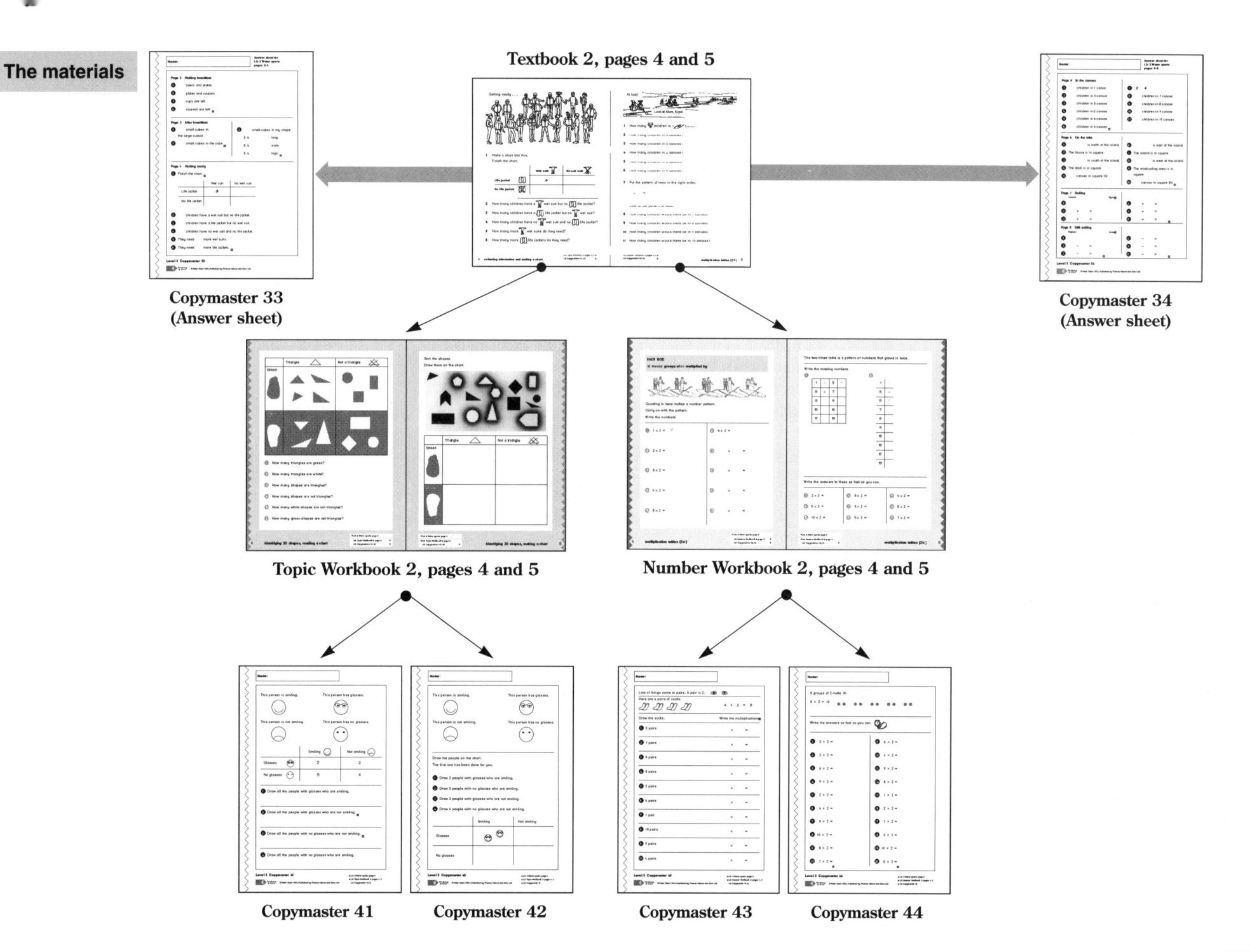

Textbook 2, pages 4 and 5

Copymaster 33 (Answer sheet)

Copymaster 34 (Answer sheet)

Topic Workbook 2, pages 4 and 5

Number Workbook 2, pages 4 and 5

Copymaster 41

Copymaster 42

Copymaster 43

Copymaster 44

L3:2 Water sports

PAGES 6 AND 7

Sailing

SKILLS, CONCEPTS AND KNOWLEDGE

- Co-ordinates and compass points
- Ordering numbers to 70
- Addition to 130

PRE-ASSESSMENT

Can the child:
- use letter and number co-ordinates to describe position?
- use the 4 compass points to describe position?
- order two-digit numbers?
- add two-digit numbers?

The story

The characters look at a map of the lake and decide they would like to try sailing next. Look at the map with the children and discuss which activities they would like to do. As an additional piece of work, ask them to draw the lake or to draw their own map of a lake.

The characters go sailing. Discuss with the children why the sails are triangles and what the numbers on the sails might mean.

Copymaster 34 provides a format for children to record their answers to questions in the textbook.

Maths content and resources

Page 6 of the textbook combines work on co-ordinates with work on compass points as children locate features on a map.

This work is reinforced on pages 6 and 7 of Topic Workbook 2 where children read a map and then draw boats in specified positions.

Copymaster 45 involves more drawing as children follow a plotted sailing course around the grid.

Copymaster 46 is about identifying compass points. (If teachers require a blank 5×5 grid for further work, Copymaster 25 may be used.)

Page 7 of the textbook develops the work on addition of two-digit numbers with the exchange of tens (when the total in the ones column is greater than 9). Many children find this difficult and base-ten apparatus is indispensable.

Page 6 of Number Workbook 2 encourages children to use base-ten blocks to find the answers, and page 7 asks them to order numbers to 70 and then to do some vertically presented additions.

For further addition practice there are two more worksheets on Copymasters 47 and 48. This is a great deal of work on one number topic, and teachers may wish to spread it over a period of time.

Collect base-ten

Use base-ten apparatus and 2 dice.

Children take turns to throw the dice and decide which number will represent the tens and which will represent the ones. They then take the appropriate rods and cubes from the base-ten apparatus to show the numbers. (They decide beforehand whether the highest or lowest numbers will win.)

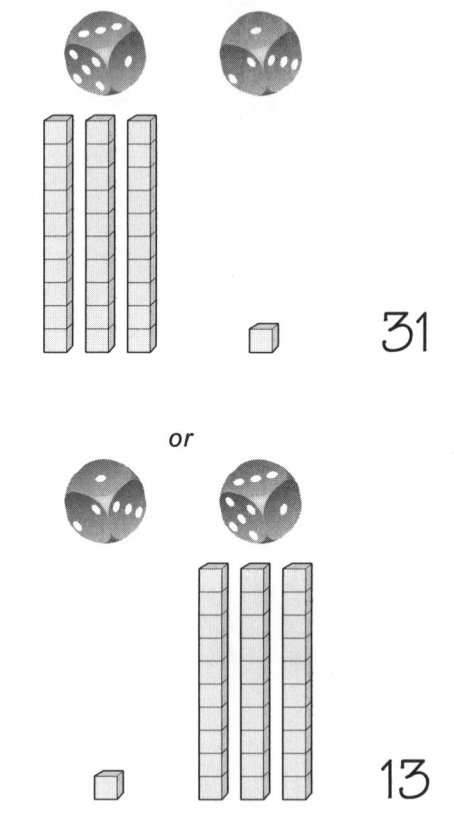

31

or

13

Another version of the game involves collecting base-ten apparatus to try to get to 100. A die representing the tens can be marked **0, 1, 2, 0, 1, 2** to restrict the number of tens available at each turn. The second die can be marked from **1** to **6** or from **5** to **10**.

Alternatively, children could start with 100 and use the dice throws to discard rods and cubes to reach 0.

52 **L3:2 Water sports**

The materials

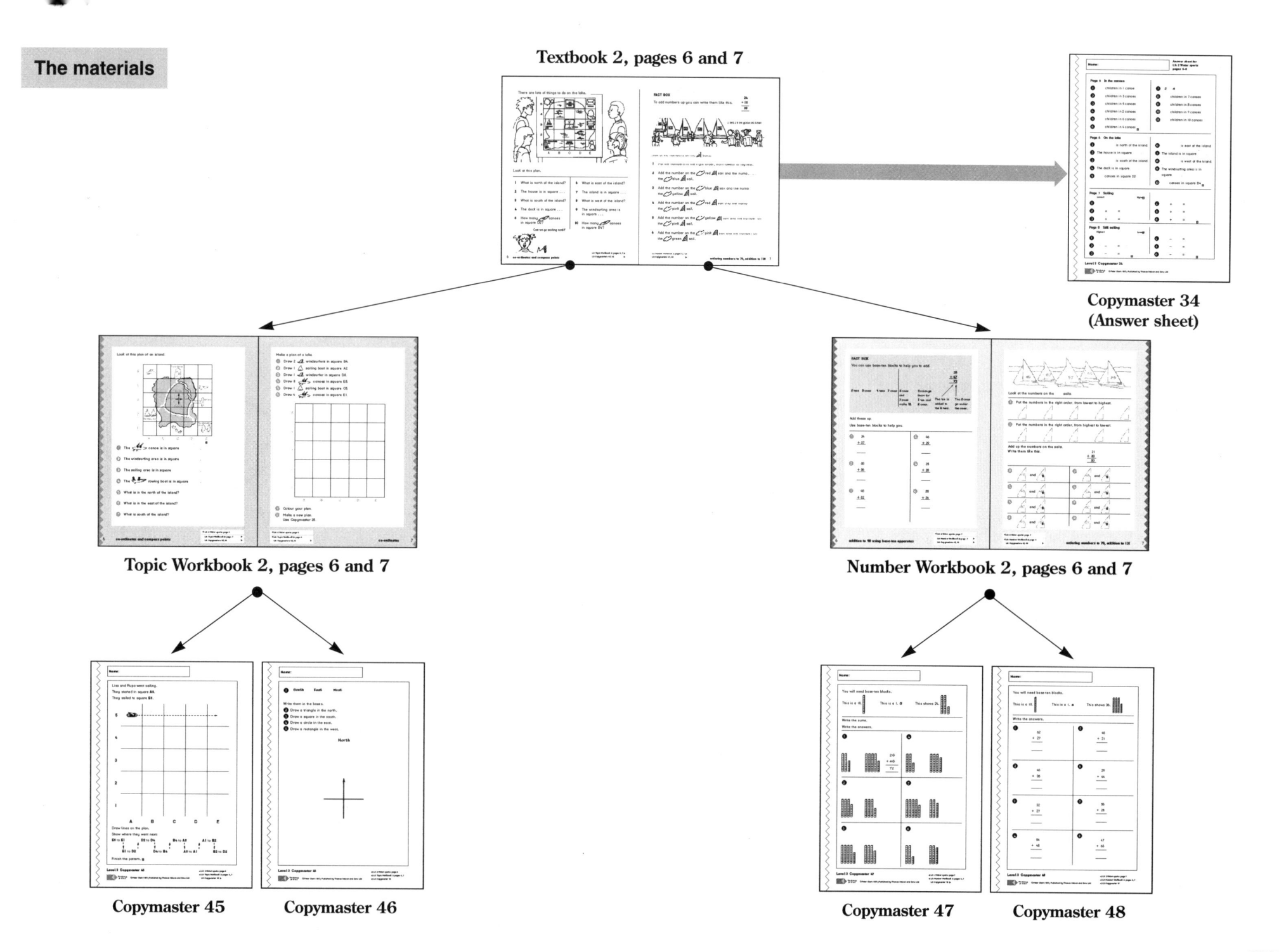

Textbook 2, pages 6 and 7

Copymaster 34 (Answer sheet)

Topic Workbook 2, pages 6 and 7

Number Workbook 2, pages 6 and 7

Copymaster 45

Copymaster 46

Copymaster 47

Copymaster 48

L3:2 Water sports 53

PAGES 8 AND 9
Still sailing!

SKILLS, CONCEPTS AND KNOWLEDGE

▶ Ordering numbers to 70
▶ Subtraction from 70
▶ Growing a number pattern of threes

PRE-ASSESSMENT

Can the child:
▶ order two-digit numbers?
▶ subtract one two-digit number from another?
▶ continue a pattern of threes?

The story

The characters are still sailing on the lake. Discuss how sailing boats use wind power and how they are steered. There are 3 people in each sailing boat. Ask the children what each crew member's job might be.

Copymasters 34 and 35 provide formats for children to record their answers to questions in the textbook.

Maths content and resources

Subtraction of two-digit numbers, including the exchange of tens, is featured on page 8 of the textbook. As with addition children should have access to base-ten apparatus to model the problems.

The use of base-ten apparatus in exchanging tens is shown on pages 8 and 9 of Number Workbook 2. Page 9 asks children to order numbers to 70 and then to do some vertically presented subtractions.

Copymasters 49 and 50 provide more examples of vertically presented subtractions.

The people in the sailing boats on page 9 of the textbook are used as a context for growing a pattern of threes, leading to the three-times table.

This is extended on page 8 of Topic Workbook 2. Page 9 looks at the three-times table in various number arrays. Children could experiment further by making their own number arrays on squared paper.

The three-times table is again practised on Copymasters 51 and 52.

This is an extensive body of work and may be spread over a period of time.

The planet of the three-legs

To focus on threes, set up a miniature project about an imaginary planet where everything is organised in threes. The inhabitants have three legs, three eyes, three arms and so on. Their vehicles have three wheels and their tables have three legs. Encourage children to suggest everyday objects and re-design them for the planet. For example, when laying the table they will need three knives, three forks and three spoons for each person.

At all times the repeating sequence of threes can be highlighted.

54 **L3:2 Water sports**

The materials

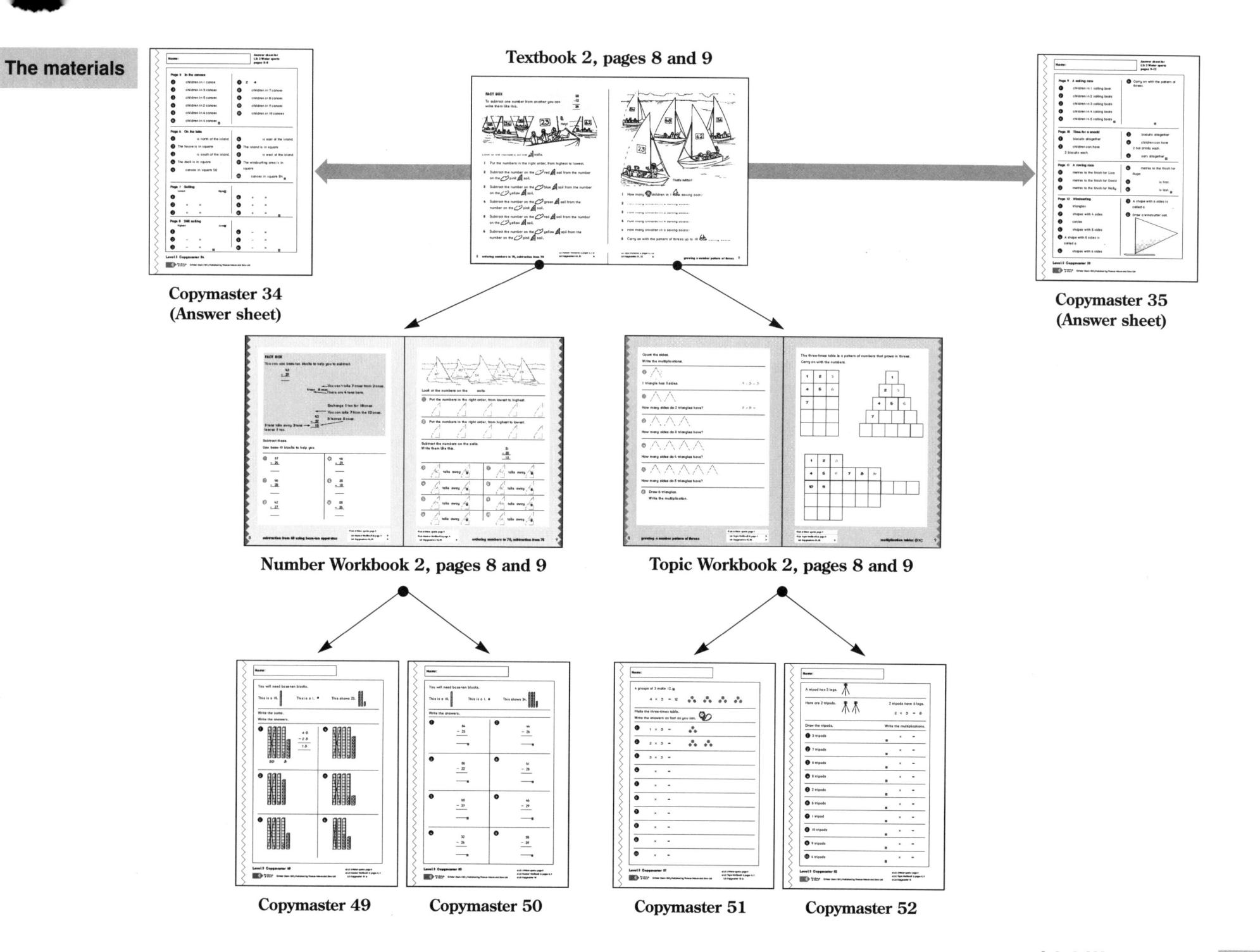

Textbook 2, pages 8 and 9

Copymaster 34 (Answer sheet)

Copymaster 35 (Answer sheet)

Number Workbook 2, pages 8 and 9

Topic Workbook 2, pages 8 and 9

Copymaster 49

Copymaster 50

Copymaster 51

Copymaster 52

L3:2 Water sports

PAGES 10 AND 11

Snacking and rowing

SKILLS, CONCEPTS AND KNOWLEDGE

- Dividing by 2
- Multiplying by 2 and 4
- Distance in metres

PRE-ASSESSMENT

Can the child:

- divide a two-digit number by 2?
- multiply a two-digit number by 2 and by 4?
- measure using metres and centimetres?

The story

After canoeing and sailing the characters are wet, cold and tired. They all take a break for a hot drink and biscuits. Ask the children which hot drinks and biscuits they like best. Some children may be allergic to milk or chocolate. They could do a survey and display their results.

After the break Lisa, Rupa, Nicky and David go back on the water for a rowing race. Ask the children if they have ever tried rowing and discuss the difficulties of keeping a rowing boat in a straight line.

Copymaster 35 provides a format for children to record their answers to questions in the textbook.

Maths content and resources

Page 10 of the textbook looks at situations where multiplying and dividing two-digit numbers occur, in the context of distributing drinks and biscuits.

The work is developed on page 10 of Number Workbook 2 where the vertical arrangement of multiplications is featured. There is no exchange of tens. Page 11 covers simple division by partitioning. Children should be encouraged to look at the problems with practical apparatus such as cubes to hand.

There are two more worksheets on Copymasters 53 and 54. The first shows the multiplication of two-digit numbers by 2, using base-ten apparatus. The second shows division in the same way. Children should use the apparatus alongside the worksheets.

Page 11 of the textbook shows a situation in which the course for a rowing race is measured in metres. All measurement is essentially practical and children should have the opportunity to set out a real course.

An idea for this may arise from page 10 of Topic Workbook 2. Instead of using canoes(!) the children could make a slalom course in the playground with cones or beanbags and see how quickly they can zigzag between them from start to finish.

Copymaster 55 is another worksheet on metres.

Measuring in centimetres is introduced on page 11 of Topic Workbook 2 and followed up on Copymaster 56. Most children will need help with the ruler for measuring and drawing, particularly if it has a small area of waste at the end.

Measuring activities

Suggest that children go into the playground and use chalk to measure and mark out some of the arrays of numbers they have used in work on tables. For example, can they make a 3-metre by 3-metre square to show the numbers from 1 to 9?

(Grids with co-ordinates can also be measured and chalked on the playground so that activities with co-ordinates may involve people rather than drawings or apparatus.)

L3:2 Water sports

The materials

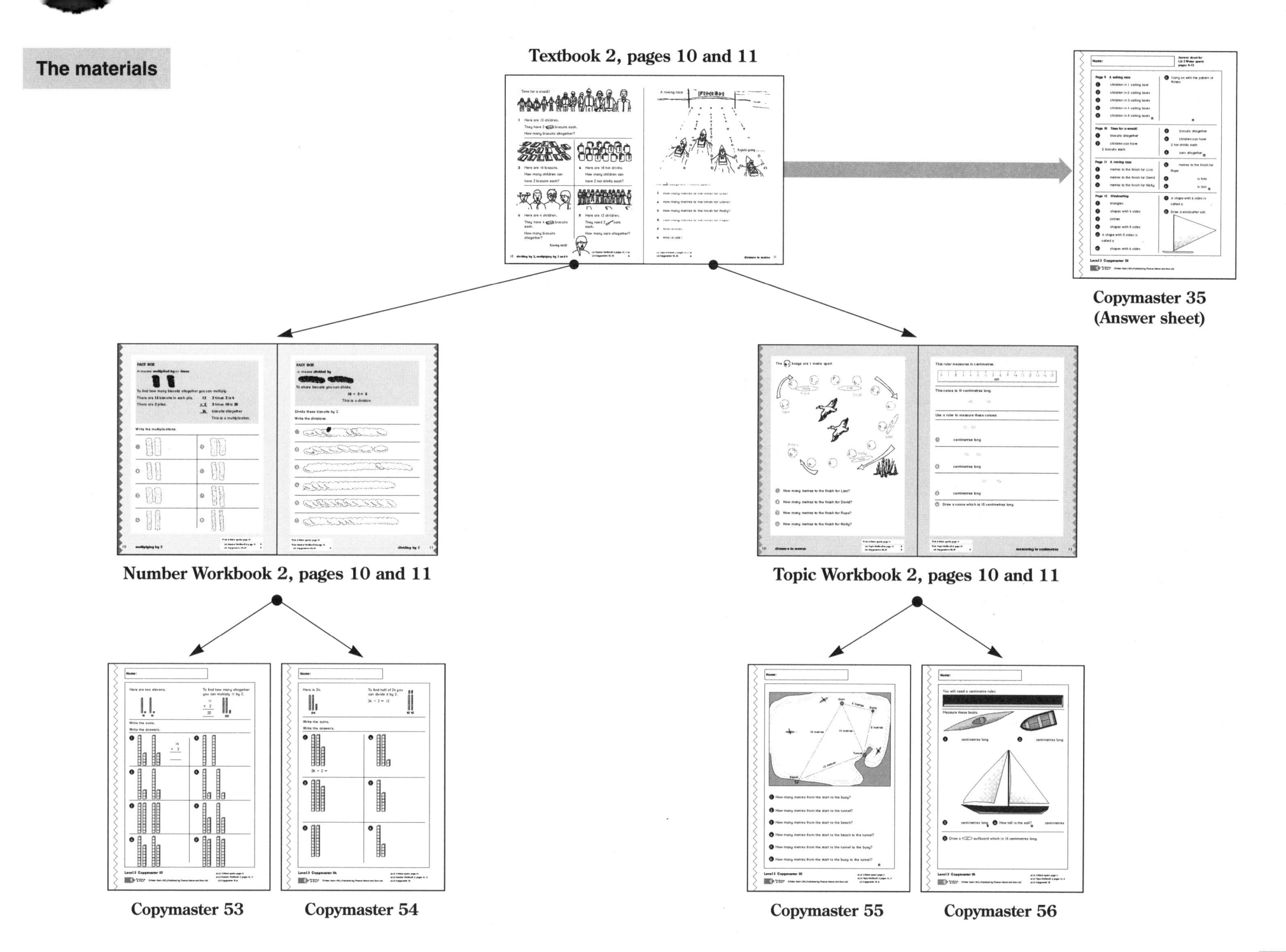

Textbook 2, pages 10 and 11

Copymaster 35 (Answer sheet)

Number Workbook 2, pages 10 and 11

Topic Workbook 2, pages 10 and 11

Copymaster 53

Copymaster 54

Copymaster 55

Copymaster 56

L3:2 Water sports 57

PAGES 12 AND 13
Windsurfing and cooking

SKILLS, CONCEPTS AND KNOWLEDGE
- Identifying 2D shapes
- Drawing 2D shapes
- Tens and ones

PRE-ASSESSMENT
Can the child:
- identify common 2D shapes including hexagons?
- organise two-digit numbers into tens and ones?

The story

The final activity of the morning is windsurfing. Ask the children if they have ever tried it and discuss the problems of keeping your balance and steering a windsurfer. Before they start on the page, talk to them about the pattern on the sail and the shapes they see. Many items of modern sports equipment and clothing use colour, shape and pattern in their design.

After windsurfing, Nicky and David make chips for lunch. It may be possible to bring some real potatoes into the classroom so the children can peel them and slice them. Can they make ten chips from a potato?

Copymasters 35 and 36 provide formats for children to record their answers to questions in the textbook.

Maths content and resources

Page 12 of the textbook uses a windsurfer sail to show the use of regular and irregular shapes in designs.

The work is extended to include quadrilaterals on page 12 of Topic Workbook 2. On page 13 children have the opportunity to design their own windsurfer sail on a background of spotty paper.

There are more examples of regular and irregular 2D shapes on Copymaster 57 which is a worksheet. These shapes may also be copied on to thin card and cut out to be used in tessellation experiments. Copymaster 58 asks children to draw quadrilaterals with a specified number of spots inside them on a background of spotty paper. This kind of work can also be tried with triangles, pentagons and hexagons.

Page 13 of the textbook revisits tens and ones.

The work on pages 12 and 13 of Number Workbook 2 extends the range of two-digit numbers and introduces numbers beyond 100. Base-ten apparatus is shown in the illustrations and children should have access to it.

Copymasters 59 and 60 ask children to shade columns of tens and ones in a hundred square to show a range of two-digit numbers, and to identify the numbers indicated by columns of tens and ones already shaded.

Tessellating and tiling

Use Copymaster 57.

Copy the shapes on to thin card, or paste the sheet on to thin card.

Children can cut out a shape and try to make it tessellate. They should be familiar with squares and rectangles forming tile and brick patterns, but do all quadrilaterals tessellate? Encourage them to rotate and slide the shapes to try to fit them together.

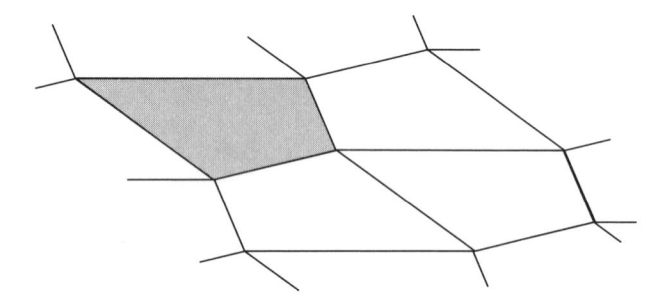

L3:2 Water sports

The materials

Textbook 2, pages 12 and 13

Copymaster 35 (Answer sheet)

Copymaster 36 (Answer sheet)

Topic Workbook 2, pages 12 and 13

Number Workbook 2, pages 12 and 13

Copymaster 57

Copymaster 58

Copymaster 59

Copymaster 60

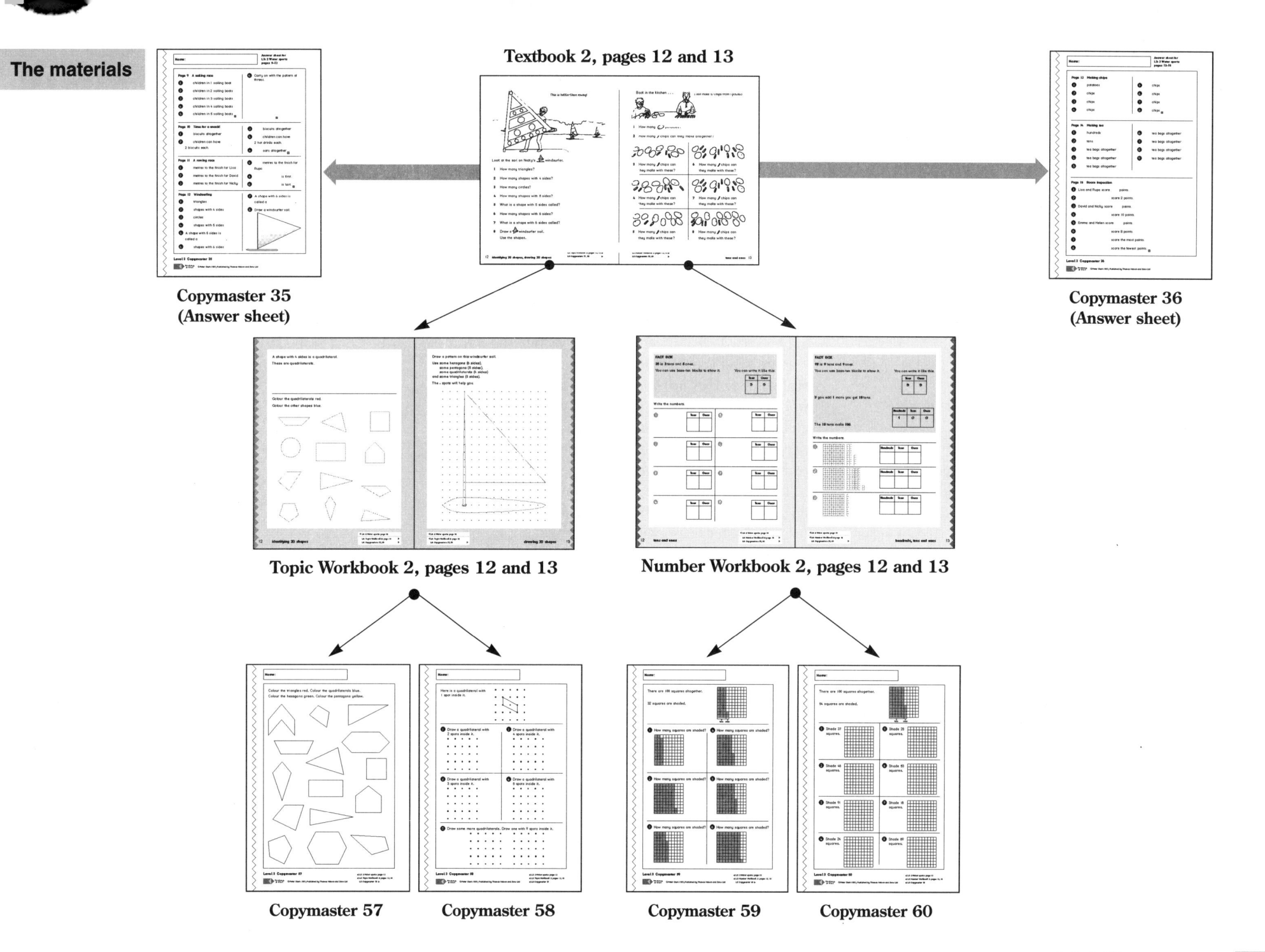

L3:2 Water sports

PAGES 14 AND 15
Tea and tidiness

SKILLS, CONCEPTS AND KNOWLEDGE

▶ Hundreds, tens and ones
▶ Reading a pictogram

PRE-ASSESSMENT

Can the child:
▶ organise three-digit numbers into hundreds, tens and ones?
▶ read a pictogram?
▶ understand scale (where one symbol stands for two things)?

Lisa and Rupa are making a cup of tea to go with lunch. Ask the children whether they make tea at home. A fascinating exercise is to ask them to write instructions on how to make a cup of tea. (If they have problems with writing they could dictate into a cassette recorder.) This is an exercise in ordering a sequence of events. The teacher can then try to make a cup of tea following their instructions literally. Children quite often leave out a key instruction such as *'boil the water'*, thus making the tea undrinkable. Exercises like this encourage them to think carefully about sequences of events and attention to detail.

After lunch the characters discover that their rooms have been inspected for tidiness. The results are shown on a chart. Discuss with children the tidiness of their own rooms and how they organise them.

Copymaster 36 provides a format for children to record their answers to questions in the textbook.

Maths content and resources

Page 14 of the textbook builds directly on the previous page by developing numbers from 100 to 300.

Place value is emphasised on pages 14 and 15 of Number Workbook 2 by the use of base-ten apparatus for children to interpret and draw.

There is further work on this on Copymasters 61 and 62. The drawings of base-ten apparatus on Copymaster 61 may be cut out for children to re-arrange to show a variety of numbers involving hundreds, tens and ones. To make further worksheets, the printed numbers on Copymaster 62 may be masked and new numbers written in.

Page 15 of the textbook introduces the idea of using scale in a pictogram. Each star in the illustration is worth 2 points. This can be linked with the work children have been doing on counting in twos and developing the two-times table. Encourage them to count 2, 4, 6 ... and so on.

There are more pictograms to interpret and draw on pages 14 and 15 of Topic Workbook 2.

Copymaster 63 provides another pictogram to interpret, and on Copymaster 64 children are asked to draw smily faces to make their own pictogram with a scale of 1:2.

Sweet pictograms

Ask children to collect and keep the wrappers from any sweets they buy regularly. When they have a collection, ask them to choose two types of sweet and use them in a survey of their friends. They ask their friends to choose between the two sweets. For every two people who like a sweet, they paste one wrapper on to a pictogram. If they end up with an odd number, they cut a wrapper in half and paste it on.

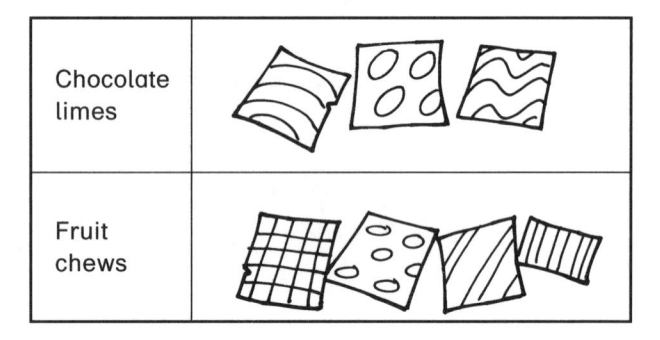

Chocolate limes	
Fruit chews	

Pictograms may also be made with pictures cut from magazines and packaging.

L3:2 Water sports

The materials

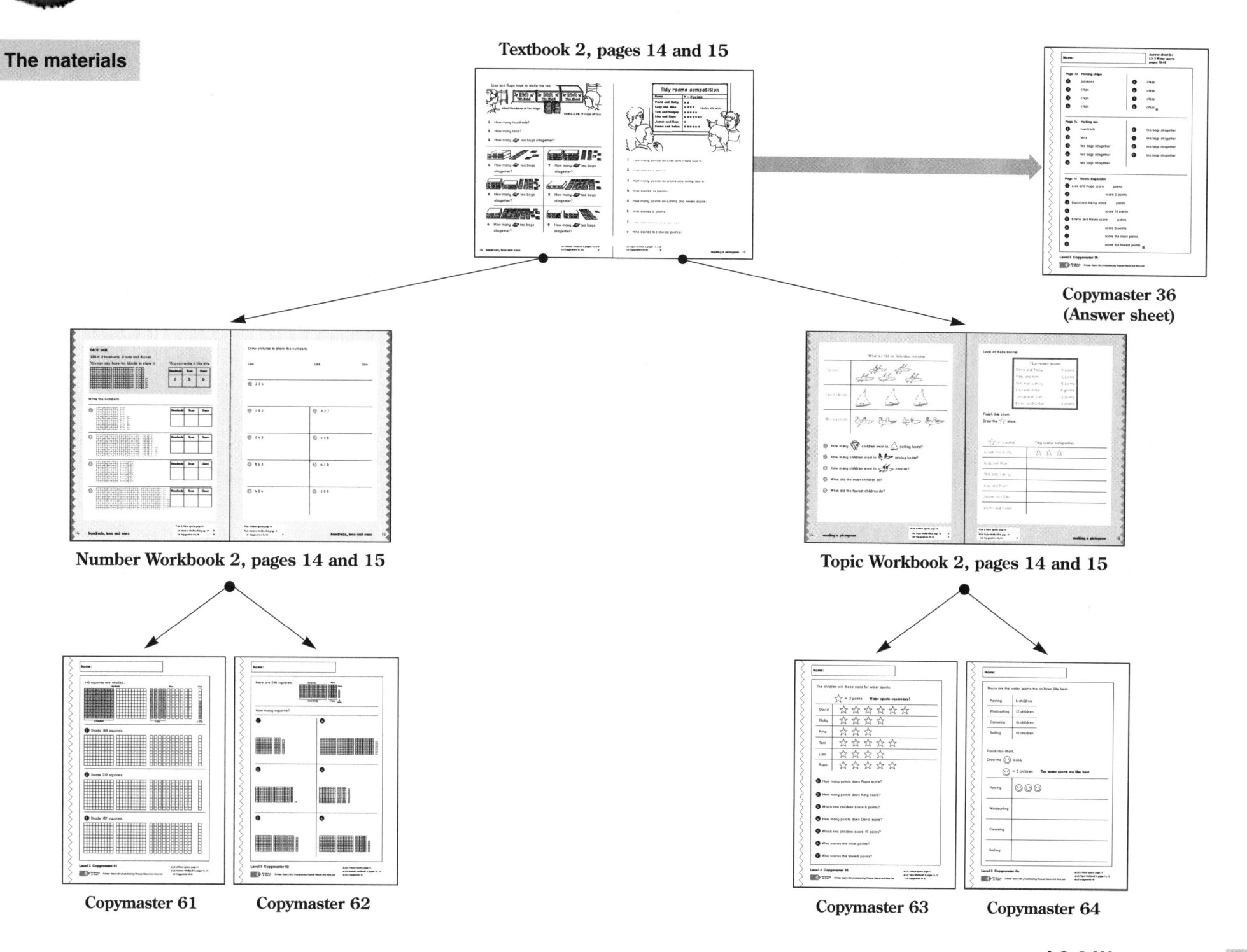

Textbook 2, pages 14 and 15

Copymaster 36 (Answer sheet)

Number Workbook 2, pages 14 and 15

Topic Workbook 2, pages 14 and 15

Copymaster 61

Copymaster 62

Copymaster 63

Copymaster 64

L3:2 Water sports 61

L3:3 The museum

PAGES 2 AND 3

At the museum

SKILLS, CONCEPTS AND KNOWLEDGE

- Identifying 2D shapes
- Making a table
- Co-ordinates and compass points

PRE-ASSESSMENT

Can the child:

- identify triangles, squares and rectangles?
- make a table?
- use letter and number co-ordinates to describe position?
- use the 4 compass points to describe position?

The story

On Saturday afternoon Rupa, Lisa, Nicky and David visit the local museum. They look at the shapes on the front of the building. Once inside, they see a plan of a Roman villa.

Much of the work in this textbook is drawn from the kinds of theme likely to be found in a small country town museum. The main themes are the Romans and Victorian Britain. All the work can be used as a starting point for discussing either of these, or as part of a History project.

Copymaster 65 provides a format for children to record their answers to questions in the textbook.

Maths content and resources

Page 2 of the textbook asks children to identify and sort the 2D shapes they see on the front of the museum. They then have to make a chart of the shapes, and draw a building using these shapes.

This work is continued on pages 2 and 3 of Topic Workbook 3 where there are two more drawing and data collecting exercises based on 2D shapes.

The work on symmetrical shapes on page 2 is developed on Copymaster 69. Copymaster 70 provides blank spotty paper with lines of symmetry for children to devise their own shapes and drawings. Copymaster 71 is another data collecting exercise based on 2D shapes.

Page 3 of the textbook looks at co-ordinates and compass points in the context of a Roman villa.

The work is supported by further exercises on pages 4 and 5 of Topic Workbook 3.

Copymaster 72 is a worksheet which asks children to follow a sequence of co-ordinates to draw a picture. This work can be developed further by using the blank grid on Copymaster 25. Children can then devise their own 'co-ordinate pictures' for their friends to try.

Copy my shape

Use copies of Copymaster 70.

Two children work together, using copies of Copymaster 70 and some coloured felt-tip pens. Each child draws two shapes on Copymaster 70, on the right- or left-hand side of the line of symmetry. They then exchange sheets and draw the reflections of each other's shapes.

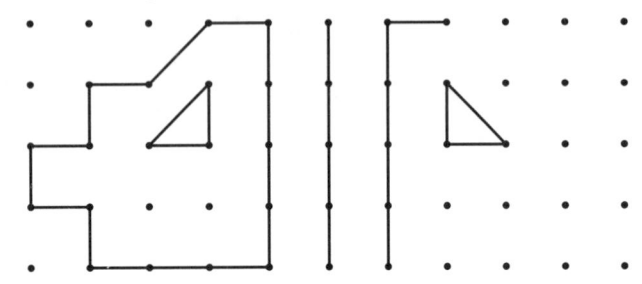

Reflecting shapes

Use Copymaster 70 and a transparent mirror (such as Mira) or a piece of transparent plastic.

Transparent mirrors reflect shapes and also allow children to see through to the other side. Children can use such a mirror to draw reflections of shapes by lining the mirror up along one edge of the shape and drawing the reflection on the other side. They can repeat this several times to make a sequence of shapes across a page.

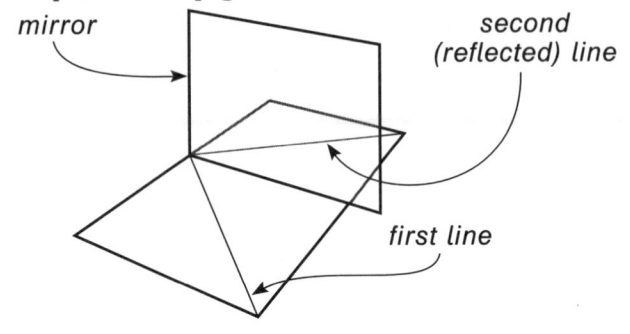

The materials

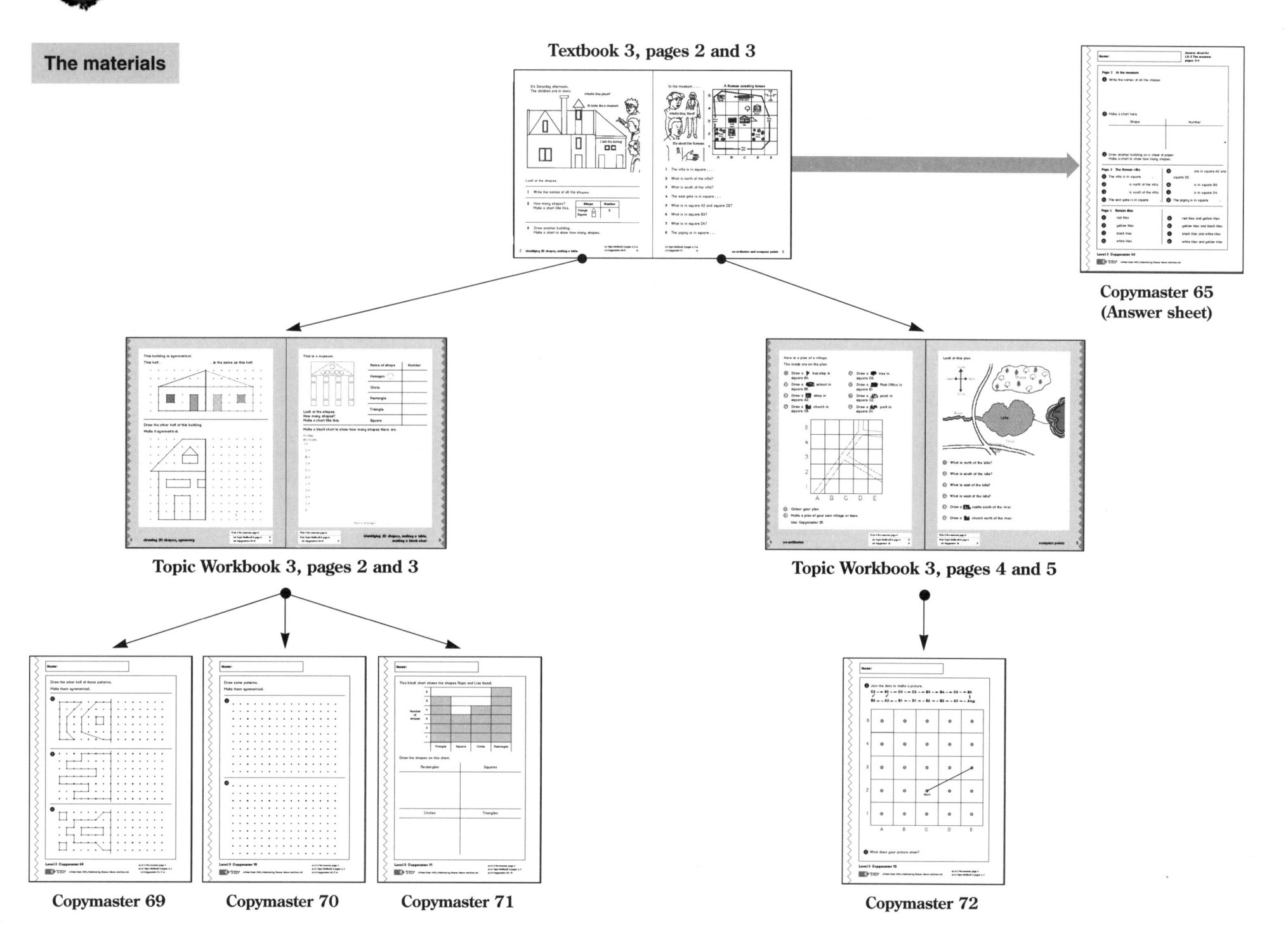

Textbook 3, pages 2 and 3

Copymaster 65
(Answer sheet)

Topic Workbook 3, pages 2 and 3

Topic Workbook 3, pages 4 and 5

Copymaster 69

Copymaster 70

Copymaster 71

Copymaster 72

L3:3 The museum   63

PAGES 4 AND 5

Roman floor tiles

SKILLS, CONCEPTS AND KNOWLEDGE

▶ Addition of two-digit numbers to 70
▶ Pentominoes

PRE-ASSESSMENT

Can the child:
▶ add two-digit numbers?
▶ subtract one two-digit number from another?
▶ continue a pattern of fives?
▶ remember any of the five-times table?

The story

As part of the display about the Romans the characters see some tile patterns based on Roman tessera. This is a useful starting point for looking at ancient and contemporary tile designs. Encourage children to look for them at school, at home and in the local environment.

Copymasters 65 and 66 provide formats for children to record their answers to questions in the textbook.

Maths content and resources

Page 4 of the textbook uses arrangements of Roman floor tiles as a context for revisiting the addition of tens and ones. The patterns of the tiles can be modelled by the children using base-ten apparatus.

The work is reinforced on page 2 of Number Workbook 3, where drawings of base-ten apparatus support the additions and children are reminded of how to set an addition out vertically. Page 3 revisits the subtraction of tens and ones in the same way.

There are further worksheets on this on Copymasters 73 and 74.

The tile theme is developed on page 5 of the textbook which looks at patterns of five and the five-times table.

This is revisited on page 6 of Topic Workbook 3 where 5-pointed stars are used as a context for the five-times table. Page 7 shows the five-times table in two different arrays of numbers.

There is further practice of the table on Copymasters 75 and 76.

This is a great deal of work on the five-times table and teachers may wish to spread it over a period of time.

Page 5 of the textbook also includes a starting point for investigating pentominoes (shapes which can be made from 5 squares) and repeating patterns which can be made from pentominoes.

Quadrominoes and pentominoes

Use squared paper and card.

Dominoes are rectangles made from 2 squares:

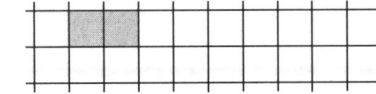

Triominoes are shapes made from 3 squares. There are 2 different triominoes – a rectangle and an L-shape:

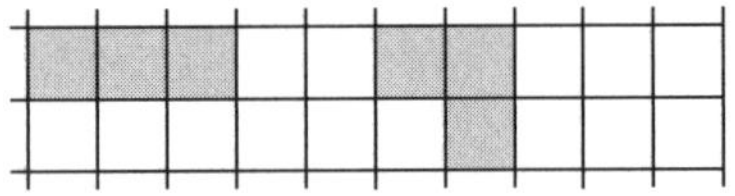

Quadrominoes are shapes made from 4 squares. Ask children to experiment with squared paper to find as many different quadrominoes as possible. They may need to try many times before they find them all, but these are all the quadrominoes:

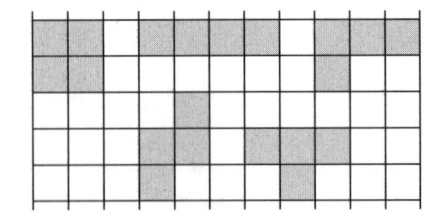

Rotations and reflections will produce shapes which are ostensibly different from these. If children paste their quadrominoes on to card and cut them out, they can rotate and reflect them to check which shapes are truly different.

Exactly the same kind of investigation can be tried with pentominoes. However, there are 12 different pentominoes and children may need many attempts to find them all and confirm that they are all different:

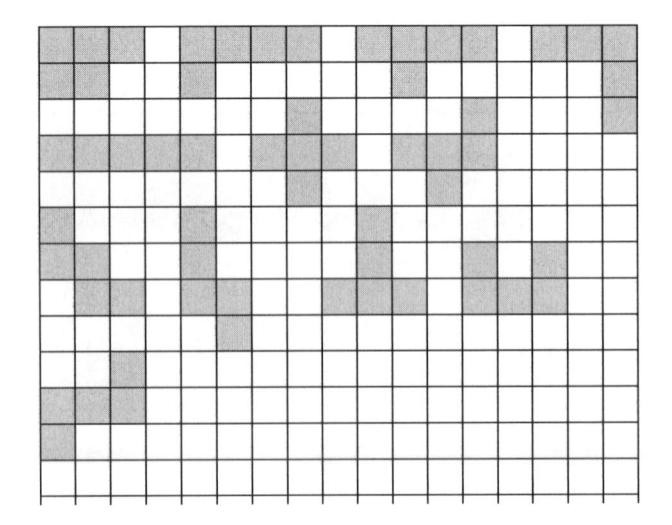

L3:3 The museum

The materials

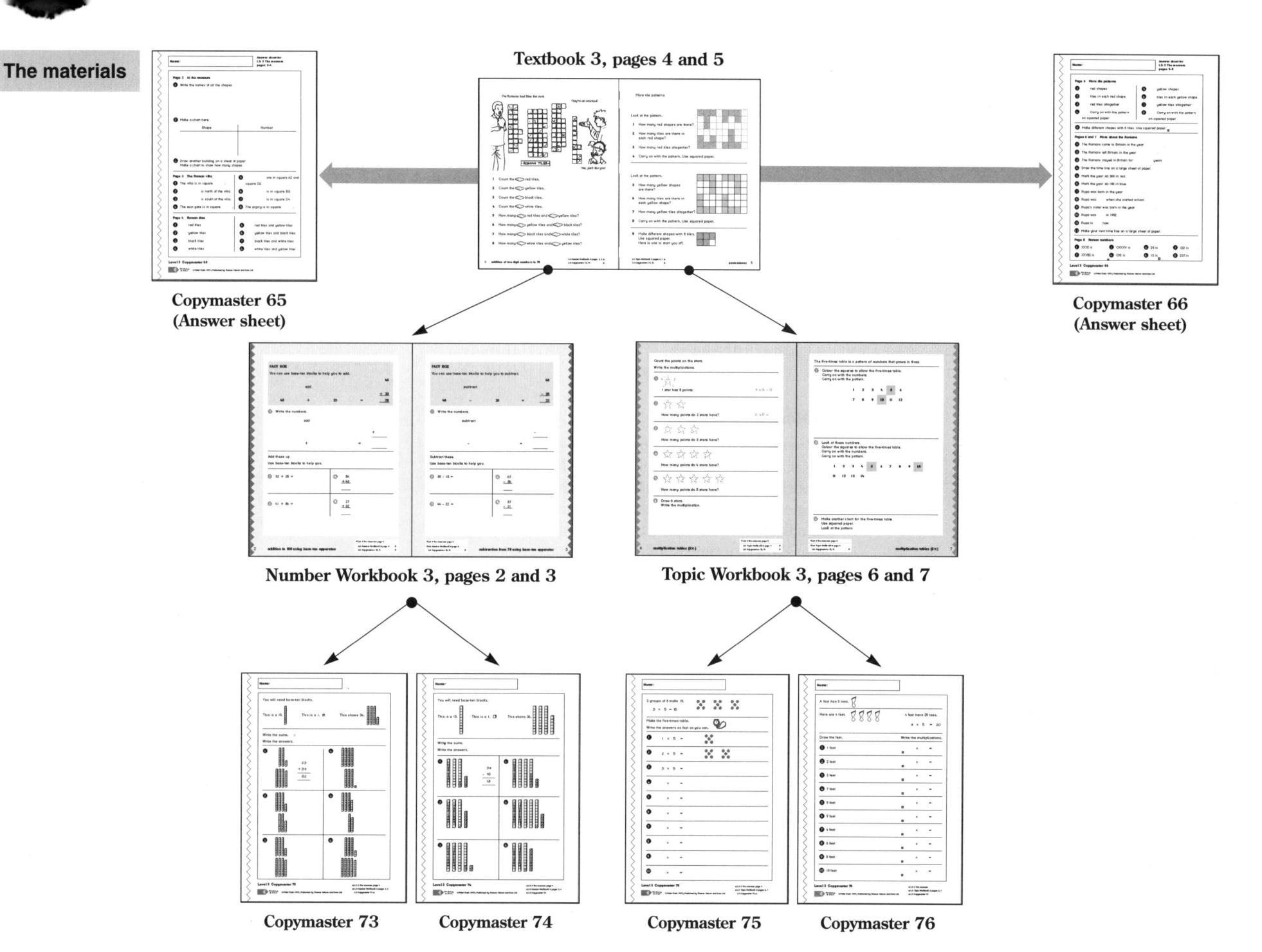

Textbook 3, pages 4 and 5

Copymaster 65
(Answer sheet)

Copymaster 66
(Answer sheet)

Number Workbook 3, pages 2 and 3

Topic Workbook 3, pages 6 and 7

Copymaster 73

Copymaster 74

Copymaster 75

Copymaster 76

L3:3 The museum

PAGES 6 AND 7
More about the Romans

SKILLS, CONCEPTS AND KNOWLEDGE
▶ Time lines (number lines)

PRE-ASSESSMENT
Can the child:
▶ use a number line?
▶ use a time line?

The story

Rupa and Lisa study a time line which shows when the Romans arrived in Britain and when they departed. There is also a time line drawn by Rupa to show events in her own life.

Children could make their own time lines, beginning with one which shows the period from when they were born to the present day. This could be extended to show events further back in the past, for example, the birth of their parents. A time line extended into the future could show a child's next birthday and the year when (s)he will leave the primary school for the secondary school.

Copymaster 66 provides a format for children to record their answers to questions in the textbook.

Maths content and resources

Pages 6 and 7 of the textbook show two time lines. The first shows the duration of the Romans' stay in Britain, and the second is a representation of the kind of time line a child might draw. The concept of time is difficult for some children and it is revisited on pages 4 and 5 of Number Workbook 3. Pages 6 and 7 develop the time line work to include counting on, counting back and counting in twos using number lines.

Copymasters 77 to 79 also cover addition, subtraction and multiplication (by 2, 3, 4 and 5) on number lines. Copymaster 80 provides blank number lines so that teachers or children can create more worksheets if they are needed.

More time lines

Use strips of 2-centimetre squared paper.

Children can develop time lines for a variety of purposes. A simple one to start with could be a time line showing a child's day. (Time lines should always indicate a continuation at the beginning and at the end to show that time is infinite.)

A logical development of this would be to make a time line showing a week. Children could include special events at home and at school. For example, they could show which days they do games or swimming at school and which evenings they go to clubs or do other activities.

Other time lines could show a month, a school term or a calendar year. It is important, though, to have a genuine reason for developing a time line.

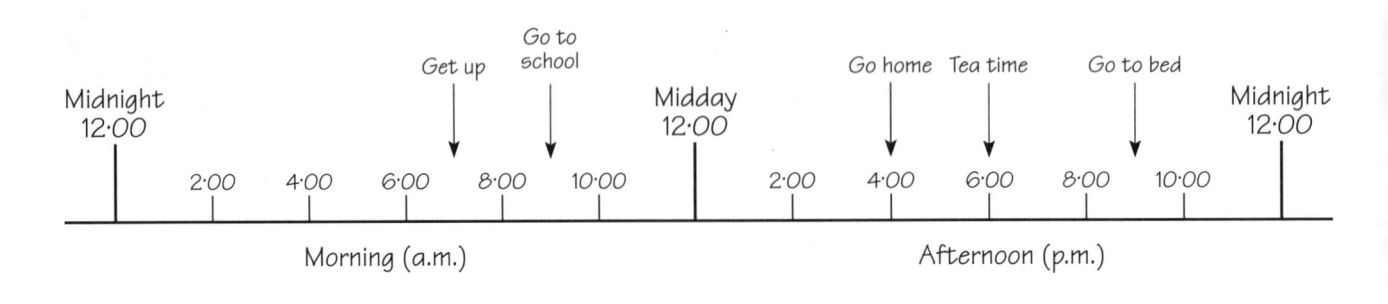

L3:3 The museum

The materials

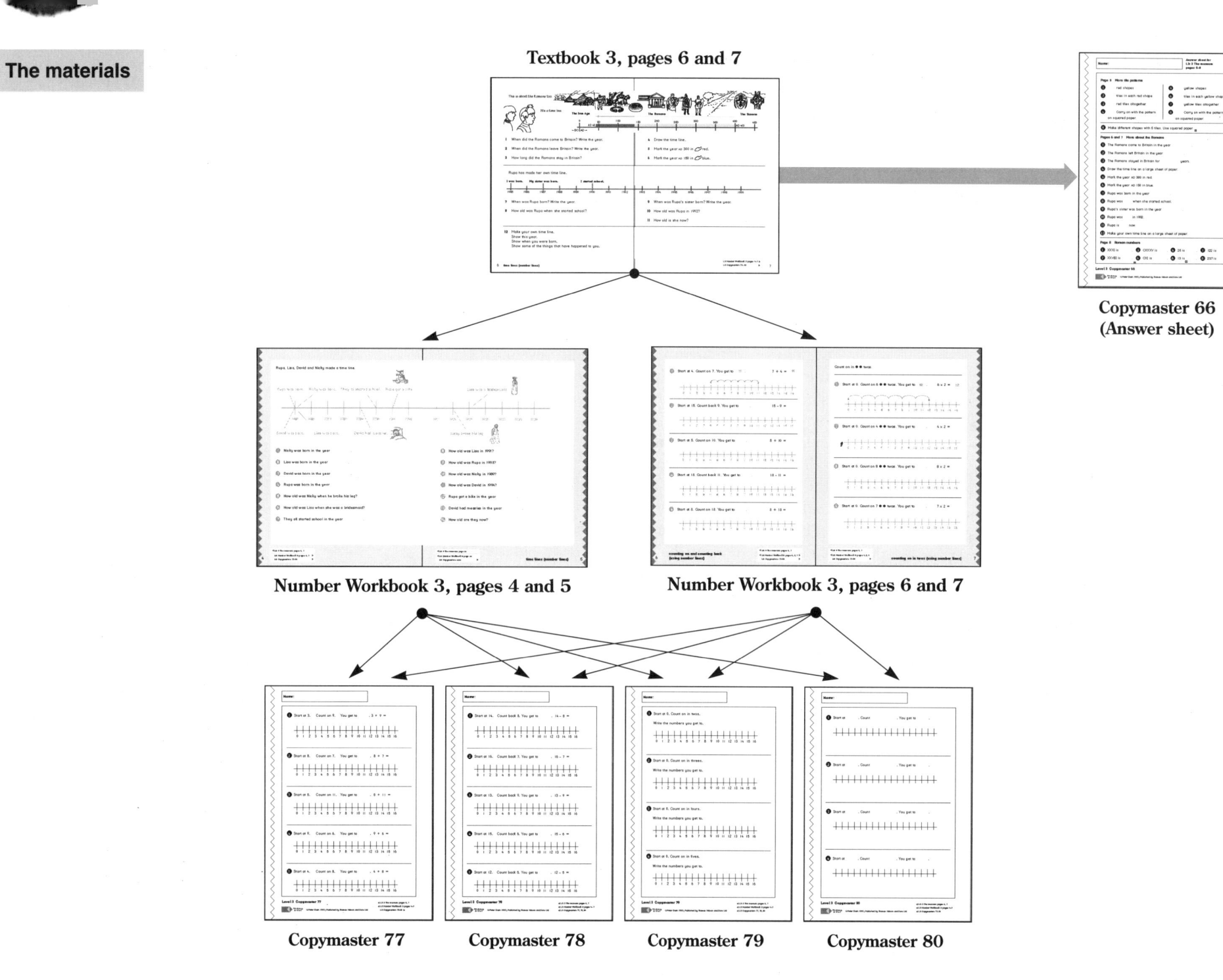

Textbook 3, pages 6 and 7

Copymaster 66 (Answer sheet)

Number Workbook 3, pages 4 and 5

Number Workbook 3, pages 6 and 7

Copymaster 77

Copymaster 78

Copymaster 79

Copymaster 80

L3:3 The museum

PAGES 8 AND 9
Roman numerals and a Victorian school

SKILLS, CONCEPTS AND KNOWLEDGE

▶ Roman numerals
▶ Multiplication tables (4×)

PRE-ASSESSMENT

Can the child:
▶ translate from Roman–Arabic–Roman numerals?
▶ continue a pattern of fours?
▶ remember any of the four-times table?

As part of the display about the Romans the characters see some examples of Roman numerals. Discuss with them how the Romans might have used these to write sums as well as simple numbers.

Next, the children see an illustration of a Victorian classroom. There are plenty of opportunities for comparison with a modern classroom; discuss the number of children in the class and the classroom organisation.

Copymasters 66 and 67 provide formats for children to record their answers to questions in the textbook.

Maths content and resources

Page 8 of the textbook looks at Roman numerals. Simple numbers have been used so that children can easily translate them into Arabic numbers and vice versa.

Some children may find this work difficult and it is supported on pages 8 and 9 of Topic Workbook 3. These pages include a key to the Roman numerals from 1 to 20. Children also look at how Roman numerals can be organised on squared paper to show the patterns they make as they grow.

Copymaster 81 is a further worksheet on Roman numerals. Copymaster 82 introduces another ancient system for writing numbers – the one developed by the Mayan people. Both of these could be used as a stimulus for children to try to devise their own ways of recording numbers. There is also the opportunity to look again at place value.

The rows of 4 children in the picture on page 9 of the textbook introduce another visit to groups of four and the four-times table.

Pages 8 and 9 of Number Workbook 3 encourage children to develop the four-times table and to look at patterns of four in arrays of numbers.

Copymaster 83 promotes quick recall of the four-times table, and Copymaster 84 provides another chance to write out the table with pictorial support.

Once again, there is a large amount of work on this concept and teachers may wish to spread it over a period of time.

Sticks and stones

Use lolly sticks and cooking ingredients such as split peas or butter beans.

Children can make their own base-ten apparatus using lolly sticks and split peas to represent tens and ones, to help with workbook pages and worksheets on number. These can be pasted on to paper to represent numbers in displays.

'Sticks and stones' could be drawn on cards to represent the numerals from 10 to 20 (or beyond). These could be used alongside a corresponding set of numeral cards for matching and for snap games.

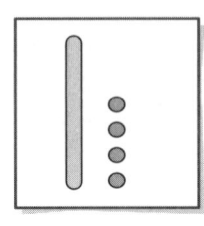

L3:3 The museum

The materials

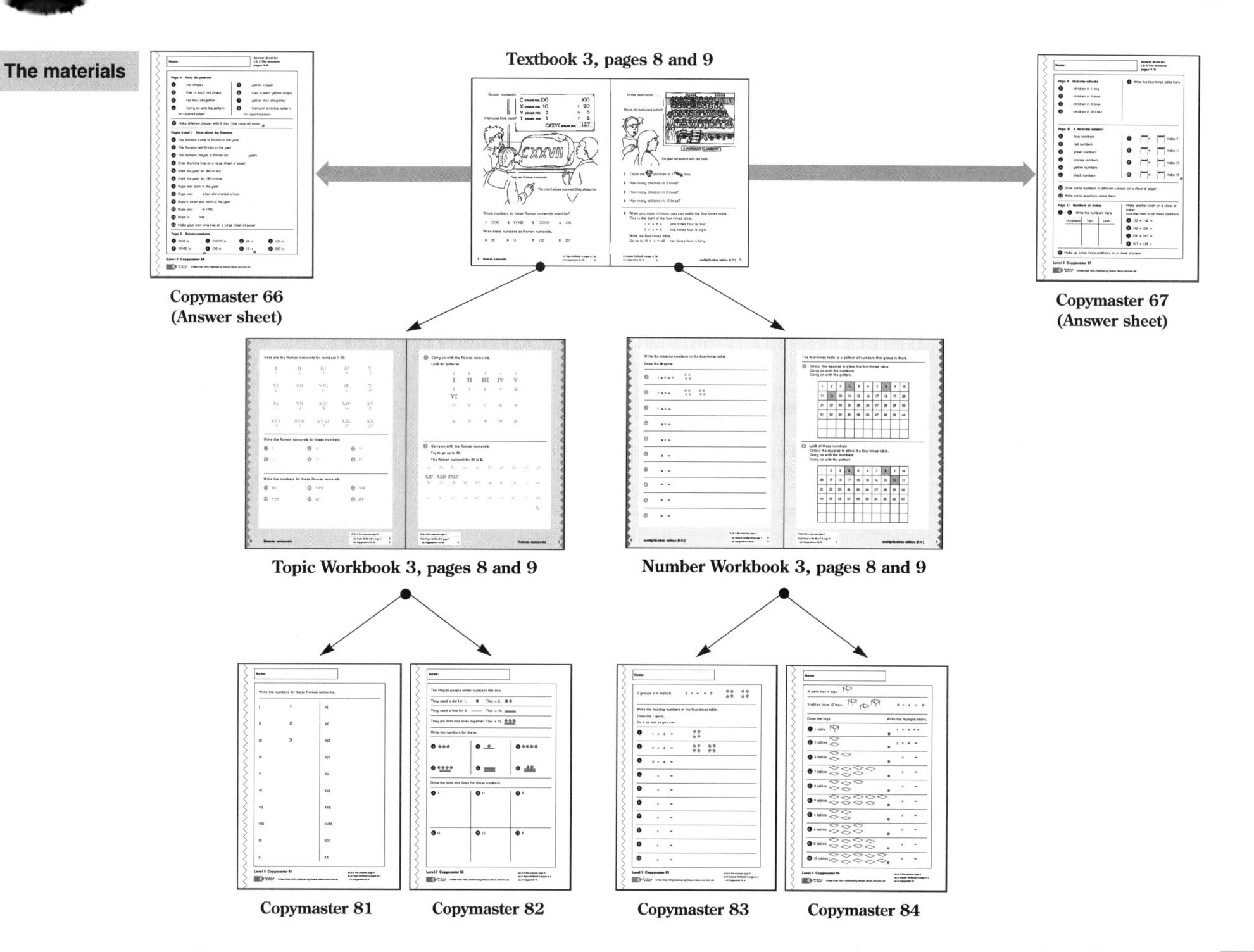

Textbook 3, pages 8 and 9

Copymaster 66
(Answer sheet)

Copymaster 67
(Answer sheet)

Topic Workbook 3, pages 8 and 9

Number Workbook 3, pages 8 and 9

Copymaster 81

Copymaster 82

Copymaster 83

Copymaster 84

L3:3 The museum

PAGES 10 AND 11
Samplers and slates

SKILLS, CONCEPTS AND KNOWLEDGE

▶ Addition facts to 20
▶ Place value
▶ Addition of three-digit numbers to 500

PRE-ASSESSMENT

Can the child:
▶ recall any number facts to 20?
▶ add three-digit numbers?
▶ understand place value in three-digit numbers?

The story

The theme of Victorian schools is continued as the characters look at a sampler. Children could try to make their own samplers, either by drawing crosses on squared paper to show the numerals and letters or by sewing in cross-stitch.

The characters then see a slate and a slate pencil showing how children recorded their mathematics. Discuss the fact that paper was expensive, and corrections could be made very quickly and easily on slates. Children could use chalk and blackboards to try to write the numerals and words in copperplate.

Copymaster 67 provides a format for children to record their answers to questions in the textbook.

Maths content and resources

Page 10 of the textbook revisits addition facts to 20 in the context of numbers embroidered on a Victorian sampler. Children are encouraged to devise their own number chart and write some questions to go with it.

This is supported by pages 10 and 11 of Number Workbook 3, which also cover subtraction facts.

Copymasters 85 and 86 give further practice in addition and subtraction facts with a number range below 20.

The number facts are revisited regularly throughout Level 3 so teachers may wish to use these sheets sparingly.

Page 11 of the textbook covers the addition of three-digit numbers, focusing on place value. The numbers on the schoolchildren's slates are headed 'hundreds,' 'tens' and 'units'. (Throughout *Breakaway Maths* the term 'ones' has been used instead of 'units'. This is to avoid any confusion with units of measurement.)

Place value is reinforced on page 12 of Number Workbook 3, and addition is revisited on page 13. This work includes the exchange of tens, and base-ten apparatus is used in the illustrations to demonstrate this process.

Copymasters 87 and 88 provide two further worksheets on place value and addition with the exchange of tens.

High, low

For 4 children, use 2 sets of numeral cards from 0 to 9, and a sheet of paper divided vertically into three sections for each player.

Label the columns 'Hundreds,' 'Tens' and 'Ones'. The children decide whether to try to make the highest or lowest number. The numeral cards are stacked or spread out face down. The children take turns to select a card and lay it down in the best place on their sheet of paper to make the highest (or lowest) number. Once a card has been placed it cannot be moved. Each child then takes a second card and decides where to place it. After placing the third set of cards they decide who has the highest or lowest number and therefore who the winner is.

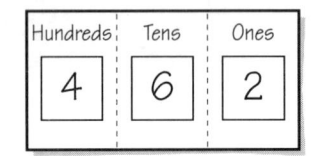

Hundreds	Tens	Ones
4	6	2

Hundreds	Tens	Ones
8	3	1

L3:3 The museum

The materials

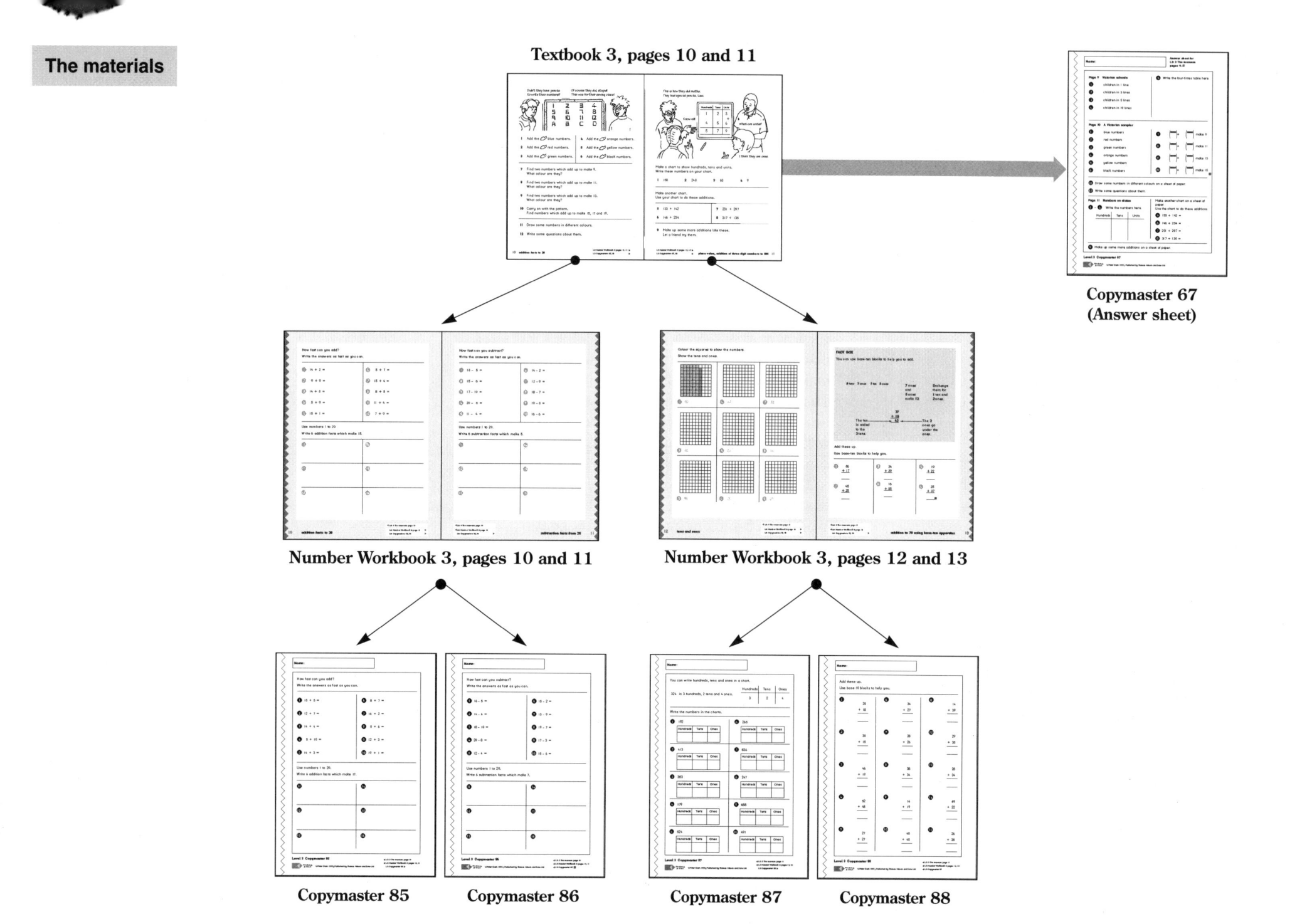

Textbook 3, pages 10 and 11

Copymaster 67
(Answer sheet)

Number Workbook 3, pages 10 and 11

Number Workbook 3, pages 12 and 13

Copymaster 85

Copymaster 86

Copymaster 87

Copymaster 88

L3:3 The museum 71

PAGES 12 AND 13
Slates and farm animals

SKILLS, CONCEPTS AND KNOWLEDGE

▶ Place value
▶ Subtraction of three-digit numbers from 400
▶ Making a table
▶ Making a block chart

PRE-ASSESSMENT

Can the child:
▶ understand place value in three-digit numbers?
▶ subtract one three-digit number from another?
▶ make a table?
▶ make a block chart?

The story

The characters see another slate from a Victorian school, this time showing subtractions. They then move on to a display showing a Victorian farmyard. An etching shows a farming couple surrounded by animals. Discuss with the children the differences between farming in Victorian times and farming now.

Copymaster 68 provides a format for children to record their answers to questions in the textbook.

Maths content and resources

Page 12 of the textbook deals with place value in three-digit numbers and subtraction with the exchange of tens. Children are encouraged to make up some subtractions of their own based on the examples shown on the Victorian slates.

Place value is reinforced on page 14 of Number Workbook 3, and subtraction is revisited on page 15.

Copymasters 89 and 90 provide two worksheets on place value and subtraction with the exchange of tens.

Page 13 of the textbook uses a Victorian farmyard scene as the context for a data collection exercise. Remind children of how to make a tally (making a vertical mark for every animal they count and a diagonal line to show each five). Children also have to make a block chart to show the animals, using scale. The idea of using 1 block to represent 2 animals could be reinforced by the use of squares of sticky paper with 2 written on each one. This allows children to count as they make their block charts.

There is more work on making and interpreting block charts with scale on pages 10 and 11 of Topic Workbook 3 and on Copymasters 91 and 92.

Build a bar chart

Use 1 or 2 dice, a sheet of paper for each player to make a tally, a bar chart with an axis showing the players' names, and some small pieces of card (or Post-it notes).

The bar chart is placed where all the players can reach it. Children throw the dice and record the score as a tally. For every 5 (4 verticals and 1 diagonal), a child can take a square of card or a Post-it note and place it on the bar chart next to his/her name. The first child to build his/her bar up to a predetermined level (e.g. 30) is the winner.

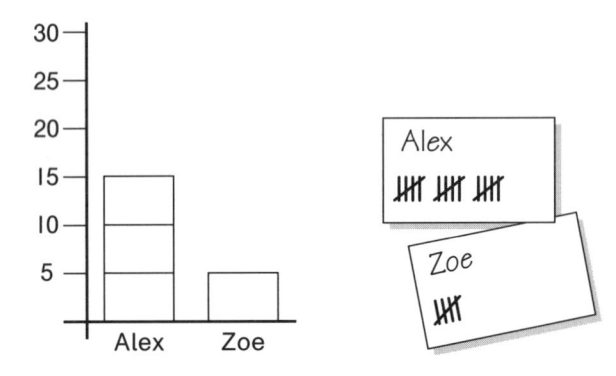

Try this game with a pictogram instead of a bar chart; one picture can stand for more than one object.

L3:3 The museum

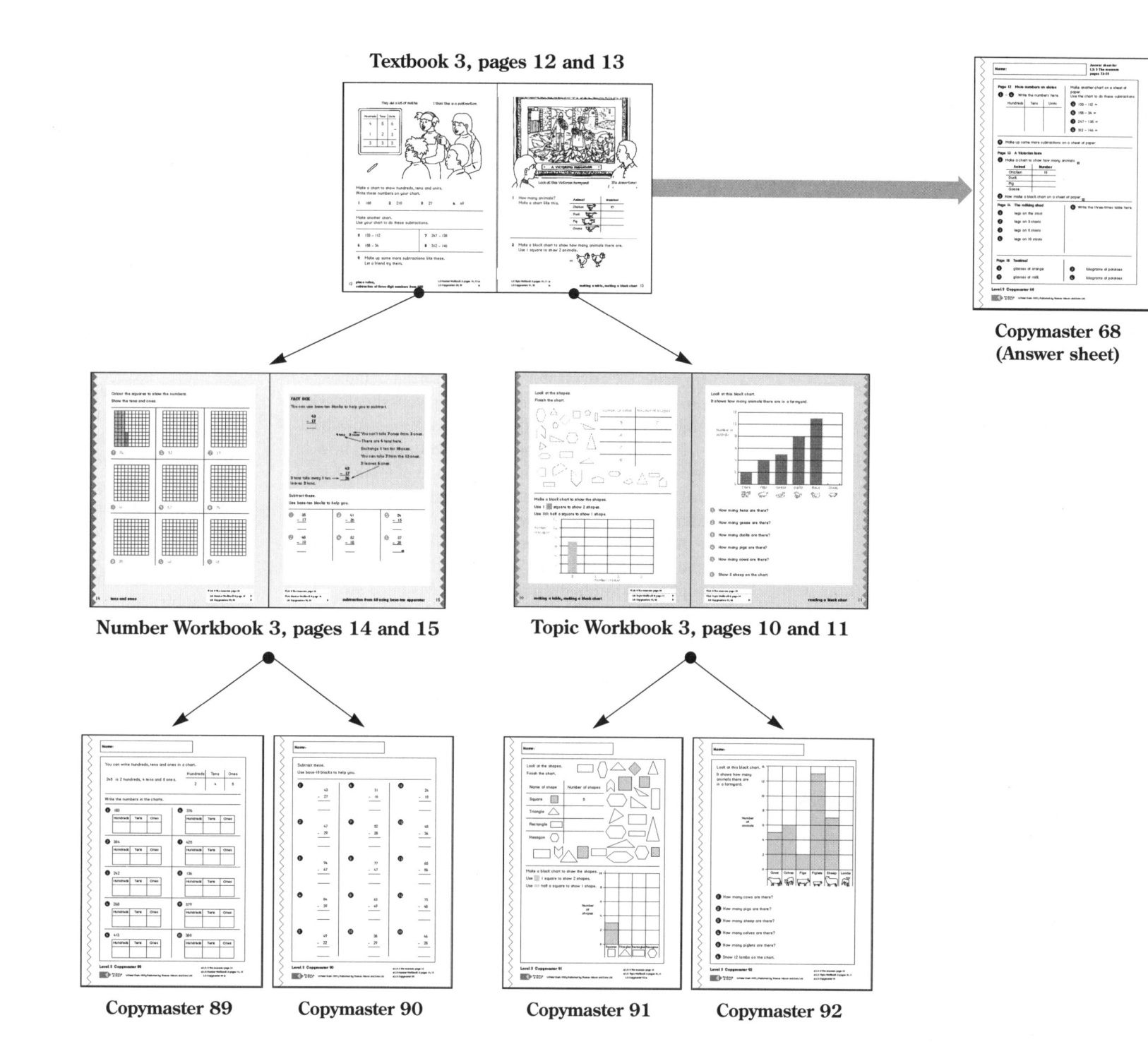

The materials

Textbook 3, pages 12 and 13

Copymaster 68 (Answer sheet)

Number Workbook 3, pages 14 and 15

Topic Workbook 3, pages 10 and 11

Copymaster 89

Copymaster 90

Copymaster 91

Copymaster 92

L3:3 The museum 73

PAGES 14 AND 15
Milking a cow, and milk for tea

SKILLS, CONCEPTS AND KNOWLEDGE

▶ Multiplication tables (3×)
▶ Litres and millilitres
▶ Kilograms and grams

PRE-ASSESSMENT

Can the child:
▶ continue a pattern of threes?
▶ recall any of the three-times table?
▶ measure in litres and millilitres?
▶ measure in kilograms and grams?

The story

The museum visit ends with a tableau showing a cow being milked by hand. This can be contrasted with pictures of a modern-day milking parlour.

After the museum visit the characters return to the Warren Study Centre to prepare their tea. Ask the children whether they help with meal preparation at home, whether they can cook and what jobs they are expected to do at home.

Copymaster 68 provides a format for children to record their answers to questions in the textbook.

Maths content and resources

The three-legged stool in the milking shed scene shown on page 14 of the textbook is used as a context for reviewing groups of three and the three-times table.

Pages 12 and 13 of Topic Workbook 3 review the two-times, three-times, four-times and five-times tables at this 'halfway stage' in Level 3. Children are reminded of how the patterns develop, asked to look for missing numbers in the tables and shown how, for example, 3×5 is the same is 5×3.

There are two further worksheets on Copymasters 93 and 94. Copymaster 93 looks at tables up to 5×5 (in order). Copymaster 94 provides a set of table problems arranged randomly. Both worksheets ask children to write the answers as quickly as possible.

Page 15 of the textbook shows examples of how measures are used in the preparation of food. Drinks are measured in litres and half-litres, and potatoes in kilograms and half-kilograms.

All work on measurement is essentially practical, and pages 14 and 15 of Topic Workbook 3 could be supported by children pouring liquids from litre bottles into half-litre cups, and weighing real potatoes or balls of plasticine in kilograms and half-kilograms.

There are more worksheets on litres and kilograms on Copymasters 95 to 98. These include a sheet of blank measuring cylinders marked in litres and half-litres, and a sheet of blank scales marked in kilograms and half-kilograms. These can be used to prepare further worksheets or to record the results of practical measuring activities.

Thumb cards

Use strips of paper or card divided into 5 equal sections about the width of a child's thumb.

Children write a fact from the three-times table on the card, putting a number or a symbol into each section. Some of the cards could show divisions by 3.

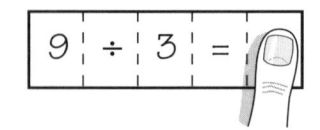

| 2 | × | 3 | = | 6 |

| 9 | ÷ | 3 | = | |

They shuffle the cards and stack them face down. One player takes the top card and looks at it without showing the others. That player then covers one of the numbers or symbols with a finger or thumb. The card is shown to the other players and they have to guess what has been covered up by the thumb. The first player to give the right answer wins the card. Play continues with the next person covering a number or symbol. The person with the most cards at the end is the winner.

These cards can be made for all the other multiplication tables, or to practise recall of addition and subtraction facts.

L3:3 The museum

The materials

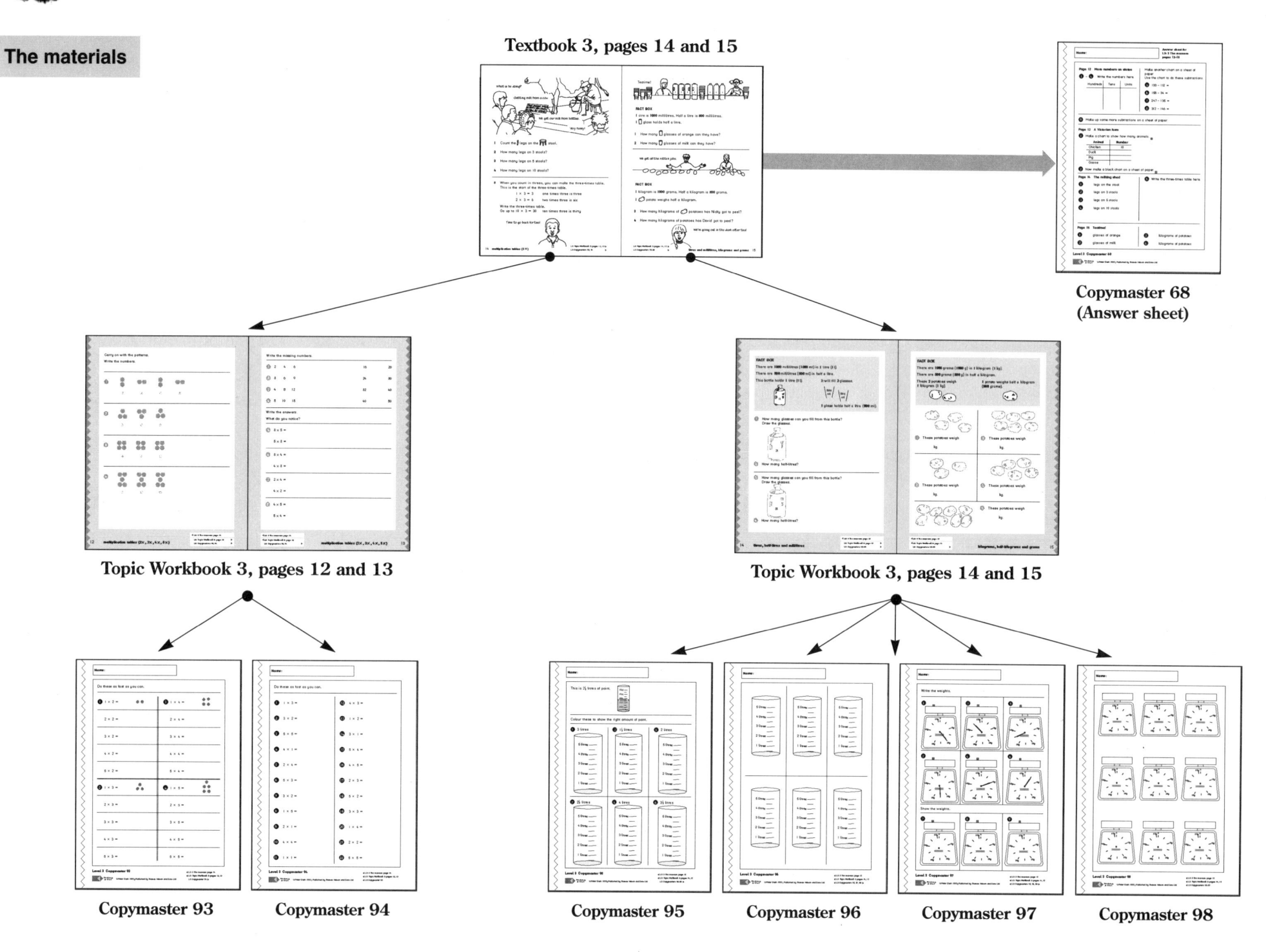

Textbook 3, pages 14 and 15

Copymaster 68
(Answer sheet)

Topic Workbook 3, pages 12 and 13

Topic Workbook 3, pages 14 and 15

Copymaster 93

Copymaster 94

Copymaster 95

Copymaster 96

Copymaster 97

Copymaster 98

L3:3 The museum

L3:4 Saturday night

PAGES 2 AND 3
A treasure hunt

SKILLS, CONCEPTS AND KNOWLEDGE

- Identifying 2D shapes
- Dividing by 5
- Finding one fifth

PRE-ASSESSMENT

Can the child:
- identify triangles, squares, rectangles, pentagons and hexagons?
- divide by 5?
- understand the concept of one fifth?

The story

It is Saturday night and Lisa, Rupa, David and Nicky are going out into the woods for an orienteering exercise and a treasure hunt. They are shown the orienteering signs they should look for. As well as finding their way round the woods, they have to collect certain items on the way.

This kind of activity can be tried in a simpler form in the school grounds, the field, the wildlife area or even the playground. Children can suggest where to put the signs, and use plans to devise routes and instructions for others to follow. Temporary signs can be made using chalk or from sheets of paper; more permanent ones can be made from squares of plywood and durable paint. The aim is to visit all the places in a predetermined order. A simple treasure hunt could be included, based on the sticks, stones or vegetation likely to be found on the course.

Copymaster 99 provides a format for children to record their answers to questions in the textbook.

Maths content and resources

Page 2 of the textbook uses orienteering signs as examples of regular 2D shapes. Children should handle and use these shapes in practical activities, as well as looking for them in the environment.

Page 2 of Topic Workbook 4 continues the orienteering theme by showing the shapes on a map of the woods. Page 3 asks children to identify shapes and write their names in a crossword.

Copymasters 103 and 104 provide drawing exercises based on spotty paper. Copymaster 103 looks at some regular tessellations using a combination of squares, and equilateral triangles with hexagons. Copymaster 104 asks children to draw shapes with 2, 3, 4, 5, 6 and 7 sides.

Page 3 of the textbook introduces fifths and dividing by 5. This can be related to work on groups of five and the five-times table.

Pages 2 and 3 of Number Workbook 4 ask children to colour a fifth of a shape, and to partition a set of spots to find the fifths.

These activities are followed up in Copymasters 105 and 106.

All this work should be accompanied by practical experiences: folding paper (particularly squared paper) into fifths and sorting counters into 5 sets.

Regular tessellations

Use plastic templates of regular shapes or gummed regular shapes.

Regular shapes tessellate in specific combinations. Encourage children to try to find some commonly used tessellations such as octagons/squares and hexagons/triangles:

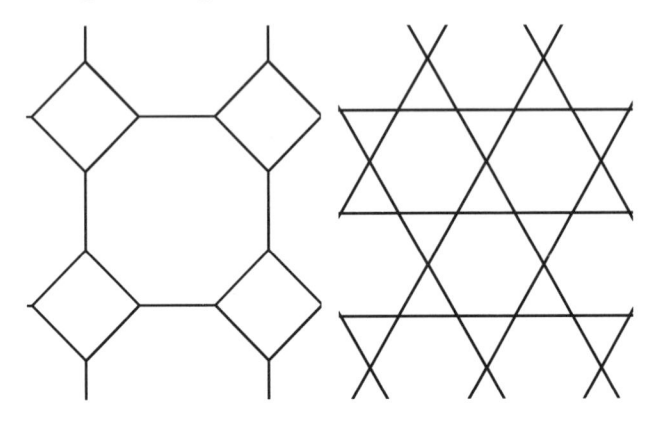

Less common combinations include those involving 12-sided shapes (dodecagons):

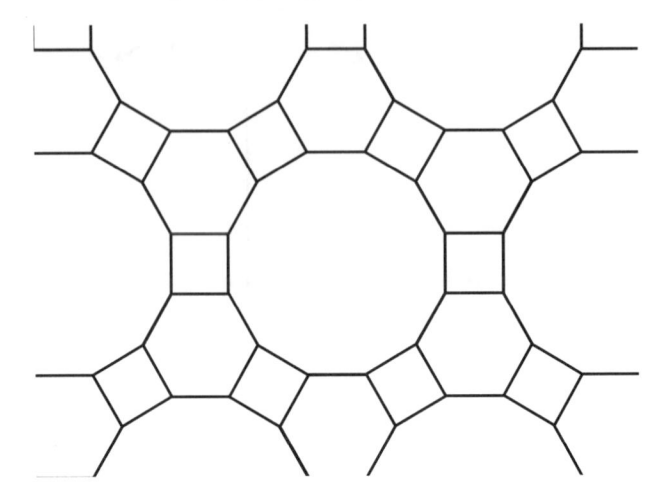

The materials

Textbook 4, pages 2 and 3

Copymaster 99 (Answer sheet)

Topic Workbook 4, pages 2 and 3

Number Workbook 4, pages 2 and 3

Copymaster 103

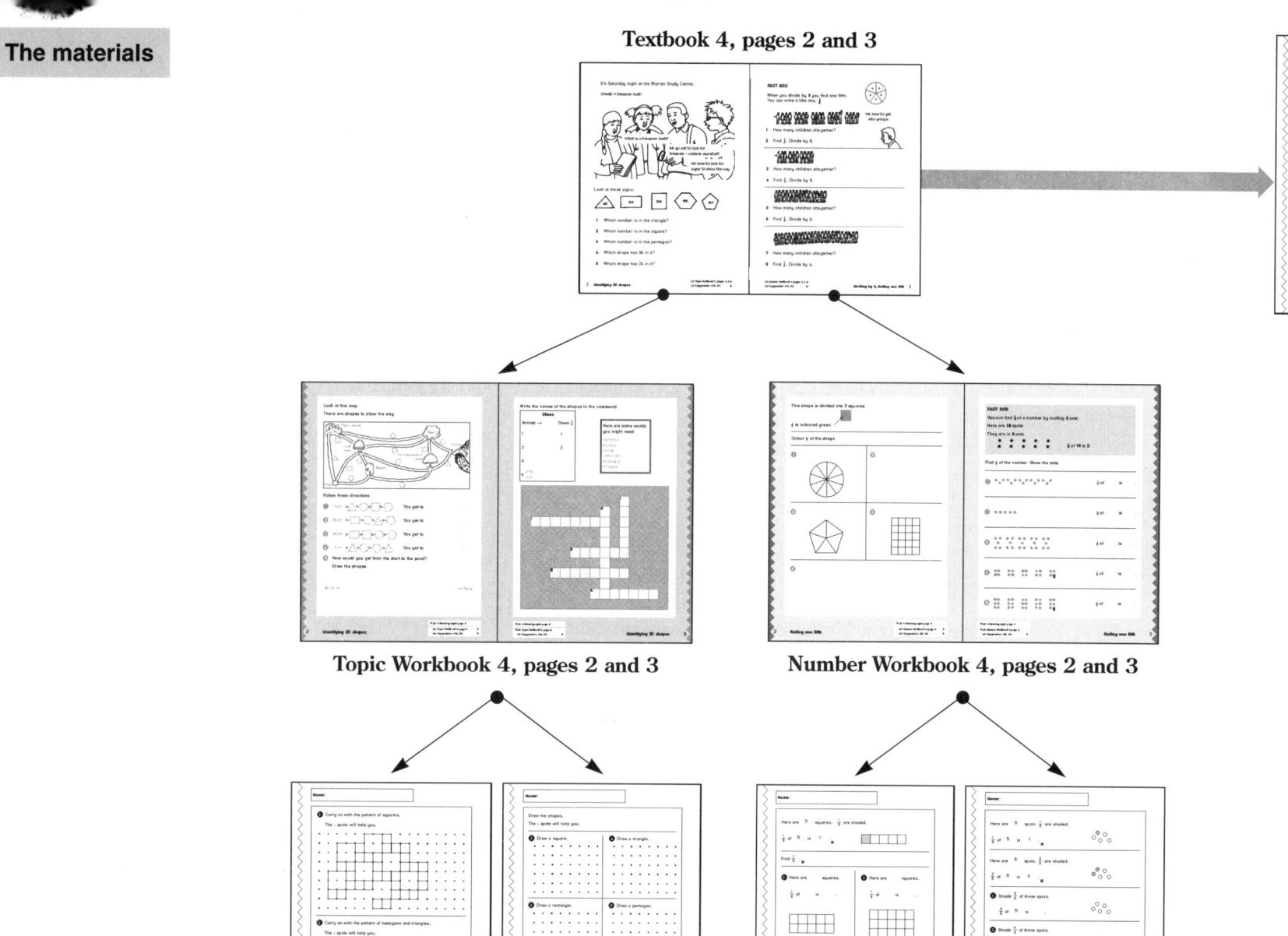

Copymaster 104

Copymaster 105

Copymaster 106

L3:4 Saturday night

PAGES 4 AND 5
Setting off

SKILLS, CONCEPTS AND KNOWLEDGE

- Addition of two-digit numbers to 130
- Subtraction of two-digit numbers from 70
- Co-ordinates and compass points

PRE-ASSESSMENT

Can the child:

- add two-digit numbers?
- subtract one two-digit number from another?
- use letter and number co-ordinates to describe position?
- use the 4 compass points to describe position?

The story

The characters set off on the orienteering course, after being reminded to collect the 'treasure' on the way. There is a map of the course showing the places they will visit. This shows how simple an orienteering course can be. To enrich the work, children could try to devise a plan of the school and mark on it all the important places.

Copymaster 99 provides a format for children to record their answers to questions in the textbook.

Maths content and resources

The orienteering signs are used again on page 4 of the textbook as a context for revisiting the addition and subtraction of two-digit numbers. The sums include examples where children need to exchange tens.

On pages 4 and 5 of Number Workbook 4 there are more additions and subtractions for children to try. They are reminded of how to set out the problems vertically to help them to organise the numbers into tens and ones. As with all the work on two-digit numbers, encourage children to use base-ten apparatus to model the situations and numbers.

The use of base-ten apparatus is emphasised again on Copymasters 107 and 108 which are two more worksheets on adding and subtracting two-digit numbers.

The map on page 5 of the textbook is based on a 6×6 grid to extend the use of co-ordinates. The work also includes the use of compass points which children would use in a real orienteering exercise.

There is more work on this larger grid on pages 4 and 5 of Topic Workbook 4. Page 4 concentrates on compass points and page 5 provides a drawing exercise involving co-ordinates.

Copymaster 109 is a blank 6×6 grid to give children more scope for drawing and playing games involving co-ordinates. Copymaster 110 is a worksheet based on compass points and co-ordinates.

Capturing squares

Use Copymaster 109, counters in two colours and two dice (one marked **1** to **6** and the other marked **A** to **F**).

Two children can play. Each takes a set of counters, and they then take turns to throw both dice. A player can place a counter on the co-ordinate indicated by the dice if the square is free. If not, the player has to wait until his/her next turn. The game ends when all squares are taken (or after a time limit). The player who has captured most squares wins.

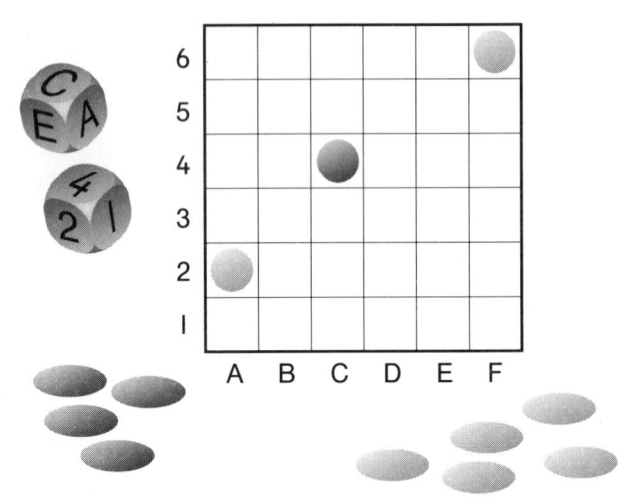

An alternative way of playing allows a player to remove a counter if (s)he throws dice to indicate a co-ordinate which is already occupied. This has the advantage that children are active after each dice throw, but the game is likely to last a little longer and may involve arguments!

L3:4 Saturday night

The materials

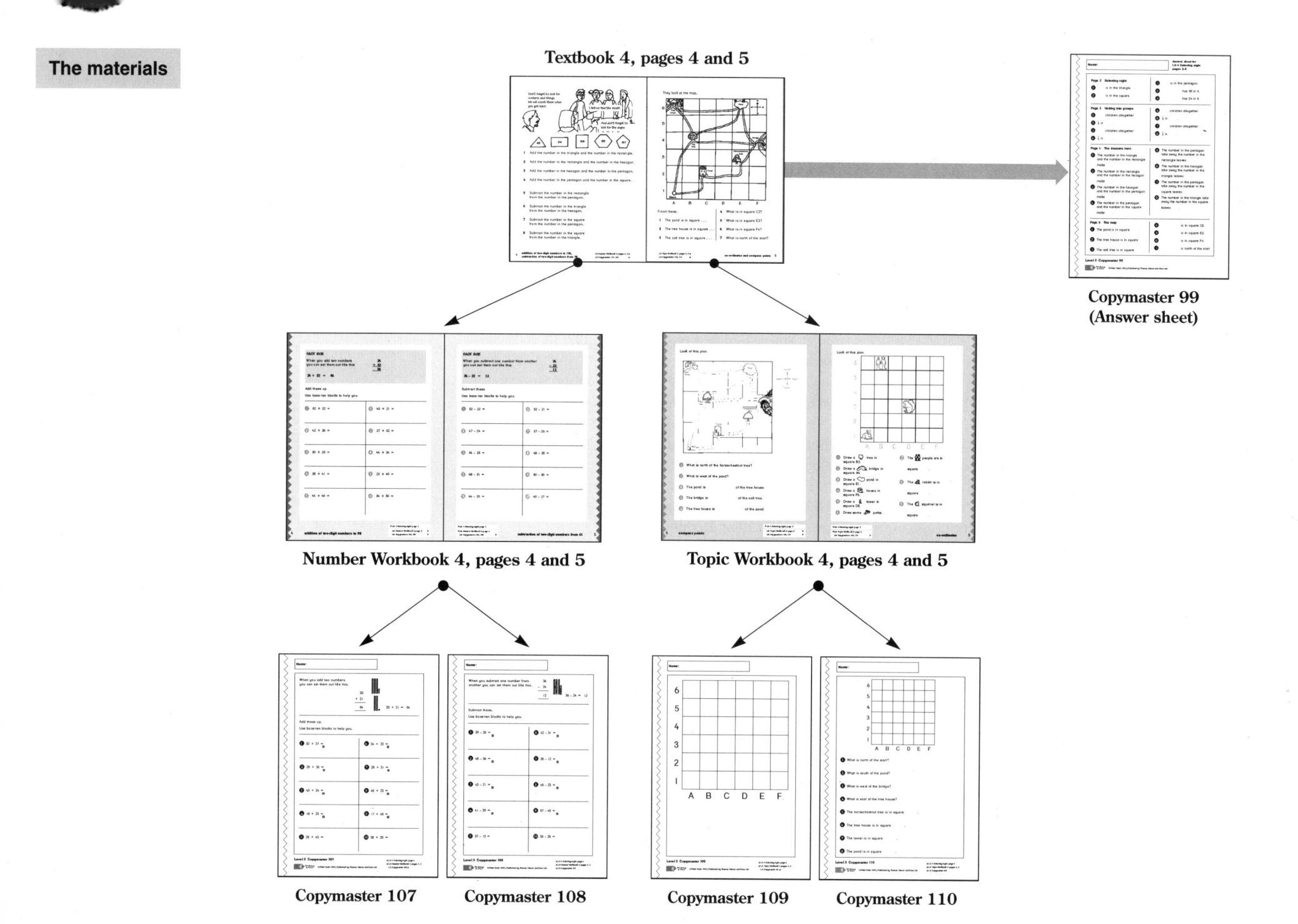

Textbook 4, pages 4 and 5

Copymaster 99
(Answer sheet)

Number Workbook 4, pages 4 and 5

Topic Workbook 4, pages 4 and 5

Copymaster 107

Copymaster 108

Copymaster 109

Copymaster 110

L3:4 Saturday night 79

PAGES 6 AND 7
Out on the course

SKILLS, CONCEPTS AND KNOWLEDGE

▶ Distance in metres
▶ Time in 5-minute intervals

PRE-ASSESSMENT

Can the child:
▶ measure in metres?
▶ tell analogue time in 5-minute intervals?
▶ tell digital time in 5-minute intervals?

The story

The map on page 6 of the textbook shows the distances between points on the orienteering course. The characters are then timed on the various legs of the journey. This work can be developed in a practial way with children trying to devise their own course. They could use metre sticks or tapes to record distances between points, and time themselves with a watch as they go from point to point.

Copymaster 100 provides a format for children to record their answers to questions in the textbook.

Maths content and resources

The work on page 6 of the textbook is about measurement using metres, but there is also the addition of two- and three-digit numbers. The numbers are kept as simple as possible (50m, 100m, 150m and so on) to allow children to focus on the map and the distances rather than being distracted by the calculations. It may be possible for them to go outside and use metre measuring equipment to show the distances.

There is more practical measurement, this time involving centimetres, on pages 6 and 7 of Topic Workbook 4. Children are reminded of the centimetre ruler and asked to measure objects and then draw some of their own.

Copymasters 111 and 112 are two more practical worksheets involving measuring in centimetres.

Page 7 of the textbook concentrates on telling the time in 5-minute intervals. Both analogue and digital clock faces are used.

There is more of this work on pages 8 and 9 of Topic Workbook 4 where children are asked to show the time 5, 10 or 15 minutes later.

To develop this work over a period of time it is helpful to draw children's attention to real clocks showing real time passing, asking questions such as, *'How long until 12 o'clock?'* or *'We have 10 minutes to clear away. What will the time be then?'*

Copymasters 113 to 116 include two further worksheets on analogue and digital time in 5-minute intervals. There are also two pro-forma worksheets, enabling teachers to prepare more materials if necessary.

Five-minute challenges

Use a classroom or kitchen timer, a stopwatch or an ordinary clock.

To help children to gain a concept of the passage of time, set up small challenges for them to complete in a set amount of time. Kitchen timers or stopwatches with alarms are ideal as they sound at the end of the period for which they are set.

Some examples of one-minute challenges are:
- How many names can you write in one minute?
- How many different additions with an answer less than 20 can you write in one minute?
- How many different pentominoes can you find in one minute?

- Some examples of five-minute challenges are:
- How many different triangles can you draw on spotty paper in five minutes?
- How many pencils can you sharpen in five minutes?
- How many times can you walk round the playground in five minutes?

Other activities which can be timed over longer periods could include problem solving on a computer.

The materials

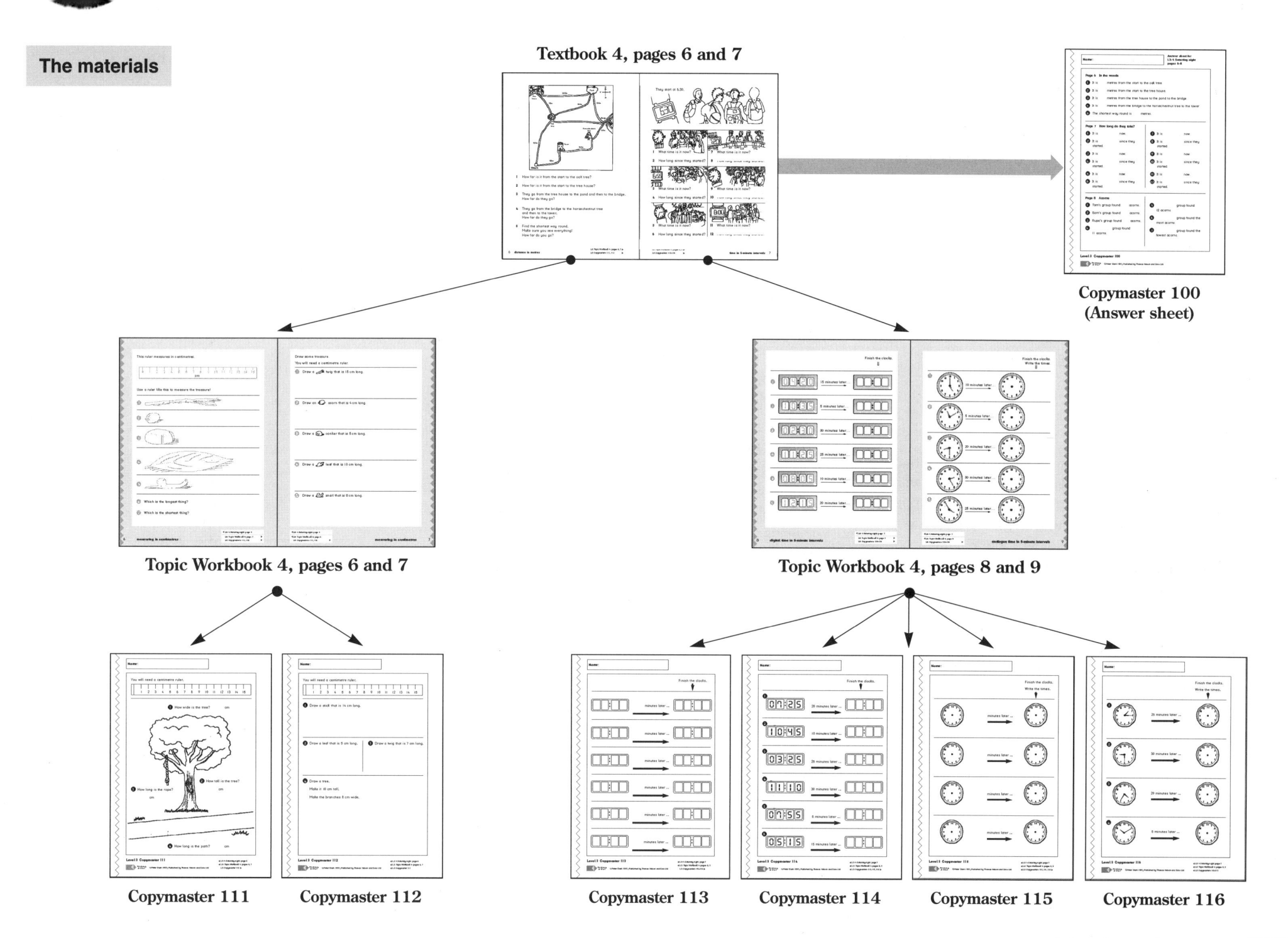

Textbook 4, pages 6 and 7

Copymaster 100
(Answer sheet)

Topic Workbook 4, pages 6 and 7

Topic Workbook 4, pages 8 and 9

Copymaster 111

Copymaster 112

Copymaster 113

Copymaster 114

Copymaster 115

Copymaster 116

L3:4 Saturday night 81

PAGES 8 AND 9
Counting the treasure

SKILLS, CONCEPTS AND KNOWLEDGE
- Reading a bar chart
- Making a bar chart

PRE-ASSESSMENT
Can the child:
- read a bar chart with a scale of 1:2?
- make a bar chart with a scale of 1:2?

The story

Out in the woods, the characters collect the 'treasure' and bring it back for sorting and counting. The work can be developed by staging a real treasure hunt in the school or classroom. Children can be asked to bring back simple things such as 4 white stones, 2 twigs shorter than their fingers, and so on. Including litter in the treasure hunt can be useful!

The work on sorting and making bar charts is much more effective if it is based on a real collection.

Copymasters 100 and 101 provide formats for children to record their answers to questions in the textbook.

Maths content and resources

On page 8 of the textbook children are asked to read a bar chart showing how many acorns each group found on the treasure hunt. This is developed on pages 10 and 11 of Topic Workbook 4. Page 9 of the textbook asks children to make a bar chart based on an illustration, and there are similar exercises on pages 12 and 13 of Topic Workbook 4. These two pages also include work on tally charts. All these pages involve the use of several skills: sorting, tallying, counting and using scale, as well as drawing and measuring skills.

There is further practice on Copymasters 117 to 120. Copymaster 117 provides a blank format for making a bar chart. There are faint lines in the background to help children to construct the bars without elaborate measuring and drawing.

A litter survey

With all data collection and presentation, the best results come from practical work such as a survey using real materials and with a real purpose. A litter survey is a good example. Asking questions such as *'What is the most common type of litter in the playground?'* can lead to some interesting research and a practical result. The litter is cleared away, and children become more aware of the kinds of rubbish they are leaving behind them.

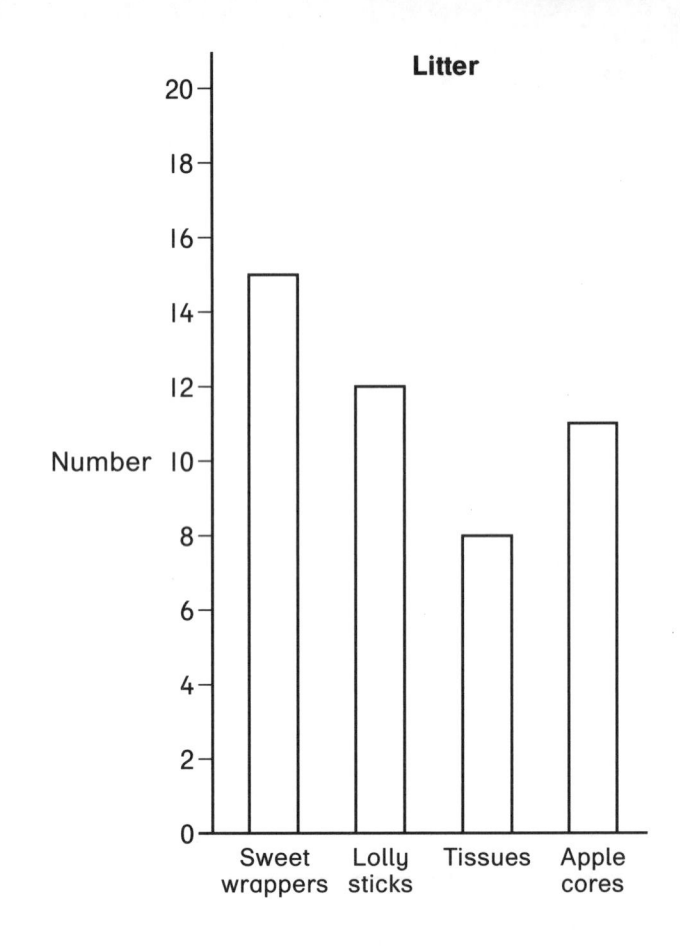

Litter

Type	Number
Sweet wrappers	15
Lolly sticks	12
Tissues	8
Apple cores	11

L3:4 Saturday night

The materials

Textbook 4, pages 8 and 9

Copymaster 100 (Answer sheet)

Copymaster 101 (Answer sheet)

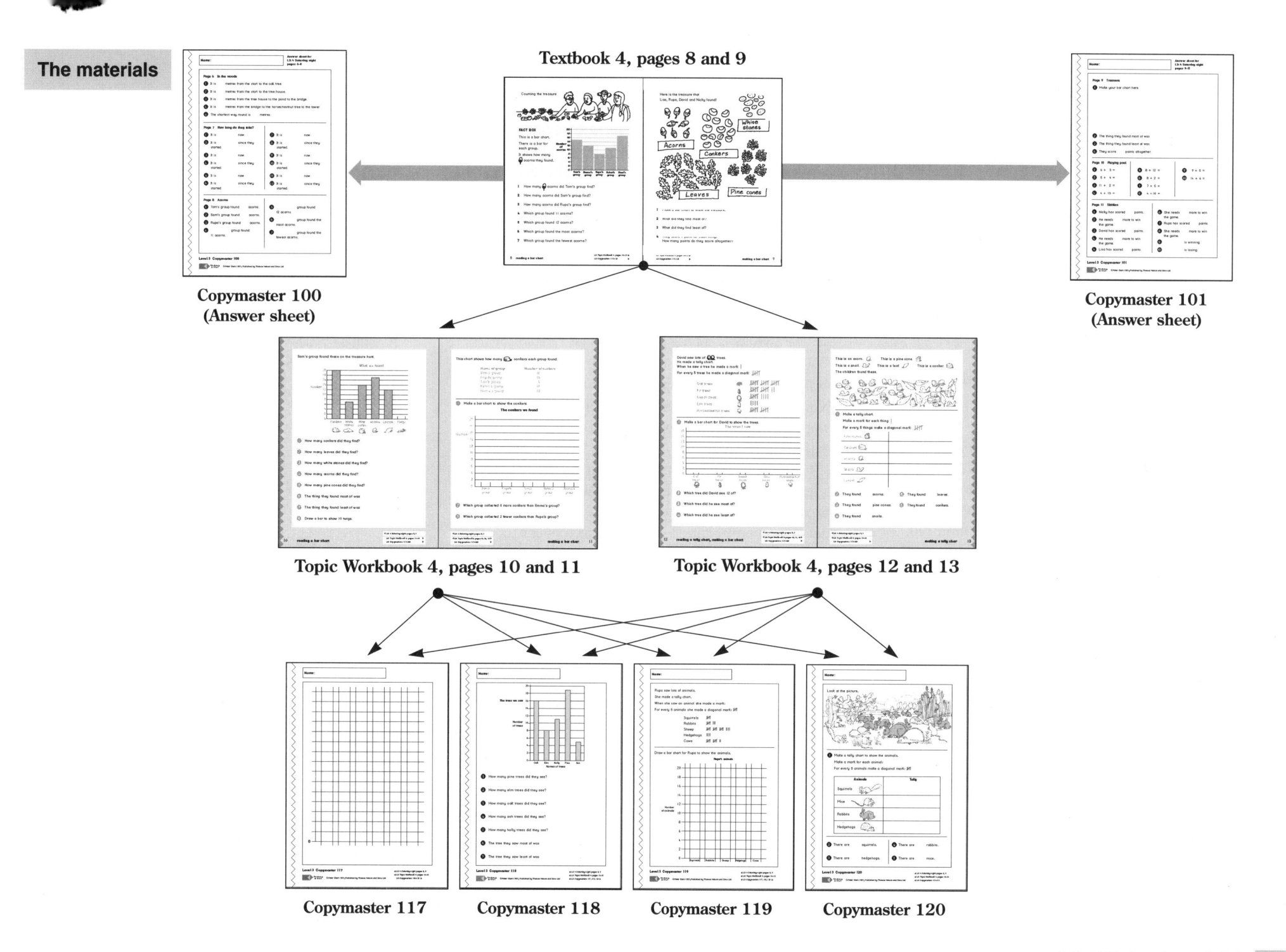

Topic Workbook 4, pages 10 and 11

Topic Workbook 4, pages 12 and 13

Copymaster 117

Copymaster 118

Copymaster 119

Copymaster 120

L3:4 Saturday night 83

PAGES 10 AND 11
Pool and skittles

SKILLS, CONCEPTS AND KNOWLEDGE
▶ Addition facts to 20
▶ Adding lists of numbers

PRE-ASSESSMENT
Can the child:
▶ recall any number facts to 20?
▶ add a list of single-digit numbers?

The story
After the exercise in the woods and the sorting resulting from the treasure hunt, the characters play some games. First of all they play pool and then they have a game of skittles. Discuss with the children the kinds of games they enjoy playing. Many children play games in clubs after school. Most of these will include some element of scoring, and therefore show real-life examples of calculation. Give children opportunities to explain the rules of different games and the ways of scoring.

Copymaster 101 provides a format for children to record their answers to questions in the textbook.

Maths content and resources
The numbers on pool balls on page 10 of the textbook are used as a context for revisiting the addition facts to 20. Many other games rely on quick recall of addition or subtraction facts, and these are ideal for classroom use.

There are two pages of work on addition and subtraction facts on pages 6 and 7 of Number Workbook 4, and a further worksheet on Copymaster 121.

Page 11 of the textbook looks at adding lists of single-digit numbers in the context of a game of skittles. This is another skill used frequently in real life for activities such as shopping.

The technique of looking for pairs of numbers which make tens is emphasised on pages 8 and 9 of Number Workbook 4 and reflects a great deal of the work on number facts which children have experienced so far.

Copymaster 122 supports this work, using 'curved stitching' to practise the number facts to 10 and produce a pleasing pattern. This work can be developed on larger sheets of squared paper to include other number facts, for example all those which make 15.

Children may need help to set up the axes, but should then be able to join all the pairs of numbers which make 15 with straight lines.

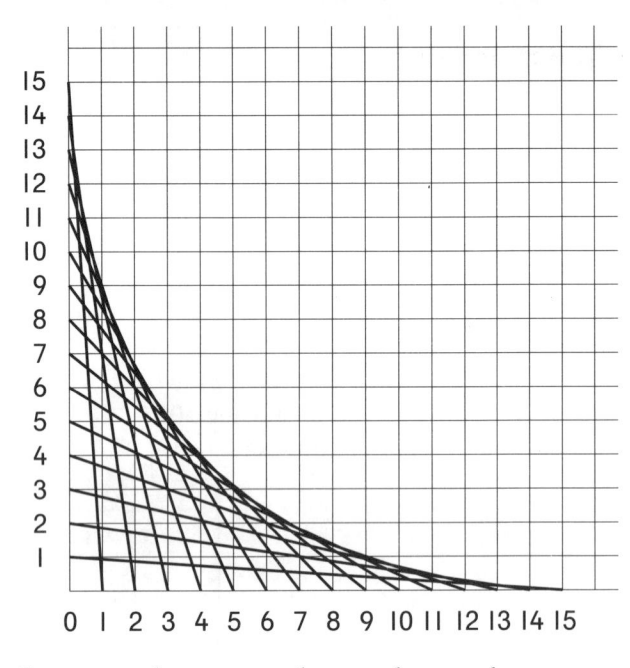

Encourage them to try other numbers, and axes which are not at right angles:

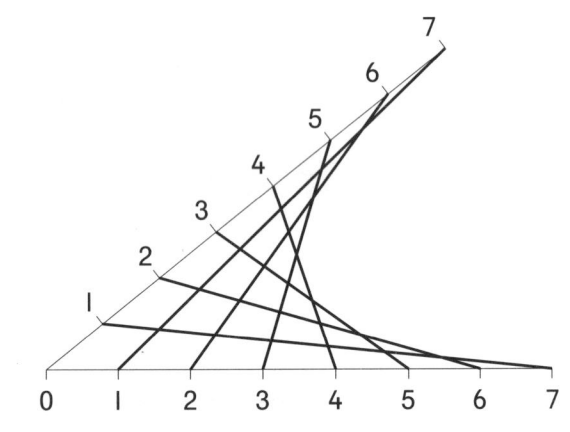

Ideally, children should play a variety of games in which they have to add lists of scores from several rounds, or throw three or more dice to make a move. In this way, adding numbers and using memorised facts will become automatic and habitual.

84 L3:4 Saturday night

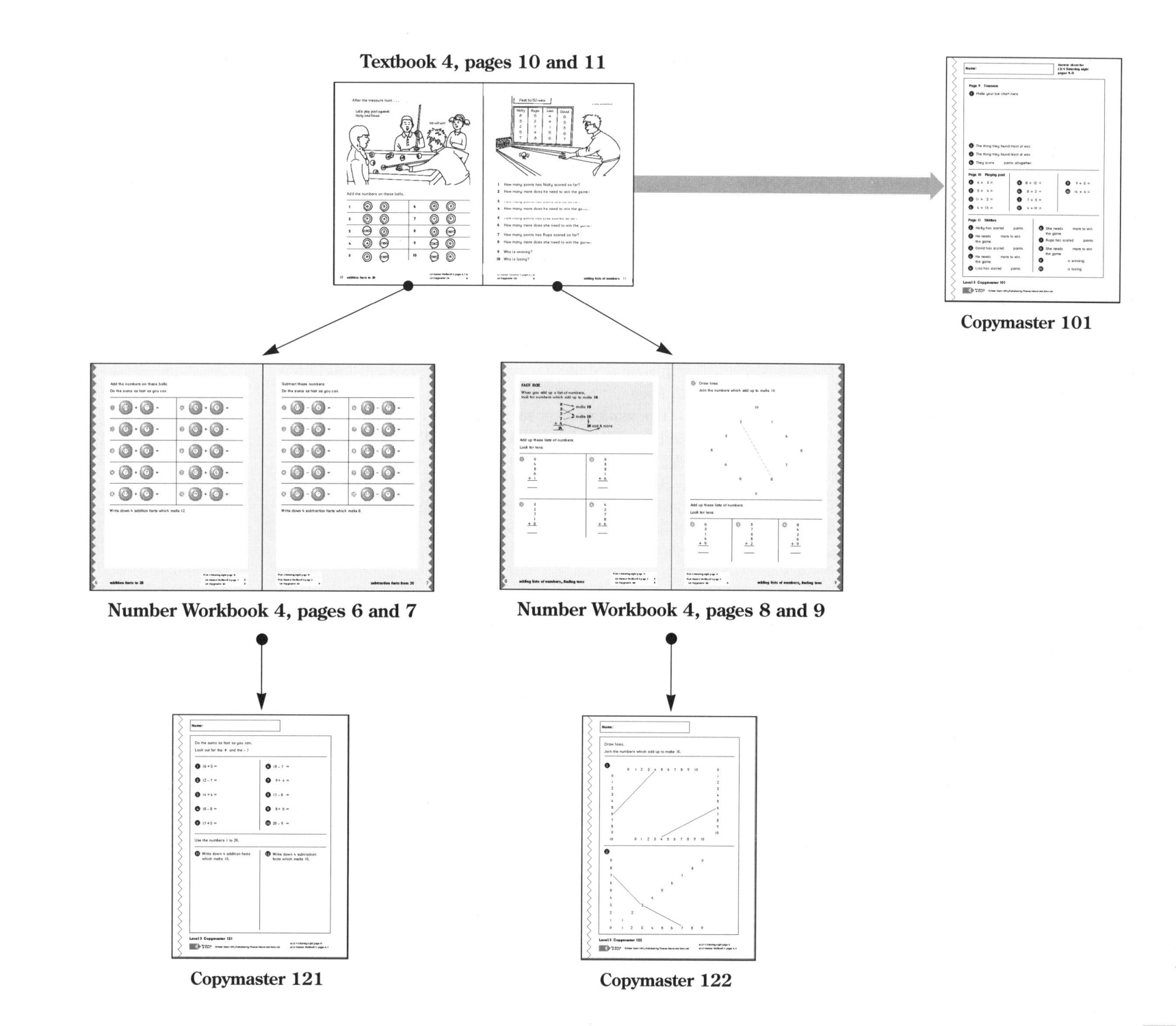

The materials

Textbook 4, pages 10 and 11

Number Workbook 4, pages 6 and 7

Number Workbook 4, pages 8 and 9

Copymaster 101

Copymaster 121

Copymaster 122

L3:4 Saturday night

PAGES 12 AND 13
Board games

SKILLS, CONCEPTS AND KNOWLEDGE

▶ Hundreds, tens and ones
▶ Thousands, hundreds, tens and ones

PRE-ASSESSMENT

Can the child:
▶ order three-digit numbers?
▶ understand place value in three-digit numbers?
▶ understand place value in four-digit numbers?

The story

The evening begins to draw to a close with the characters playing a board game. These games are very popular with children and they often have a strong mathematical content, particularly if money is involved. There are some good strategy games on the market as well. Encourage children to describe their favourite board games and ask them to bring them to school. Many basic skills can be practised painlessly through games. Children may want to try to devise a game of their own. This will involve designing a baseboard and the playing pieces and compiling the rules. All these activities are rich sources for mathematical experience.

Copymaster 102 provides a format for children to record their answers to questions in the textbook.

Maths content and resources

Page 12 of the textbook reviews the work on place value using hundreds, tens and ones. The context is a board game, and useful classroom materials may be collected from old board games found in jumble sales.

Pages 10 and 11 of Number Workbook 4 use the 'Hundreds, tens and ones' chart for setting out three-digit numbers.

There are two supporting worksheets on Copymasters 123 and 124.

Thousands are introduced on page 13 of the textbook. Show children the large base-ten cube which represents 1000 as ten hundreds, and then compare it to the flat 100 square, the 10 rod and the 1 cube.

The work on thousands is reinforced on pages 12 and 13 of Number Workbook 4 and on Copymasters 125 and 126.

All this work can be enhanced by the use of base-ten materials to model the numbers before children write them down.

Who has most?

Use cards marked **1000**, **100**, **10** and **1**.

The number of cards needed will depend on the number of players and the number of cards they take each time. For two or three players, five of each card should be enough.

The cards are shuffled and then spread out or stacked face down. Children take turns to take five cards, one at a time. They add up their cards as they take them, tell other players what their current total is and check each other's totals. The person with the highest (or lowest) total is the winner. The cards are returned and shuffled, and play starts again.

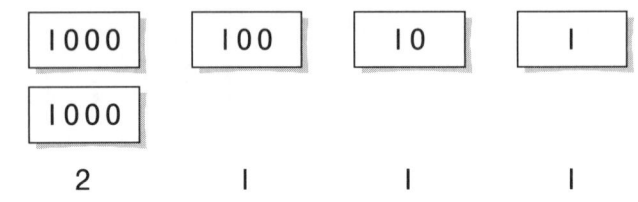

1000	100	10	1
1000			
2	1	1	1

The mathematical value of the game lies in the discussion, the checking and the need to keep a running total of the score.

Thousand place value cards

Children can try building numbers alongside base-ten apparatus using cards which overlap each other:

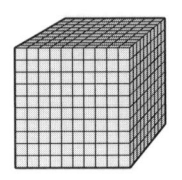

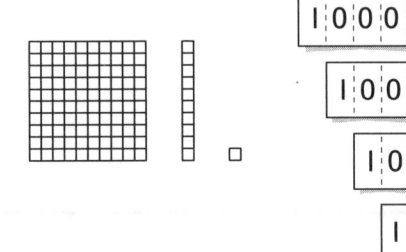

L3:4 Saturday night

The materials

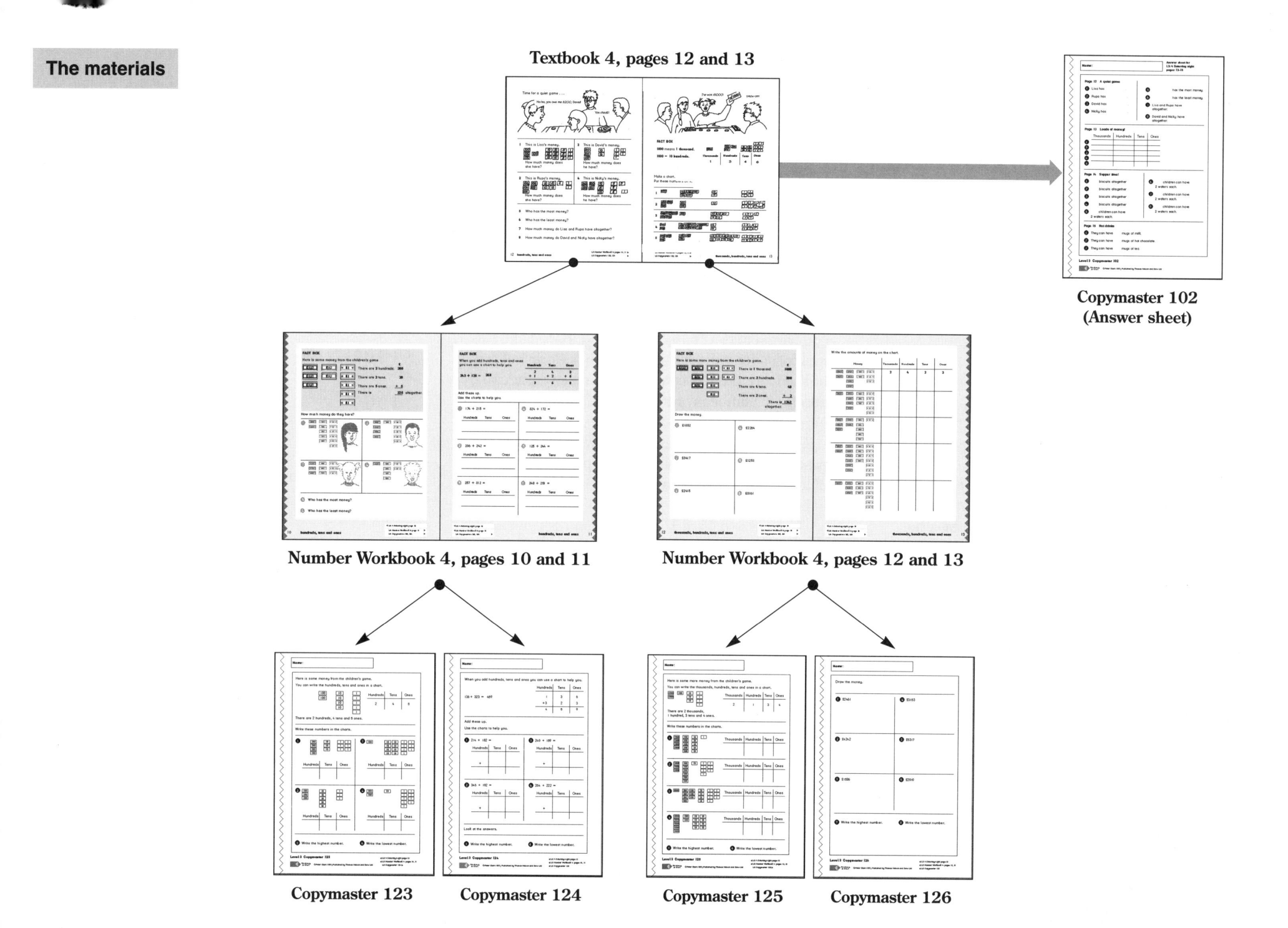

Textbook 4, pages 12 and 13

Copymaster 102
(Answer sheet)

Number Workbook 4, pages 10 and 11

Number Workbook 4, pages 12 and 13

Copymaster 123

Copymaster 124

Copymaster 125

Copymaster 126

L3:4 Saturday night 87

PAGES 14 AND 15
Supper time

SKILLS, CONCEPTS AND KNOWLEDGE

▶ Multiplying by 2
▶ Dividing by 2
▶ Litres and millilitres

PRE-ASSESSMENT

Can the child:
▶ multiply a two-digit number by 2?
▶ divide a two-digit number by 2?
▶ measure using litres and millilitres?

The story

Saturday evening ends with supper – a hot drink and biscuits. Ask the children whether they have a hot drink at bedtime. It may be possible to make a survey of which drinks and biscuits children prefer. Some children may find that certain foods keep them awake or give them bad dreams.

Copymaster 102 provides a format for children to record their answers to questions in the textbook.

Maths content and resources

Page 14 of the textbook uses the context of the sharing out of biscuits for the multiplication and division of two-digit numbers. The number range is below 30 so that children can concentrate on the processes rather than the problems of large numbers. The vertical presentation of multiplications and the use of a box for divisions are also featured.

The work is followed up on pages 14 and 15 of Number Workbook 4, where illustrations of biscuits demonstrate the processes. Children should have access to base-ten apparatus to model the numbers in the problems.

Copymasters 127 and 128 provide more multiplications and divisions. Further worksheets may be made from these by masking the two-digit numbers, photocopying the sheets and inserting new numbers.

This textbook finishes with work on measuring capacity in litres and millilitres on page 15. A quarter of a litre, or 250 millilitres, is introduced in the context of bedtime drinks.

Pages 14 and 15 of Topic Workbook 4 revise half a litre (or 500 millilitres) and then develop the idea of measuring in steps of 100 millilitres. This work should be fully supported by practical measuring activities – pouring liquids or sand into measuring cylinders. Children could begin by checking the capacity of large containers against the information printed on cans of drink and yoghurt pots.

Copymasters 129 and 130 are two more worksheets on litres, half-litres and millilitres. Copymaster 129 can be modified and used by children to record the results of their practical measuring work.

Hide the number

To support the work on multiplying and dividing two-digit numbers, children can use a calculator to 'hide' a multiplication or division. One child sets up a constant, for example ×2. On most calculators this is done by pressing **2**, **×**, **×**. The child then presses **0** to 'hide' the **2** before passing the calculator to another child.

The other child presses any number, and then presses **=**. (S)he looks at the display and tries to decide what the calculator has done to the number. For example, if (s)he pressed **9** and **=** (s)he would get **18**; if (s)he pressed **5** and **=** (s)he would get **10**. Children will need plenty of attempts before they begin to see a pattern. They can then exchange roles and play again.

This activity can be adapted for division, addition and subtraction:

2, **÷**, **÷** will set up 'divide' by 2 as a constant.
2, **+**, **+** will set up 'add 2' as a constant.
2, **−**, **−** will set up 'subtract 2' as a constant.

L3:4 Saturday night

The materials

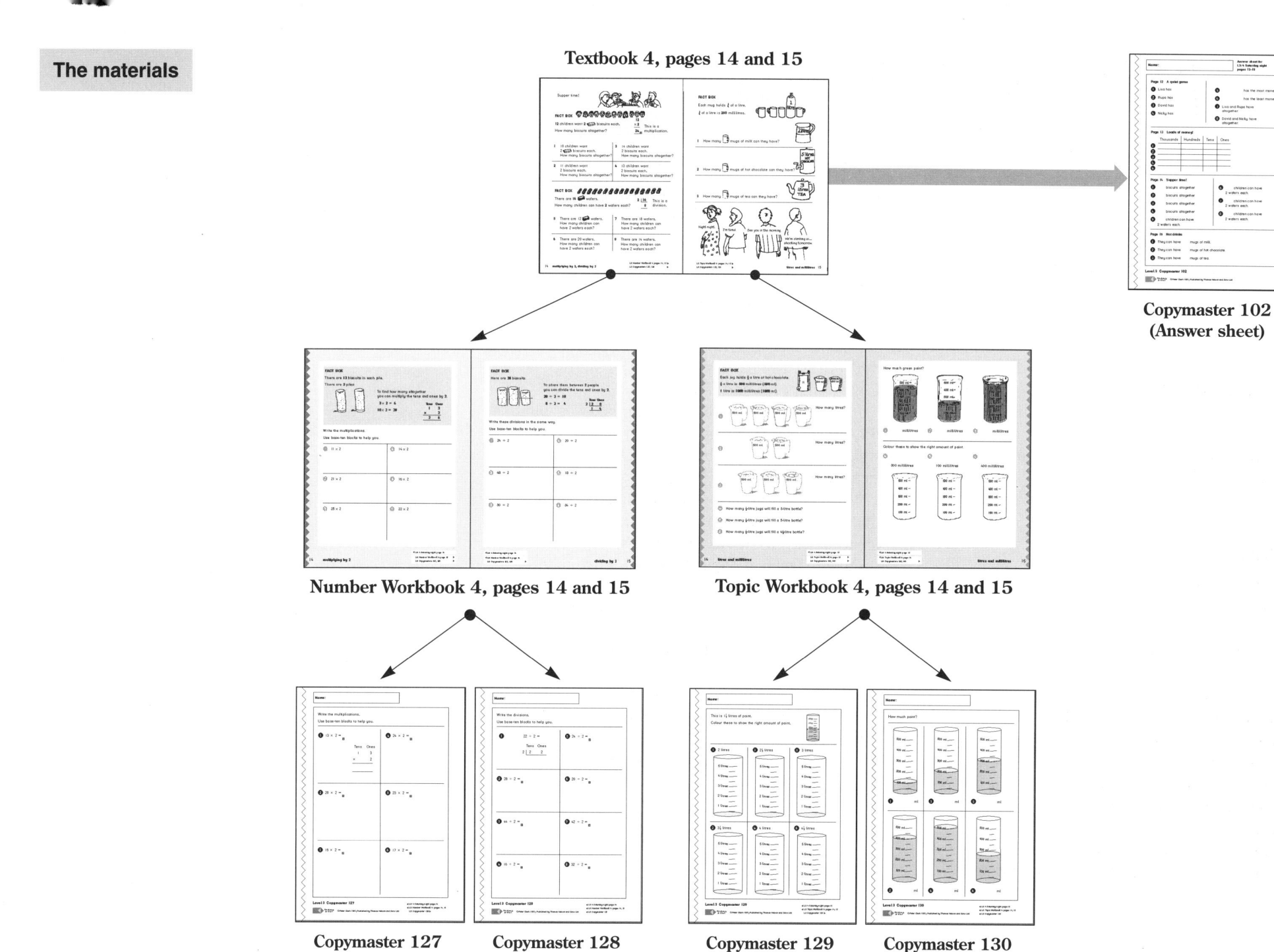

Textbook 4, pages 14 and 15

**Copymaster 102
(Answer sheet)**

Number Workbook 4, pages 14 and 15

Topic Workbook 4, pages 14 and 15

Copymaster 127 **Copymaster 128** **Copymaster 129** **Copymaster 130**

L3:4 Saturday night 89

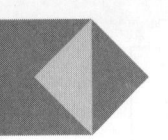

L3:5 Climbing and shooting

PAGES 2 AND 3

Getting up

SKILLS, CONCEPTS AND KNOWLEDGE
- Identifying 3D shapes
- Kilograms and grams

PRE-ASSESSMENT
Can the child:
- identify cuboids, cylinders, spheres and prisms?
- measure in kilograms and grams?

The story

It is Sunday morning, and the characters Nicky, David, Rupa and Lisa are getting up and having breakfast. The two boys are shown getting up and getting washed, and the two girls are shown choosing their breakfast cereal.

David tells Nicky that they will be climbing and shooting that morning. Ask the children what they think this will involve. Find out whether any of them take part in any similar sports.

Discuss what the children eat for breakfast. It may be possible to make a class survey of favourite breakfast cereals.

Copymaster 131 provides a format for children to record their answers to questions in the textbook.

Maths content and resources

Page 2 of the textbook uses the packaging of the boys' toiletries as a context for looking at commonly used 3D shapes. Children should have access to a set of 3D shapes, and could collect packages and containers to match to them.

The work is supported on pages 2 and 3 of Topic Workbook 5 where children look again at common 3D shapes including hexagonal and triangular prisms.

There are two more worksheets on this on Copymasters 135 and 136.

Page 3 of the textbook also features boxes, but this time they contain cereals and the emphasis is on weight in kilograms. 1 box of cereal weighs 100 grams (a tenth of a kilogram). Many scales are calibrated in 100-gram divisions and children should have the opportunity to use these. Classroom cooking is an ideal vehicle for this, as well as for work on capacity.

Pages 4 and 5 of Topic Workbook 5 ask children to calculate the weights of various numbers of boxes, and to draw the hands on scales to show specified weights.

There is another worksheet on Copymaster 138. Copymaster 137 may be used to make further worksheets if required, or children could use it to show the results of practical measurement activities using 100-gram units.

The unit of measurement is 100 grams in all this work.

Shape game cards

Use rectangles of card, Copymasters 135 and 136, and scissors and glue.

Ask the children to make some shape cards for playing games.

If they are making dominoes, they cut out a 3D shape and paste it at one end of the card. They draw a line down the middle and write the name of a different shape at the other end. They can copy out the words on the copymasters, or cut them out and paste them on.

If they are making playing cards for snap or matching games, give them a pair of cards. They paste a cut-out shape on one card and write or paste its name on the other. In this way they can quickly build up a pack of 3D shape cards.

The materials

Textbook 5, pages 2 and 3

Copymaster 131 (Answer sheet)

Topic Workbook 5, pages 2 and 3

Topic Workbook 5, pages 4 and 5

Copymaster 135

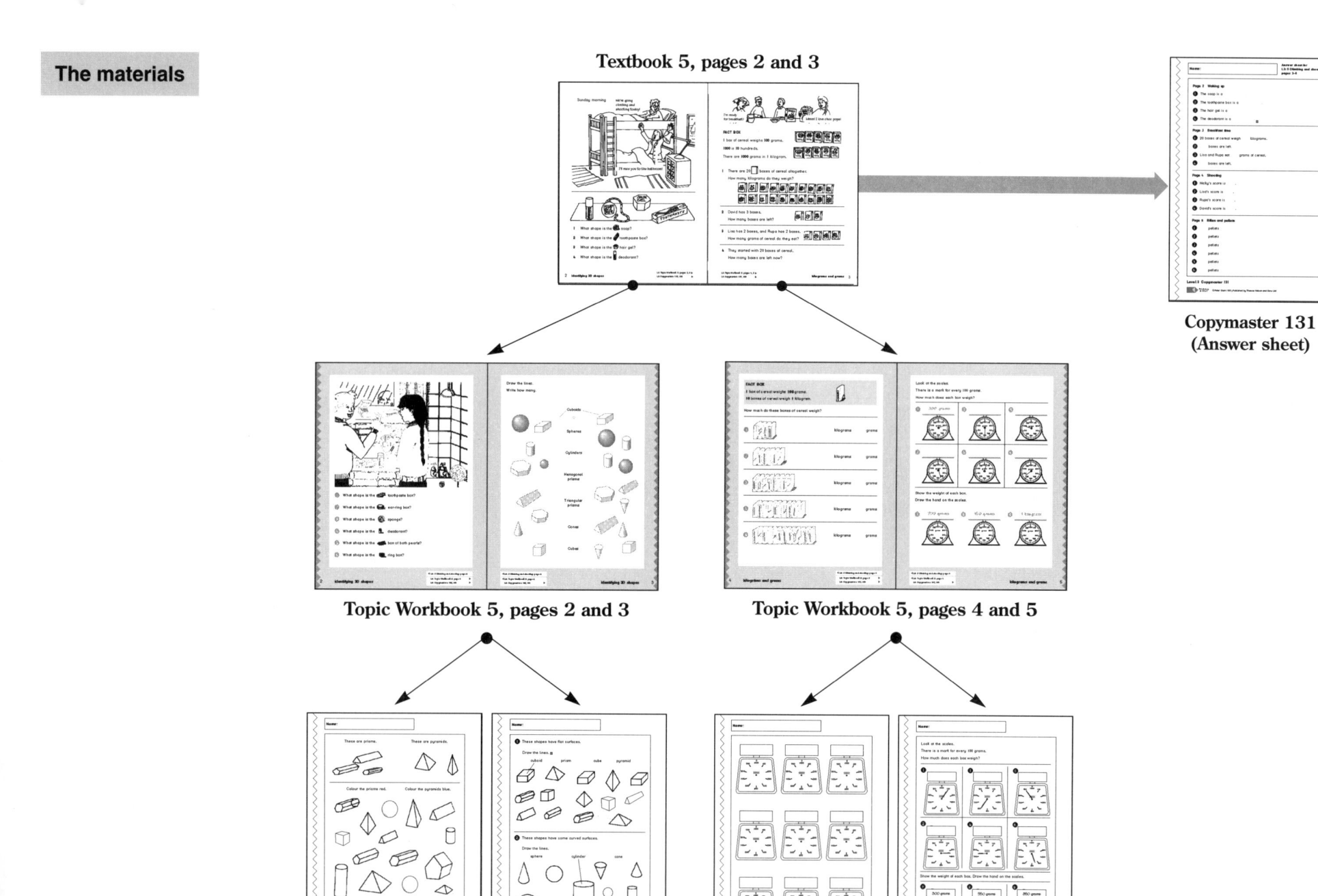

Copymaster 136

Copymaster 137

Copymaster 138

L3:5 Climbing and shooting 91

PAGES 4 AND 5
Shooting

SKILLS, CONCEPTS AND KNOWLEDGE

▶ Adding lists of numbers
▶ Hundreds, tens and ones

PRE-ASSESSMENT

Can the child:
▶ add a list of single-digit numbers?
▶ understand place value in three-digit numbers?

The story

The characters go out on to the rifle range, where they use air rifles to shoot at targets. It is important to discuss the safety aspects of shooting and climbing activities with children. These are emphasised in the textbooks, but need reinforcement. Some children may have used an air rifle at a fairground or at home. Discuss with them how their parents or others made sure they were safe.

Copymaster 131 provides a format for children to record their answers to questions in the textbook.

Maths content and resources

The targets on page 4 of the textbook provide an ideal way of revising the addition of lists of numbers. Children play many games in which they accumulate scores and should be familiar with this idea. Remind them to look for tens as a first strategy for adding lists. Page 2 of Number Workbook 5 gives more examples of targets with scores to add. Page 3 asks children to mark targets with 5 bullet holes to make a particular score. There are several possible answers to the questions.

Copymaster 139 is a large blank target that children could use for their own games. Copymaster 140 could be used for scoring those games, or for making more target worksheets. Copymasters 141 and 142 echo the Number Workbook pages.

Page 5 of the textbook uses tins of 100 pellets as a context for revising hundreds, tens and ones. This is developed on pages 4 and 5 of Number Workbook 5, where children are encouraged to relate three-digit numbers to base-ten materials. There are two parallel worksheets on Copymasters 143 and 144. There is a pro-forma worksheet on Copymaster 145 for teachers or children to create more examples.

Target games

Use paperclips, cubes or counters, and Copymasters 139 and 140.

Place the large target on Copymaster 139 on the floor. Children have 5 paperclips each, and drop them on to the target. They record their hits (or misses) on Copymaster 140. If a paperclip falls across a line they can score either the higher number or the number with most of the paperclip in its section of the target.

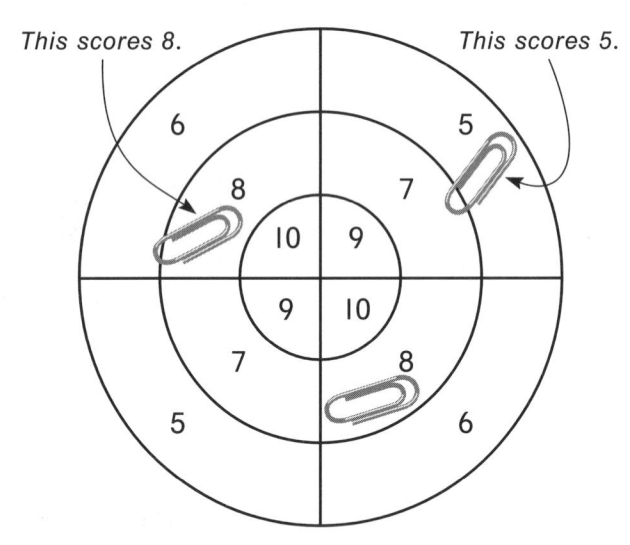

This scores 8.   *This scores 5.*

A player has all 5 turns before the next player tries. Encourage the children to help each other to add up the scores as they go along. Encourage them to try to predict the scores they need to equal or beat each other.

As an alternative to dropping paperclips, children could flip counters or toss cubes.

L3:5 Climbing and shooting

The materials

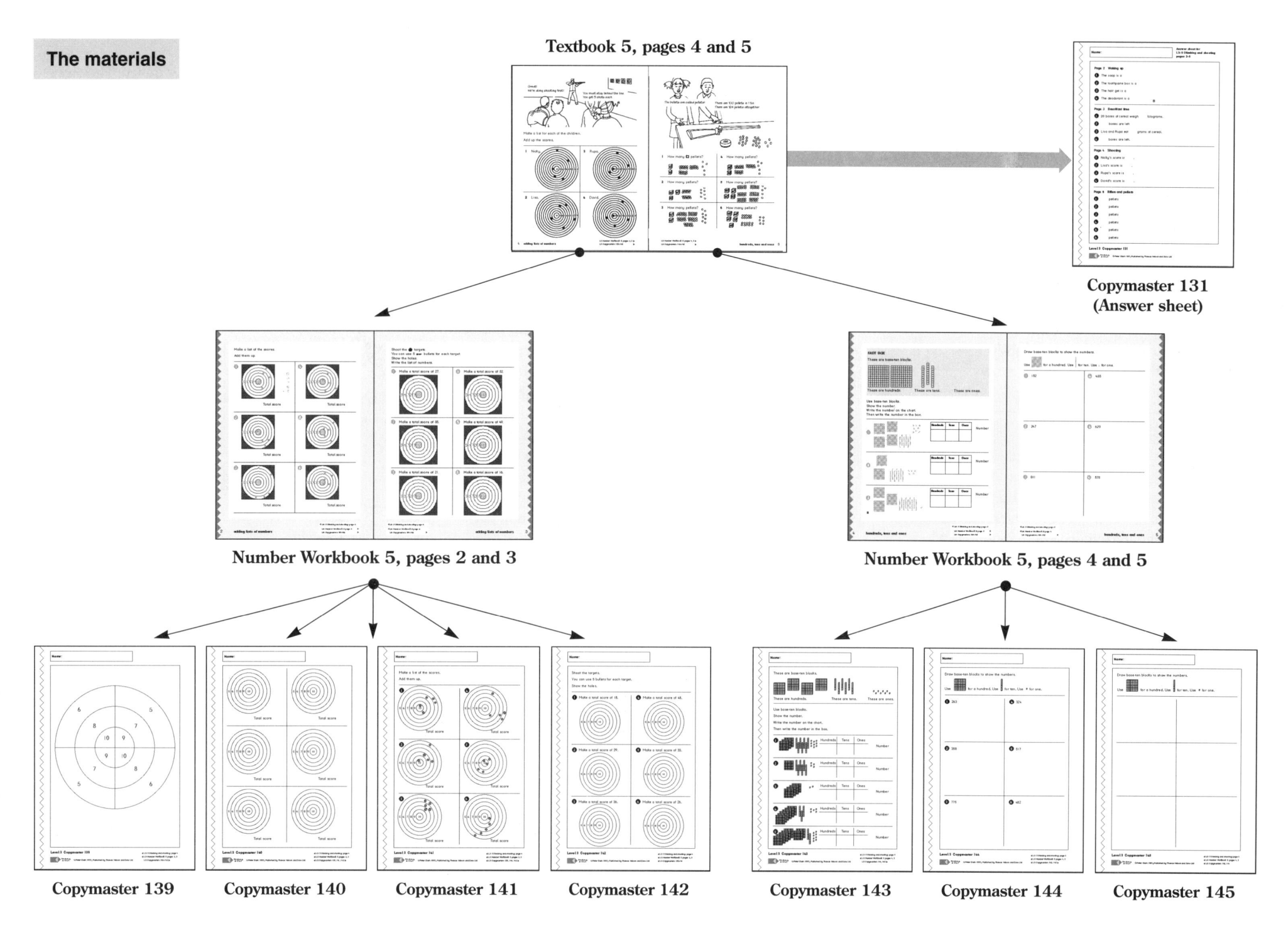

Textbook 5, pages 4 and 5

Copymaster 131
(Answer sheet)

Number Workbook 5, pages 2 and 3

Number Workbook 5, pages 4 and 5

Copymaster 139

Copymaster 140

Copymaster 141

Copymaster 142

Copymaster 143

Copymaster 144

Copymaster 145

L3:5 Climbing and shooting 93

PAGES 6 AND 7

Archery

SKILLS, CONCEPTS AND KNOWLEDGE

▶ Multiplication tables (3×)
▶ Making a tally chart
▶ Making a bar chart

PRE-ASSESSMENT

Can the child:
▶ recall any of the three-times table?
▶ make a tally chart?
▶ make a bar chart?

The story

The characters move on to archery, and once again the safety rules are emphasised. The children look at the three flights on each arrow.

Archery targets are organised into concentric circles, and the bull's eye is called the 'gold'. Ask children whether they have ever tried to fire a bow and arrow and then discuss the difficulties involved in aiming such a weapon.

Copymaster 132 provides a format for children to record their answers to questions in the textbook.

Maths content and resources

The three-times table is revisited on page 6 of the textbook, exploiting the fact that archers fire arrows in sets of three. There are also three feathers on an arrow's flight, and these could also be used to generate groups of three.

There is further work on making groups of three, patterns of three, missing numbers and the three-times table on pages 6 and 7 of Number Workbook 5.

Copymaster 146 allows children to generate any of the multiplication tables up to 5×5. Teachers could also use it to create worksheets. Copymaster 147 provides work on patterns of three, missing numbers and the three-times table.

The colours of arrow flights are the context for a tallying exercise on page 7 of the textbook. Children then make a bar chart to show the results of the tally. Arrow flights are arranged with two the same colour and the third a different colour, so children will need to take care with their tallying.

More work on tally charts and bar charts using archery as a theme can be found on pages 6 and 7 of Topic Workbook 5.

There is a further worksheet on Copymaster 148.

Fizz buzz

This is a good game for reinforcing tables. The children sit in a circle and the first child says *'One'*. The second child says *'Two'*, and so on. (They may need to practise straightforward counting before they play the game.) Every time they come to a number which features in the table they have to say *'Fizz'* (or *'Buzz'*) instead of the number.

For the three-times table the counting would go: *'One, two, fizz, four, five, fizz, seven, eight, fizz ...'*

This is quite difficult for some children, so encourage them to count slowly at first.

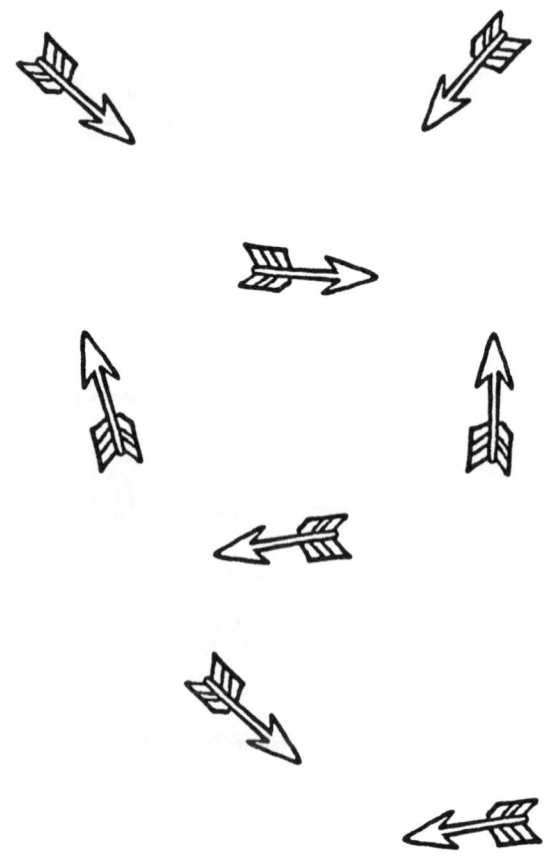

L3:5 Climbing and shooting

The materials

Textbook 5, pages 6 and 7

Copymaster 132 (Answer sheet)

Number Workbook 5, pages 6 and 7

Topic Workbook 5, pages 6 and 7

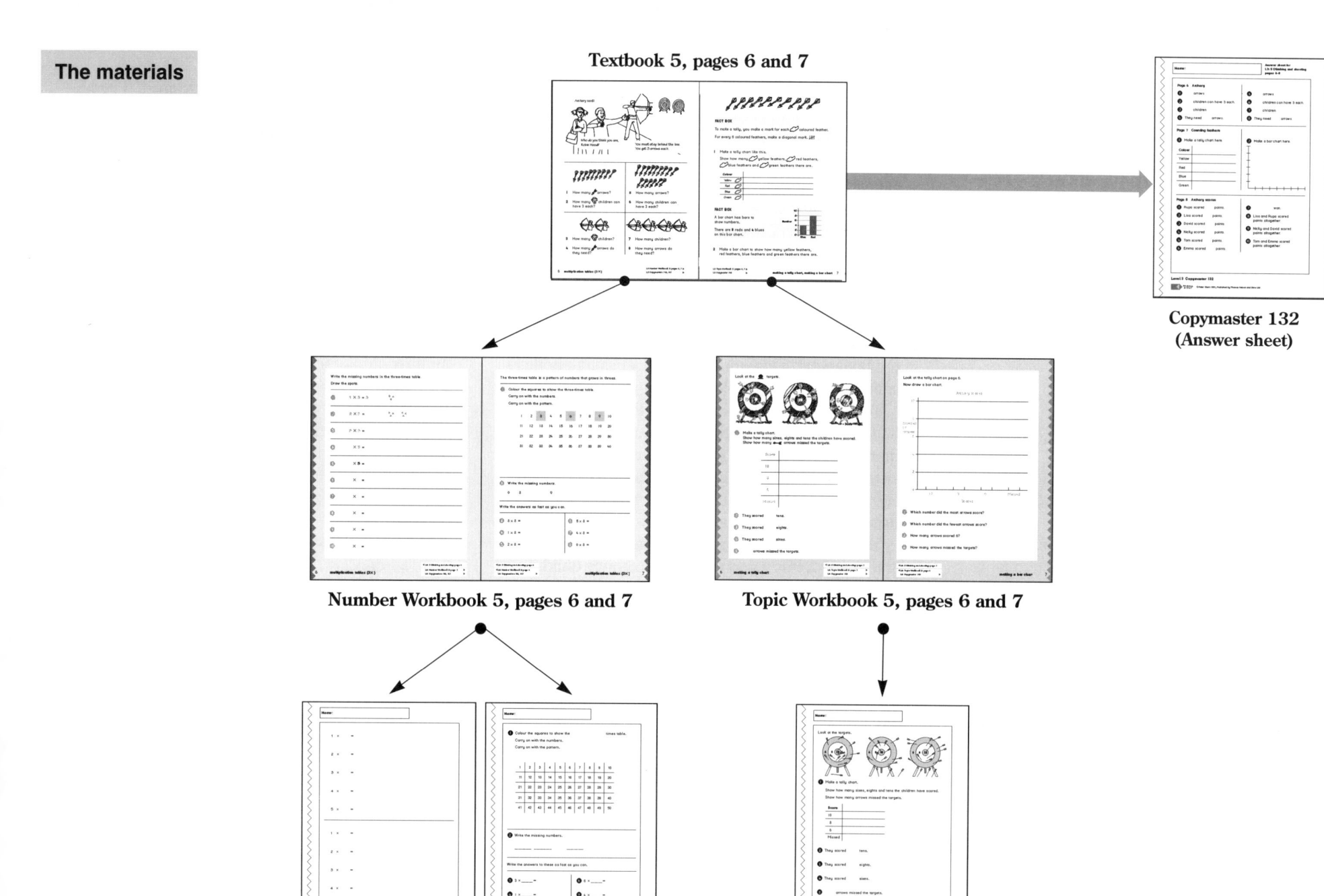

Copymaster 146

Copymaster 147

Copymaster 148

L3:5 Climbing and shooting 95

PAGES 8 AND 9
Archery scores and a climbing net

SKILLS, CONCEPTS AND KNOWLEDGE

▶ Reading a bar chart
▶ Multiplying by 2
▶ Multiplying by 3

PRE-ASSESSMENT

Can the child:
▶ read a bar chart?
▶ identify a situation requiring multiplication?
▶ multiply by 2?
▶ multiply by 3?

The story

At the end of the archery session the characters add and compare their scores, and then move on to an assault course. The first thing they see is a climbing net.

Intersecting ropes produce number arrays and patterns. Discuss where these can be found in real life, for example, in the columns and rows of goods on shelves in supermarkets.

Nets also provide examples of shapes such as squares, rectangles and parallelograms. These are not exploited here (see page 98), but may be worth discussing in the context of a climbing net in the school.

Copymasters 132 and 133 provide formats for children to record their answers to questions in the textbook.

Maths content and resources

Page 8 of the textbook is about interpreting a bar chart which shows the archery scores. Children also have to add some scores. This kind of chart could be made in the classroom and used to score any competitive activity. The bar chart on this page and the one on page 8 of Topic Workbook 5 have scales marked in twos. Children have to draw a bar chart on page 9, but this time with a scale marked in fives.

Copymaster 149 provides another bar chart with a scale marked in twos, and related questions.

The intersections made by ropes in a net are used on page 9 of the textbook as a context for multiplication. This work relates to the multiplying of columns and rows to find area. It is developed on pages 8 and 9 of Number Workbook 5 where children have to write the multiplications indicated by intersecting ropes, and draw intersecting ropes to show multiplications. To support the work practically, they could model the intersections using strips of paper or pieces of string.

There are two further worksheets on Copymasters 150 and 151. It is a good idea to encourage children to investigate intersections they find for themselves in real life.

Investigating intersections

Use strips of paper or lengths of string.

Children can investigate the intersections made by strips of paper in an organised way. For example, they could start with two horizontal strips and add the vertical strips one at a time, recording the number of intersections as the pattern develops:

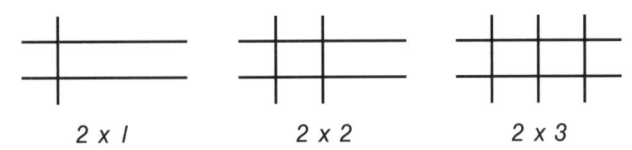

2 x 1   2 x 2   2 x 3

An alternative investigation is to compare the number of intersections with the number of squares they make and the number of strips used altogether. It is unlikely that children will be able to generalise, but they may begin to see that the number of strips added to the number of squares totals one more than the number of intersections.

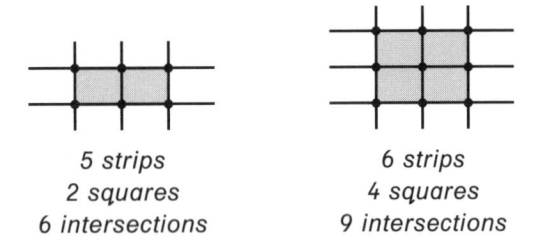

5 strips   6 strips
2 squares   4 squares
6 intersections 9 intersections

L3:5 Climbing and shooting

The materials

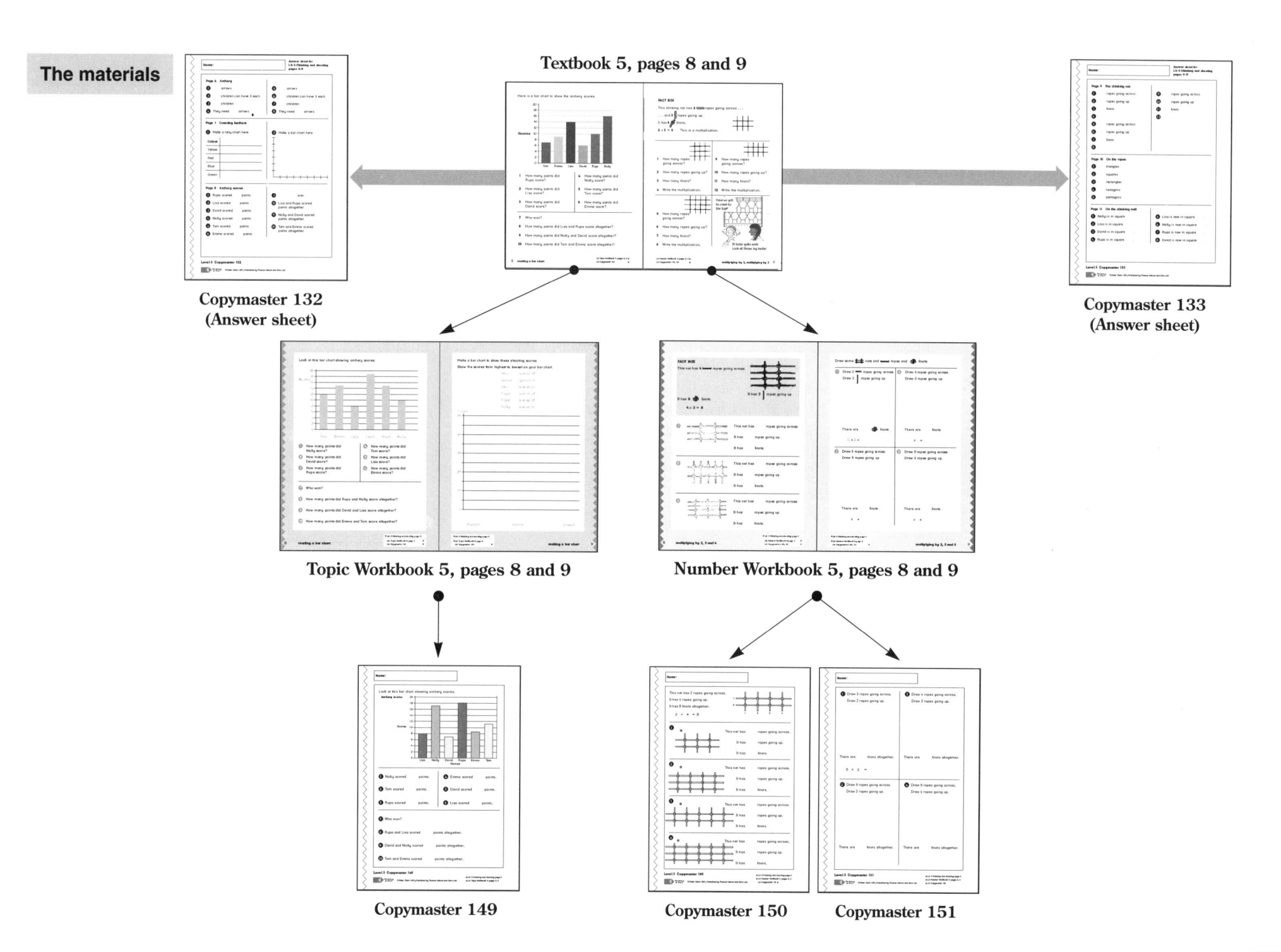

Textbook 5, pages 8 and 9

Copymaster 132 (Answer sheet)

Copymaster 133 (Answer sheet)

Topic Workbook 5, pages 8 and 9

Number Workbook 5, pages 8 and 9

Copymaster 149

Copymaster 150

Copymaster 151

L3:5 Climbing and shooting 97

PAGES 10 AND 11

On the ropes

SKILLS, CONCEPTS AND KNOWLEDGE

▶ Identifying 2D shapes
▶ Co-ordinates

PRE-ASSESSMENT

Can the child:

▶ identify triangles, squares, rectangles, hexagons and pentagons?
▶ use letter and number co-ordinates to describe position?

The story

The characters are about to climb the climbing net. This time, the shapes the ropes make are the focus of the page. Ask children to look for and identify similar shapes in school. They should be encouraged to look for irregular shapes as well as regular ones.

The characters move on to the climbing wall. Climbing is an activity in which planning, as well as physical strength, is important. Children can gain a lot of enjoyment from climbing without necessarily climbing very high. Climbing walls often provide interesting routes without taking the climber more than a few metres above the ground. Discuss with children the safety aspects of climbing.

Copymaster 133 provides a format for children to record their answers to questions in the textbook.

Maths content and resources

On page 10 of the textbook the arrangement of ropes in a climbing net demonstrates combinations of regular and irregular 2D shapes. Children could try to make these with Geostrips or strips of card and paper fasteners. They could also design their own nets.

Pages 10 and 11 of Topic Workbook 5 ask children to draw 2D shapes. First they carry on with some patterns, and then they draw as many different hexagons and pentagons as possible on spotty paper.

There is more work on shapes and symmetry in Copymaster 152.

More work on co-ordinates can be found on page 11 of the textbook. Children have to describe the characters' positions on the climbing wall, and then describe their new positions when they move. To help them with this they could place counters on the page to identify the new positions before writing the answers.

Page 12 of Topic Workbook 5 provides another exercise like this, and page 13 asks children to plot the characters' movements on a chart.

Copymasters 153 and 154 are two parallel worksheets; the shapes plotted on Copymaster 154 are the common 2D shapes. Children may notice that a square needs five instructions, and a triangle needs four. Copymaster 155 provides an arrangement of spots in a 6×6 grid for children or teachers to devise patterns, shapes or pictures and write down the co-ordinates for others to try.

Shape game cards

Use rectangles of card, Copymaster 57 (see page 58), and scissors and glue.

2D shape cards can be made in the same way as the 3D shape cards described on page 90.

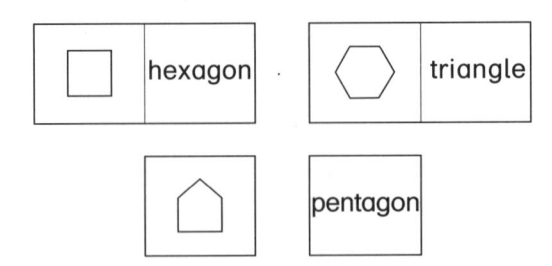

Treasure hunt

Use Copymaster 155.

Children can play a variation on the game of battleships. One child places or draws items of 'treasure' on Copymaster 155, without showing his/her opponent. The treasure could be cubes, shells, acorns, conkers or any other small items. The other child tries to guess where the treasure is by suggesting a pair of co-ordinates. If there is treasure in that square, (s)he takes it. Allow them five guesses before they exchange roles. The winner is the person with the most treasure when both players have had five guesses.

The materials

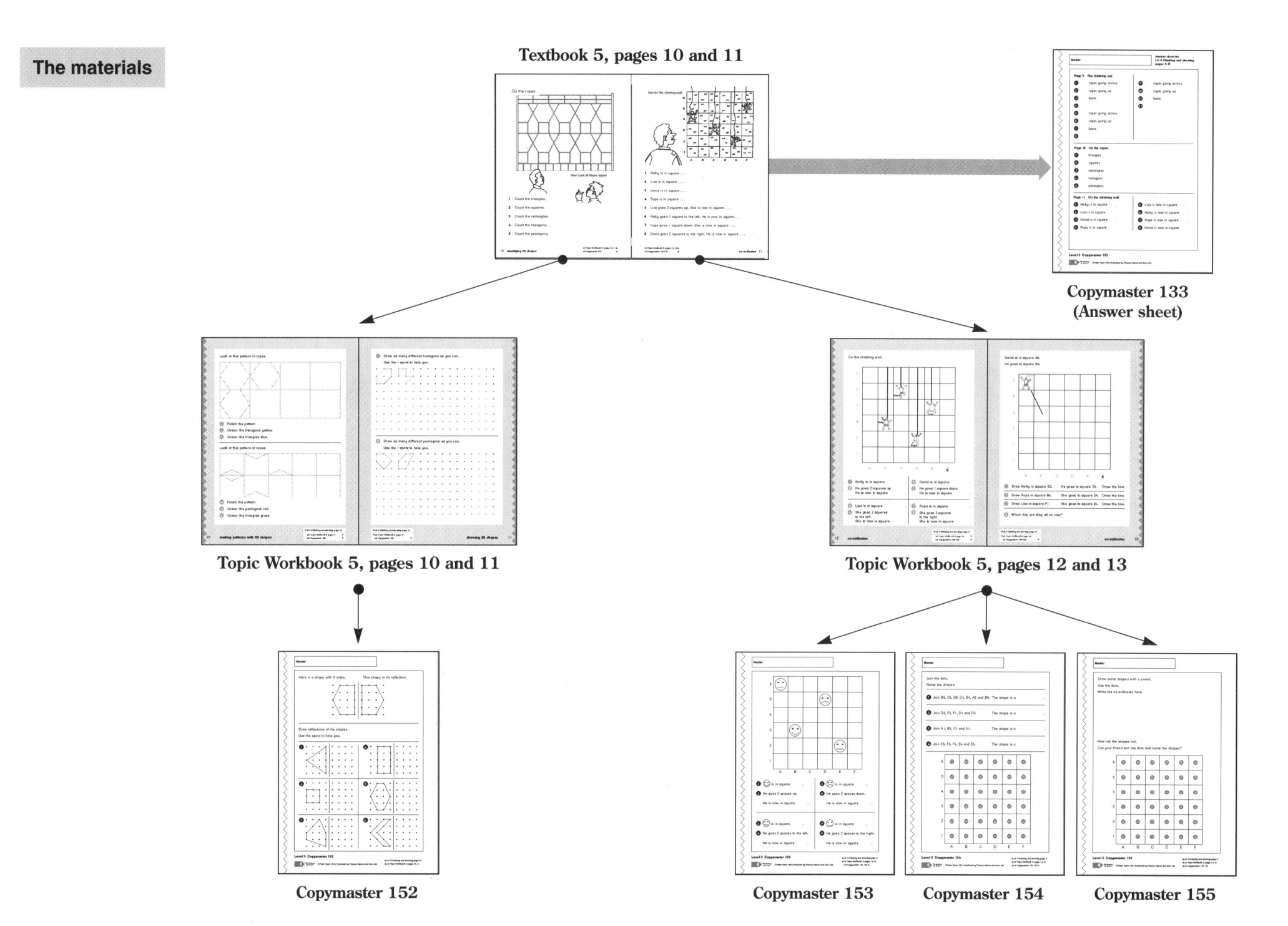

Textbook 5, pages 10 and 11

Copymaster 133 (Answer sheet)

Topic Workbook 5, pages 10 and 11

Topic Workbook 5, pages 12 and 13

Copymaster 152

Copymaster 153

Copymaster 154

Copymaster 155

L3:5 Climbing and shooting

PAGES 12 AND 13
The obstacle course

SKILLS, CONCEPTS AND KNOWLEDGE

▶ Time in 5-second intervals
▶ Subtraction of three-digit numbers from 300

PRE-ASSESSMENT

Can the child:

▶ tell analogue time in 5-second intervals?
▶ subtract one three-digit number from another?

The story

The characters move on to an obstacle course where they are timed as they go round. Children enjoy the challenge of climbing, running and crawling through tunnels. Similar activities could be tried in PE lessons, and children could time each other. Encourage them to try to plan their own obstacle courses using PE apparatus. As with all physical activities, discuss the safety aspects of the courses they devise.

Copymaster 134 provides a format for children to record their answers to questions in the textbook.

Maths content and resources

Page 12 of the textbook introduces timing in 5-second intervals as the characters go round the obstacle course. Children should be encouraged to time a variety of activities in the classroom and in games lessons.

There are analogue and digital stopwatches to read on pages 14 and 15 of Topic Workbook 5, and children also have to draw hands and write numbers to show specified times.

Copymasters 156 and 158 are two worksheets to support the textbook and workbook pages. Copymasters 157 and 159 provide blank analogue and digital clock faces which can be used to make more worksheets, or for children to record the results of practical timing activities. There are some blank analogue clocks on Copymaster 160; this sheet can be modified for any necessary revision of work on time.

Page 13 of the textbook uses time as a context for another visit to hundreds, tens and ones. Children have to find the difference between times in seconds.

There are more subtractions on page 10 of Number Workbook 5, and additions on page 11.

Two more worksheets are available to support this work on Copymasters 161 and 162.

TV times

Use copies of television guides.

Ask the children to look at the television guides and work out the duration of their favourite programmes. A good way to help them with this is to ask them to make a time line for the period between, say, 4·00 and 6·00. This can be marked in half hours or quarter hours. If the line is long enough they can try to show divisions of 5 minutes. They can shade the span of time for each programme in a different colour and write the names underneath.

The time line can be displayed or cut up to make a bar chart which shows the longest and shortest programmes.

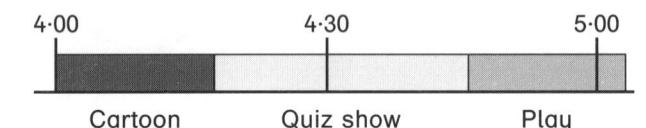

4·00	4·30	5·00
Cartoon	Quiz show	Play

100   L3:5 Climbing and shooting

The materials

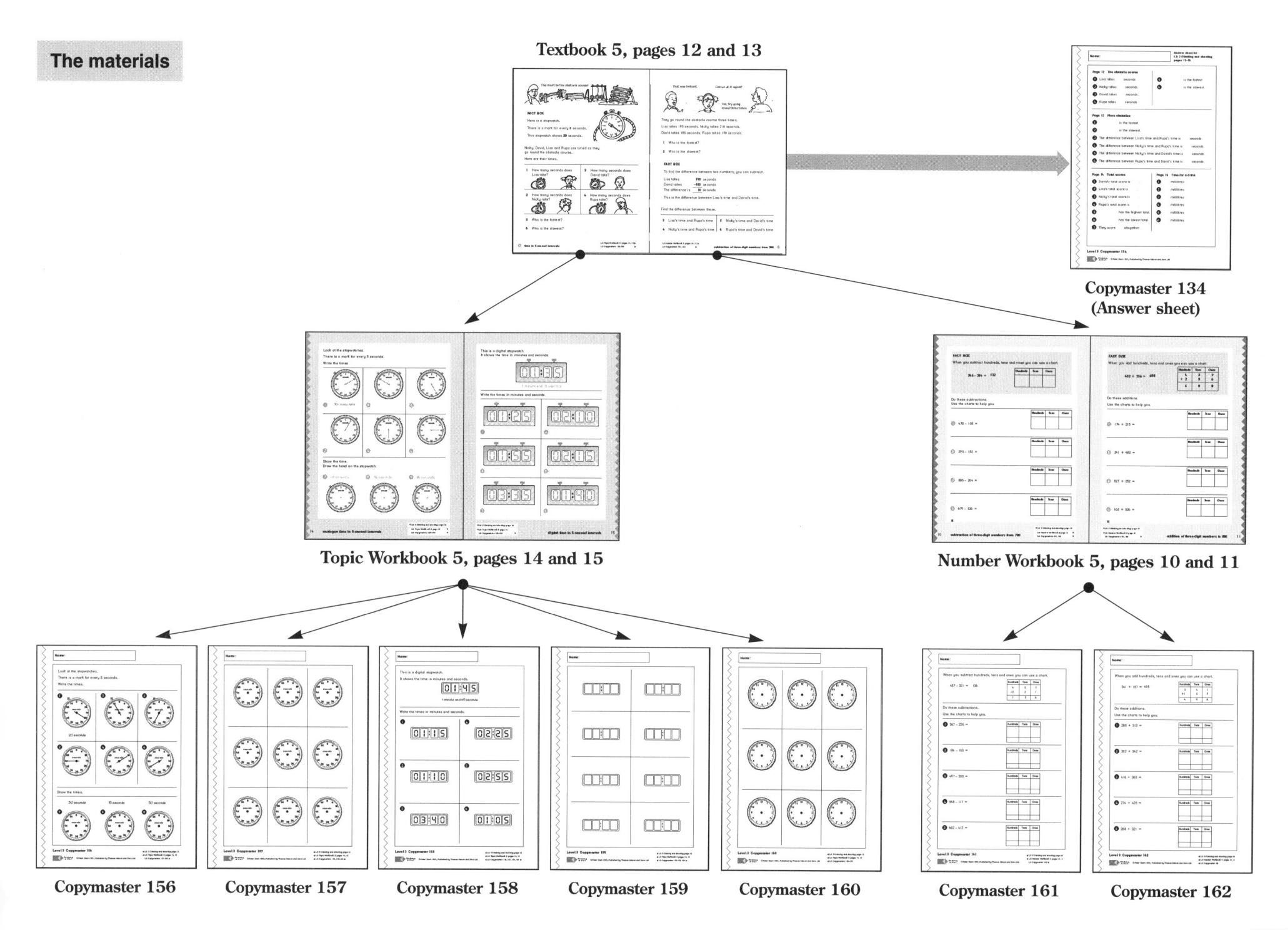

Textbook 5, pages 12 and 13

Copymaster 134 (Answer sheet)

Topic Workbook 5, pages 14 and 15

Number Workbook 5, pages 10 and 11

Copymaster 156

Copymaster 157

Copymaster 158

Copymaster 159

Copymaster 160

Copymaster 161

Copymaster 162

L3:5 Climbing and shooting 101

PAGES 14 AND 15

Scores and soft drinks

SKILLS, CONCEPTS AND KNOWLEDGE

▶ Addition of two-digit numbers to 70
▶ Thousands, hundreds, tens and ones (millilitres)

PRE-ASSESSMENT

Can the child:
▶ add two-digit numbers?
▶ understand place value in three-digit numbers?
▶ measure in millilitres?

The story

After the morning's activities, Lisa, Rupa, Nicky and David review their total scores. Discuss with the children how practising a sport or activity improves performance over a period of time. Many children may be involved in sports and activities outside school such as dancing or gymnastics. These often involve a system of certificates of achievement. Teachers can support children by acknowledging their interests and successes outside school.

At the end of the textbook the characters have a soft drink before packing and setting off for home.

Copymaster 134 provides a format for children to record their answers to questions in the textbook.

Maths content and resources

Page 14 of the textbook provides another opportunity for children to develop their skills in adding two-digit numbers. At this stage all the examples involve the exchange of tens.

There are more additions of two- and three-digit numbers on pages 12 and 13 of Number Workbook 5, which also remind children of how to exchange tens. They should still have access to and be encouraged to use base-ten apparatus, especially to check their answers.

Copymasters 163 and 164 provide further additions of two- and three-digit numbers, but teachers may wish to introduce them over a period of time to give children regular practice.

Page 15 of the textbook uses the context of measuring in millilitres to revise place value involving thousands. Children are asked to add thousands, hundreds and tens of millilitres to measure capacity. The page could be supported in a practical way using a variety of measuring cylinders.

The page is extended by the use of base-ten apparatus and thousands, hundreds, tens and ones charts on pages 14 and 15 of Number Workbook 5.

There are two more worksheets on Copymasters 165 and 166.

Reverse the digits

Use numeral cards from 0 to 9 and sheets of paper.

Children can work co-operatively to investigate the addition of three-digit numbers. The cards are stacked or spread out face down. A child takes three cards from the pack and uses them to make the highest three-digit number possible. (S)he writes this on a piece of paper. (S)he then re-arranges the same three cards to make the smallest three-digit number possible. (S)he writes this below the first number and adds them up.

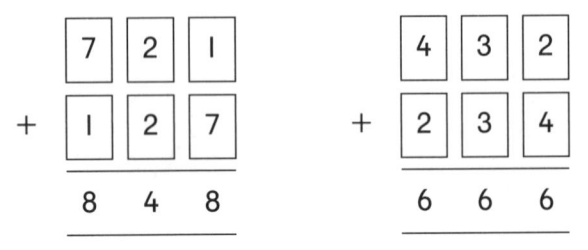

```
  7 2 1          4 3 2
+ 1 2 7        + 2 3 4
-------        -------
  8 4 8          6 6 6
```

Ask the children what they notice, and whether they think this happens with all three-digit numbers. Encourage them to test their theories, and to try the same process with two-digit numbers and with subtractions.

The materials

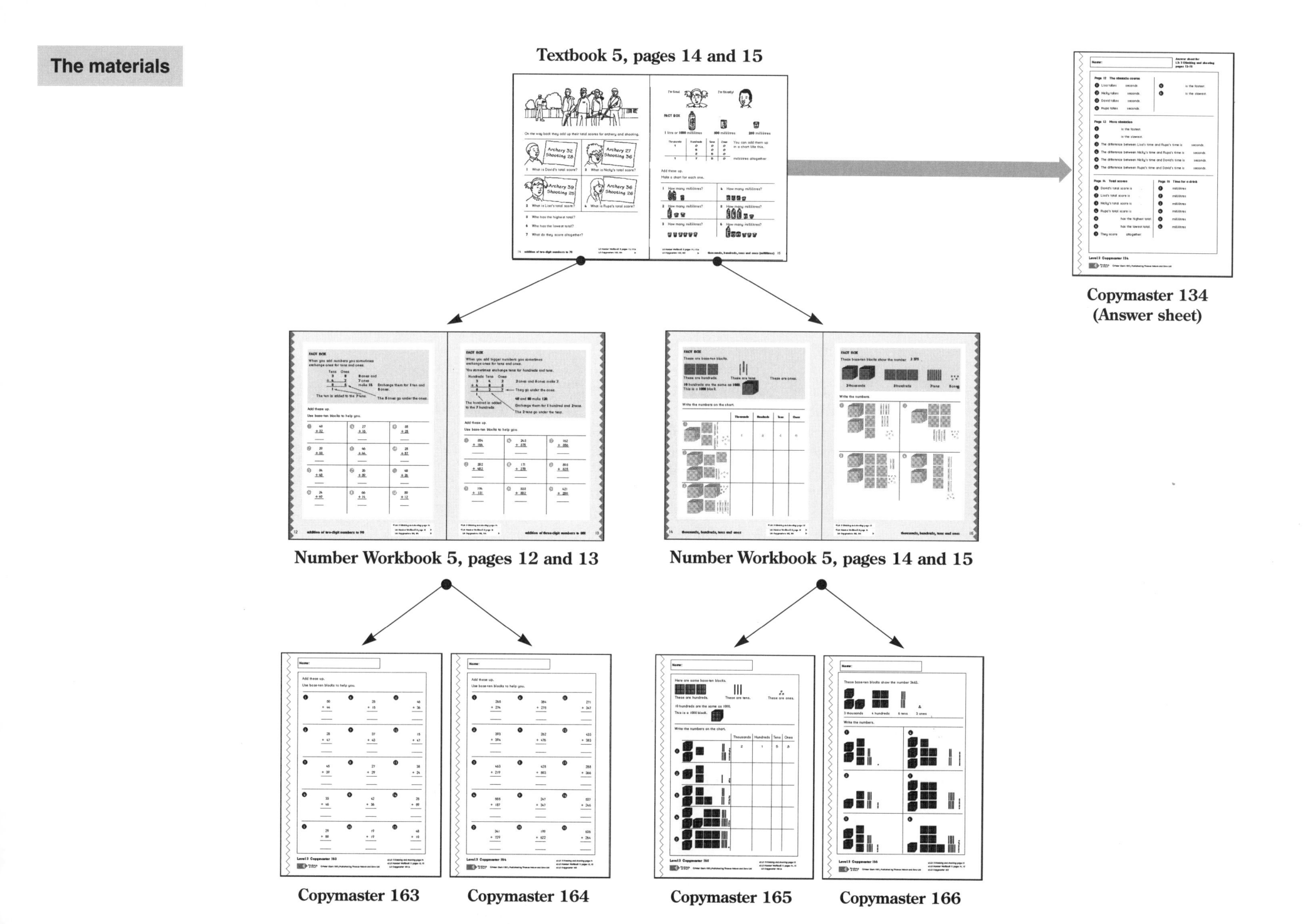

Textbook 5, pages 14 and 15

Copymaster 134
(Answer sheet)

Number Workbook 5, pages 12 and 13

Number Workbook 5, pages 14 and 15

Copymaster 163

Copymaster 164

Copymaster 165

Copymaster 166

L3:5 Climbing and shooting 103

L3:6 Going home

PAGES 2 AND 3
Packing up

SKILLS, CONCEPTS AND KNOWLEDGE

- ▶ Making a tally chart
- ▶ Making a bar chart
- ▶ Half of a set (division)

PRE-ASSESSMENT

Can the child:
- ▶ make a tally chart?
- ▶ make a bar chart?
- ▶ find half of a set?
- ▶ divide by 2?

The story

The characters are packing their bags in preparation for going home. David is particularly keen to take some 'souvenirs', things he collected on the treasure hunt. Discuss with children any things they have kept from past holidays. Collections of shells or pebbles can be useful for sorting and data handling.

Then it is time to load the minibuses, dividing people and luggage equally between the two.

Copymaster 167 provides a format for children to record their answers to questions in the textbook.

Maths content and resources

Page 2 of the textbook shows David packing his bags. Children are asked to make a tally chart to show the things he is packing. They then make a bar chart with scale to show the results of the tally.

The work is followed up on Pages 2 and 3 of Topic Workbook 6 which provide two more pages of tallying and drawing a bar chart with scale. Children could use real classroom collections to make further tallies and bar charts.

There are no further copymasters on tallying and drawing bar charts, but Copymaster 117 may be used whenever necessary.

Page 3 of the textbook returns to finding halves and dividing, using the theme of loading the two minibuses.

There is more work on finding halves and quarters on pages 4 and 5 of Topic Workbook 6. These involve partitioning, but children can also share materials such as counters to support the work in a practical way.

Copymasters 171 to 175 are worksheets covering halves, quarters, thirds, fifths and tenths. All the work can be modelled with practical materials.

The materials

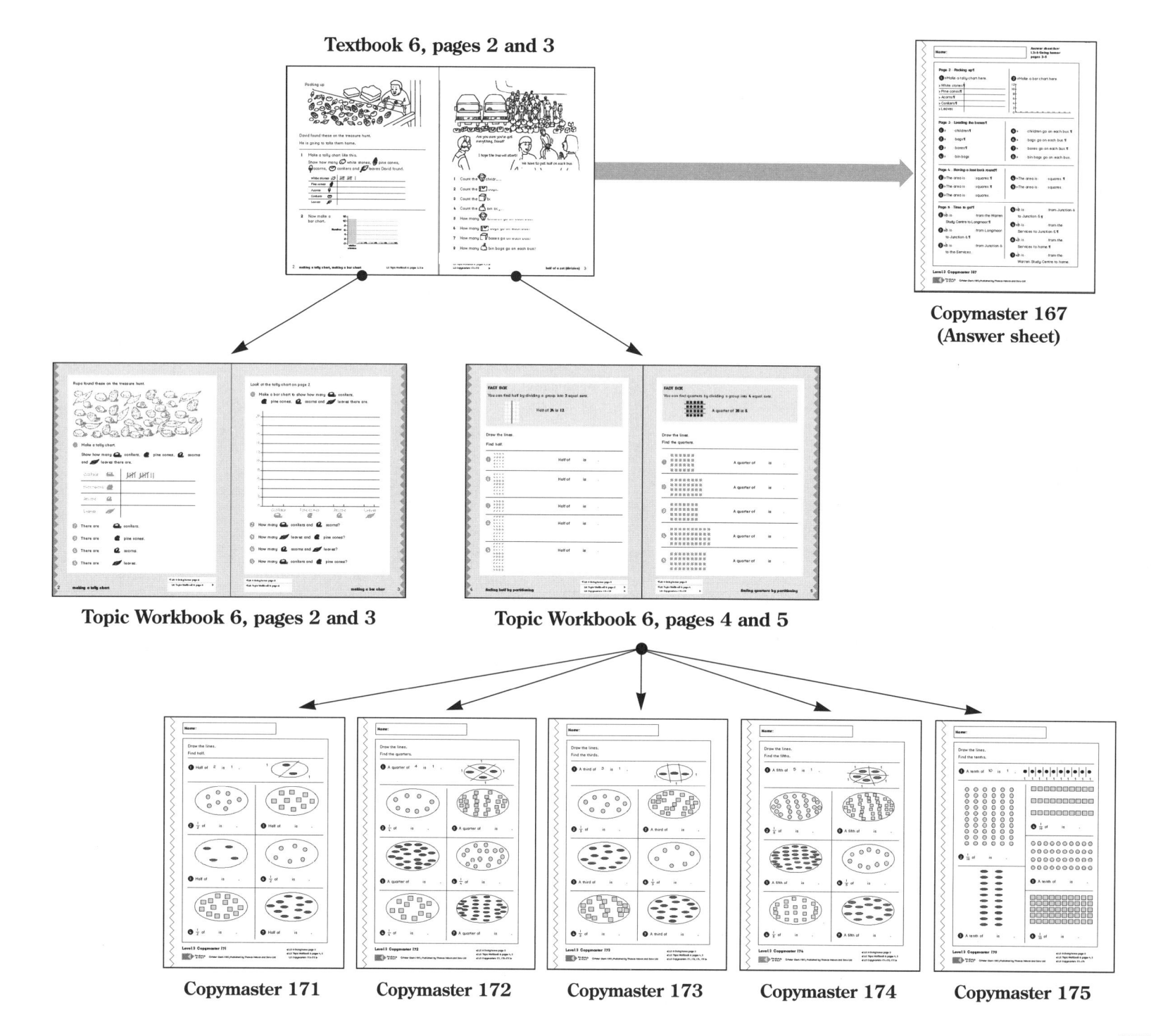

Textbook 6, pages 2 and 3

Copymaster 167 (Answer sheet)

Topic Workbook 6, pages 2 and 3

Topic Workbook 6, pages 4 and 5

Copymaster 171

Copymaster 172

Copymaster 173

Copymaster 174

Copymaster 175

L3:6 Going home 105

PAGES 4 AND 5
Time to go!

SKILLS, CONCEPTS AND KNOWLEDGE
- Area
- Distance in miles

PRE-ASSESSMENT
Can the child:
- find area in squares and square centimetres?
- understand and use the term *'miles'*?

The story

The characters have a last look round the Warren Study Centre and notice that the climbing net has been taken down. Then they look at a map of the journey home. Discuss with the children how they travel when they go on holiday and whether they use motorways. Look at local maps and ask the children how they would get to certain places. Talk about the scale, and how far away the places really are. Most motoring atlases have the mileage between towns and junctions marked on them.

Copymaster 167 provides a format for children to record their answers to questions in the textbook.

Maths content and resources

Page 4 of the textbook uses the context of the climbing net for measuring area in squares.

This is extended on page 6 of Topic Workbook 6 where children are asked to investigate the areas of irregular shapes. Page 7 goes on to consider measuring area in square centimetres. This work may be reinforced by using transparent square-centimetre grids, which can be used to overlay objects such as books to find the area of their surface.

There is no attempt at this level to introduce *'length × width'* as a formula for area. However, some children may begin to see this, particularly if they have had experience of developing multiplication tables as arrays of squares.

There are two further worksheets on Copymasters 176 and 177. These can easily be modified to create further worksheets if required.

Page 5 of the textbook uses the map of the route home as a context for revisiting addition, and the concept of miles is introduced. There is a mixture of single- and two-digit numbers.

Pages 2 and 3 of Number Workbook 6 provide more additions and some subtractions.

There is further work on Copymasters 178 and 179, with children being asked to write the answers as fast as they can. As always, encourage children to relate the written work to base-ten materials, especially when dealing with two- and three-digit numbers.

Distances on road atlases

Pages of a road atlas can be used to generate addition situations. Give children a route (preferably near to where they live), for example, Basingstoke to Newbury to Didcot. They then have to list the mileages shown beside the roads on the map and add them up to find the total distance. This is a good opportunity to discuss the fact that measurement is an approximate activity at this kind of scale, and there is no exact distance between two towns.

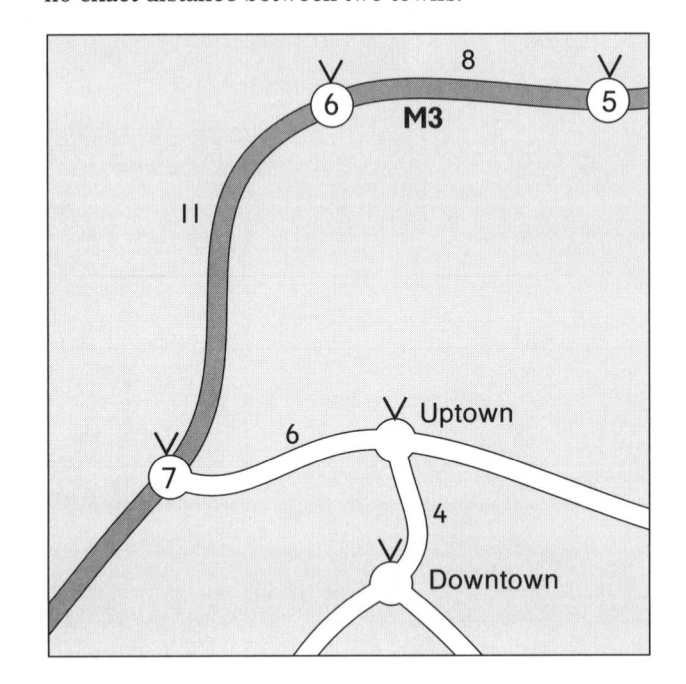

The materials

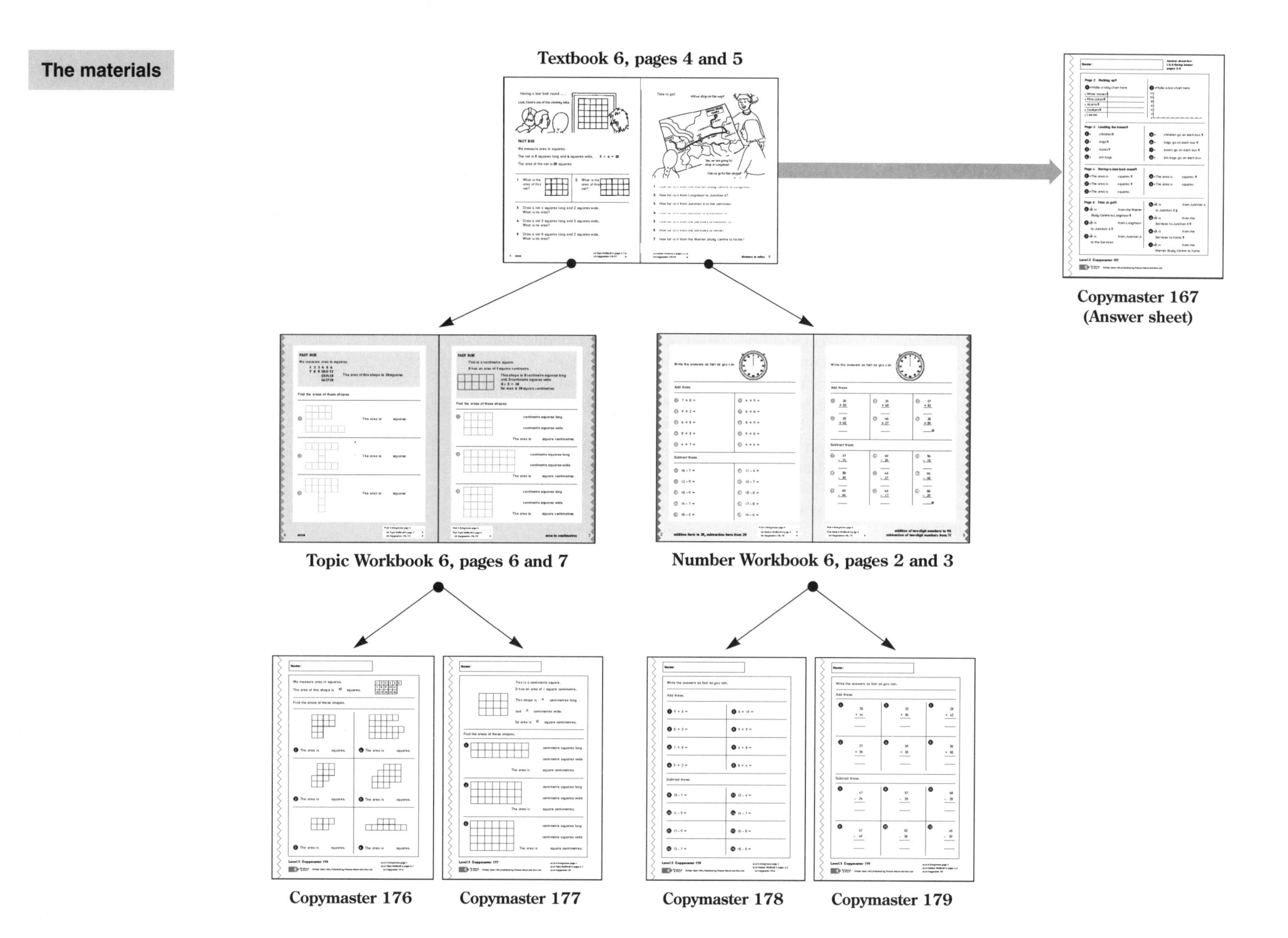

Textbook 6, pages 4 and 5

Copymaster 167
(Answer sheet)

Topic Workbook 6, pages 6 and 7

Number Workbook 6, pages 2 and 3

Copymaster 176

Copymaster 177

Copymaster 178

Copymaster 179

L3:6 Going home 107

PAGES 6 AND 7
The village

SKILLS, CONCEPTS AND KNOWLEDGE

▶ Subtraction of four-digit numbers from 2000
▶ Identifying 2D shapes

PRE-ASSESSMENT

Can the child:
▶ understand the concept of historical dates?
▶ subtract one four-digit number from another?
▶ identify triangles, squares, rectangles, pentagons and hexagons?

The story

On the way home they stop briefly in the village of Longmoor. They see the local graveyard and try to work out when and for how long the people lived. They then head towards the village shop to spend their pocket money on souvenirs.

Children could look at old gravestones in a local churchyard. They could try to make time lines (see Textbook 4) to show people's life spans and how long ago they lived. They could place old buildings on a time line, particularly those which have dates carved on the front.

Copymaster 168 provides a format for children to record their answers to questions in the textbook.

Maths content and resources

On page 6 of the textbook, the gravestones in the local churchyard are used as a context for the subtraction of four-digit numbers.

Page 8 of Topic Workbook 6 uses the context of money for identifying the thousands, hundreds, tens and ones in four-digit numbers. Base-ten apparatus and the number cards described on page 86 can help to support the work practically. Page 7 of the workbook returns to the theme of old gravestones. Children could make time lines and use them to help them to count on and back.

Copymasters 180 and 181 organise thousands, hundreds, tens and ones into charts, to show children how to present additions and subtractions of large numbers vertically. There are some examples where the exchange of tens or hundreds is necessary.

Page 7 of the textbook focuses on 2D shapes in the environment. There is more work on identifying and drawing 2D shapes on pages 10 and 11 of Topic Workbook 6. Children should also be using shape templates for their own drawings and designs.

Time lines

This is a time line showing someone's life span. Time lines do not need to be very accurate or detailed. It is more important to develop an understanding of the passage of time and its numerical representation.

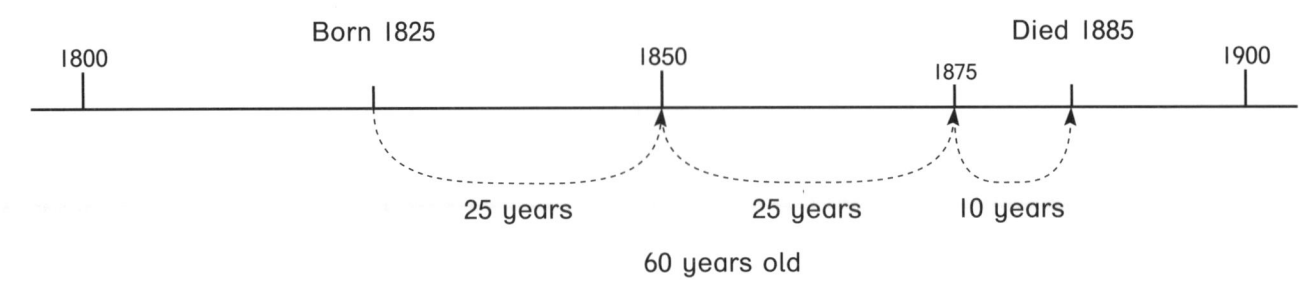

L3:6 Going home

The materials

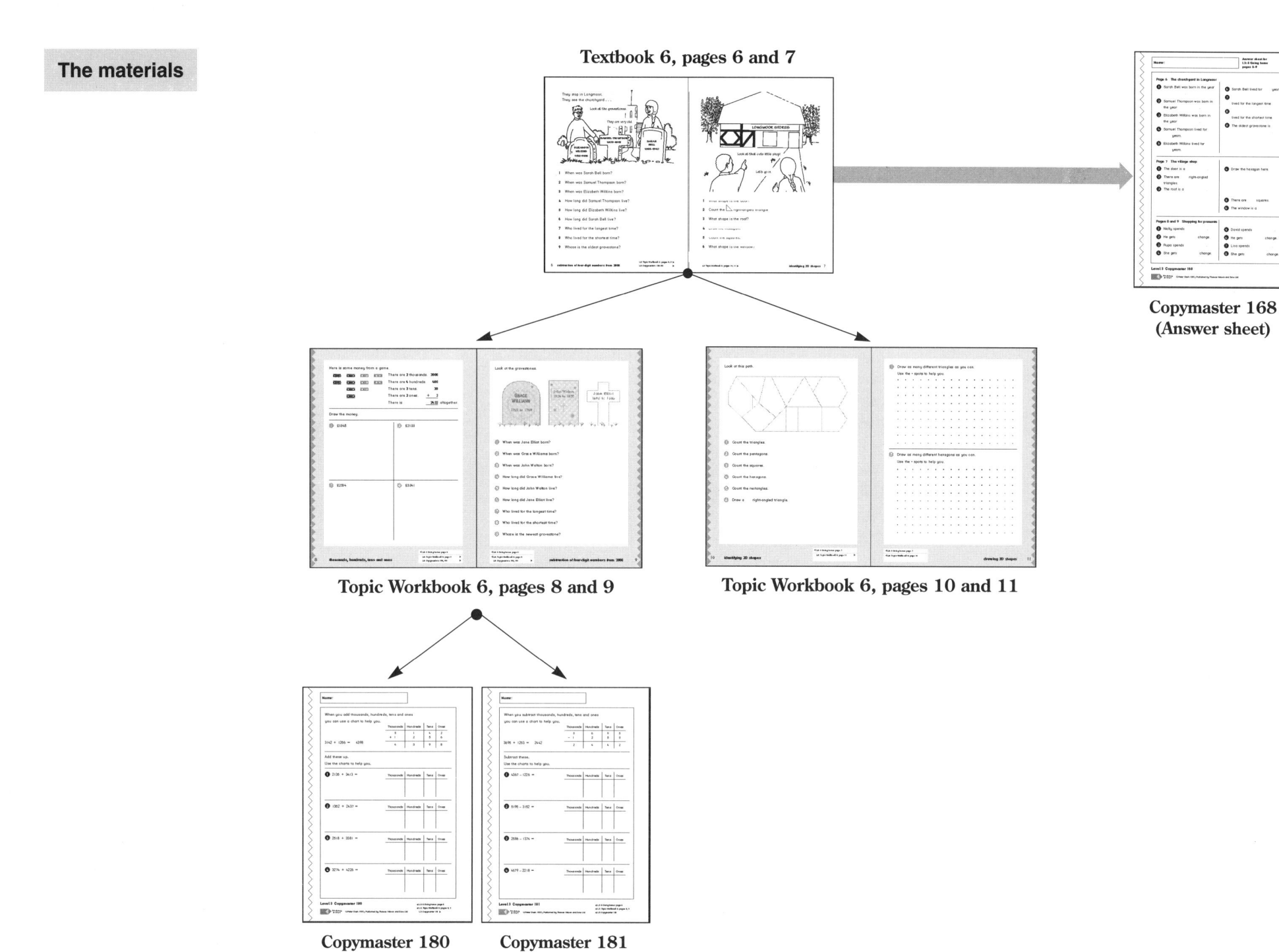

Textbook 6, pages 6 and 7

Copymaster 168
(Answer sheet)

Topic Workbook 6, pages 8 and 9

Topic Workbook 6, pages 10 and 11

Copymaster 180

Copymaster 181

L3:6 Going home 109

PAGES 8 AND 9
Buying souvenirs

SKILLS, CONCEPTS AND KNOWLEDGE

▶ Change from £5.50

PRE-ASSESSMENT

Can the child:
▶ add money up to £5.50?
▶ subtract money from £5.50?

The story

The characters are in the village shop. They are buying small model animals, sweets, postcards and other souvenirs. Discuss pocket money or holiday money with the children. How do they spend it? What kinds of present do they buy and for whom?

Copymaster 168 provides a format for children to record their answers to questions in the textbook.

Maths content and resources

Pages 8 and 9 of the textbook are a double-page spread based on shopping for souvenirs. There is plenty of work here, using the addition of money to work out total cost, and the subtraction of money to calculate change. Children should have access to plastic coins to model the amounts of money. It may be helpful to encourage them to work co-operatively and act out the situations, with one child playing the shopper and the other the shopkeeper.

This work is extensively reinforced on pages 4 to 7 of Number Workbook 6. They are asked to write sums of money in decimal notation, and to show sums of money by drawing coins. There are also two pages parallel to the work in the textbook on total cost and calculating change.

All these activities are revisited on Copymasters 182 to 184.

Coin combination investigations

Use plastic coins.

Children can investigate the different combinations of coins they can use to make specified amounts of money. It is wise to start simply and develop the work in an organised way. For example, give children 1p and 2p coins only, and ask them to find all the ways of making amounts up to 5p. Encourage them to make a chart:

Amount	Coins		
1p	1p		
2p	1p+1p	2p	
3p	1p+1p+1p	2p+1p	
4p	1p+1p+1p+1p	2p+1p+1p	2p+2p
5p	1p+1p+1p+1p+1p	2p+1p+1p+1p	2p+2p+1p

Slowly increase the amounts and the value of the coins used.

An extension of the investigation is to ask the children to use the smallest possible number of coins to make larger amounts of money. Once again, making a chart will help to organise the work.

L3:6 Going home

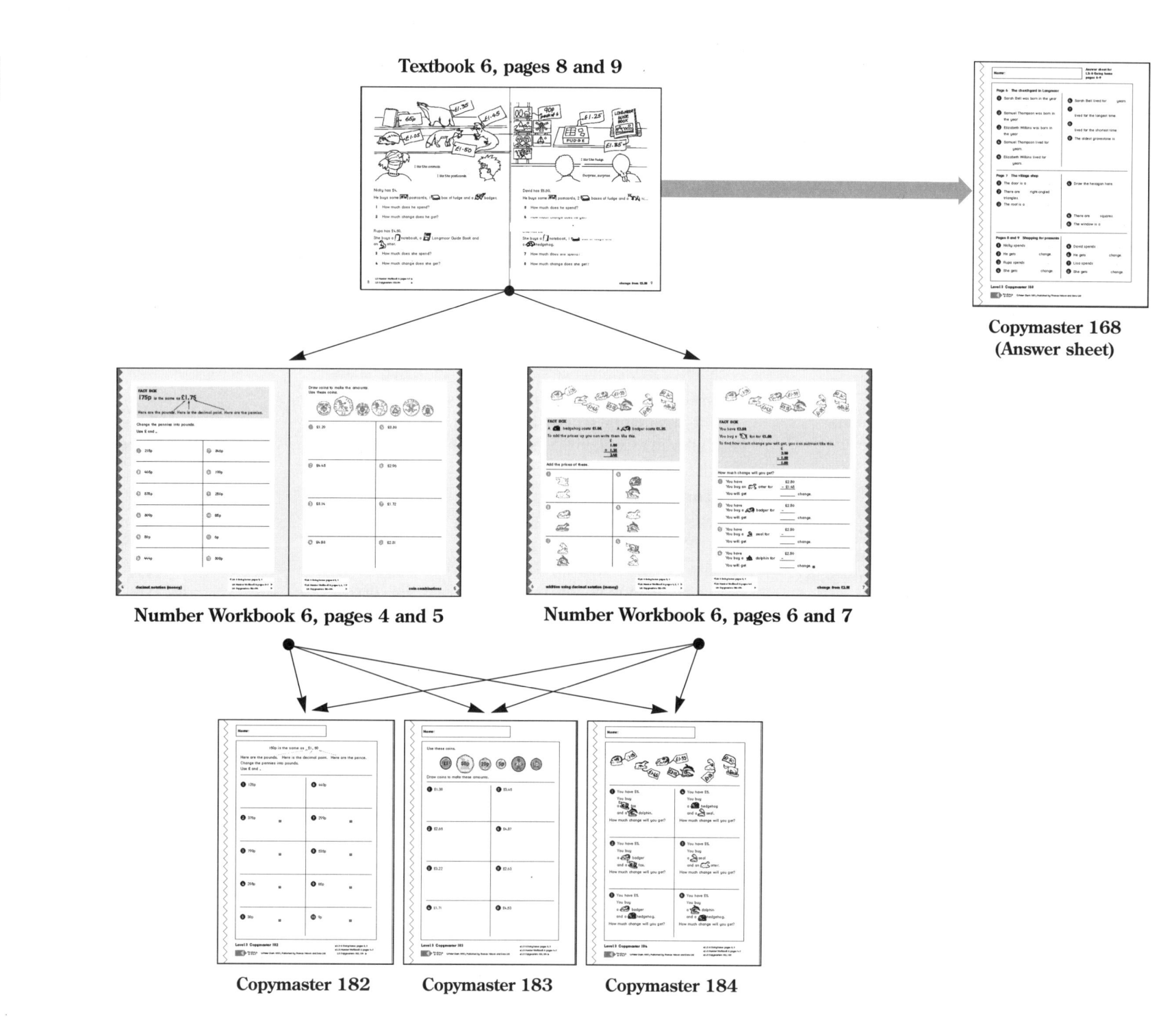

The materials

Textbook 6, pages 8 and 9

Copymaster 168
(Answer sheet)

Number Workbook 6, pages 4 and 5

Number Workbook 6, pages 6 and 7

Copymaster 182

Copymaster 183

Copymaster 184

L3:6 Going home

PAGES 10 AND 11

Seeds and speedometers

SKILLS, CONCEPTS AND KNOWLEDGE

▶ Multiplication tables (2×, 3×, 4×, 5×)
▶ Reading instruments

PRE-ASSESSMENT

Can the child:
▶ recall any of the multiplication tables (2×, 3×, 4×, 5×)?
▶ take readings from dials and instruments?

The story

Outside the shop, the characters decide to collect some fallen leaves and seeds to take back to school. Children could do this, but suggest that they do not remove them from trees and shrubs, but try to find fallen ones as the characters do.

Back on the bus, the characters look at the instruments on the dashboard. Discuss with the children all the dials and gauges they have at home and in family vehicles. If it is possible and safe, show them the utilities cupboards at school and the dials that meter water, gas and electricity. Many children are familiar with displays on computer games, videos and sound systems, and are often more comfortable with them than adults are!

Copymaster 169 provides a format for children to record their answers to questions in the textbook.

Maths content and resources

Page 10 of the textbook revises the multiplication tables to 5 × 5. Children will have visited these many times before, and any relevant worksheets not used so far may be used in conjunction with this page. Copymasters 93 and 94 are particularly useful for any work on the tables. There are 'speed trials' for the two-, three-, four- and five-times tables on pages 8 and 9 of Number Workbook 6.

Page 11 of the textbook uses the dashboard of the minibus as a context for looking at dials and gauges. These include the speedometer and the mileometer as well as the clock and the fuel and temperature gauges.

Pages 12 and 13 of Topic Workbook 6 look at speedometers and mileometers again, and introduce thermometers, scales and stopwatches. Encourage children to look for dials and gauges in the school.

Turnover tables

Use 4 sets of numeral cards from 1 to 5.

Three or more children can play. One child is the dealer. The dealer turns up two cards, and the first player to multiply the numbers and say the correct answer wins the cards. Encourage children to discuss and check their answers. Play continues until all the cards have been won. The player with the most cards is the winner and becomes the dealer for the next round.

This game has several advantages. It gives everyone a chance to be the dealer, but the new dealer is by definition the most successful player, and is taken out of the game for the next turn. Children of similar ability can play this regularly, to help them to remember facts from the multiplication tables. Even children who still need to count on their fingers can play with others of similar ability.

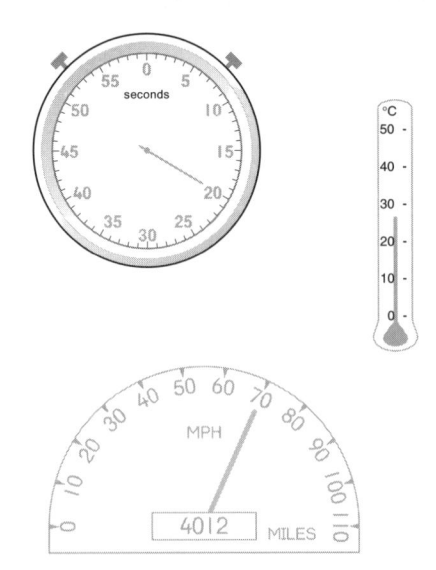

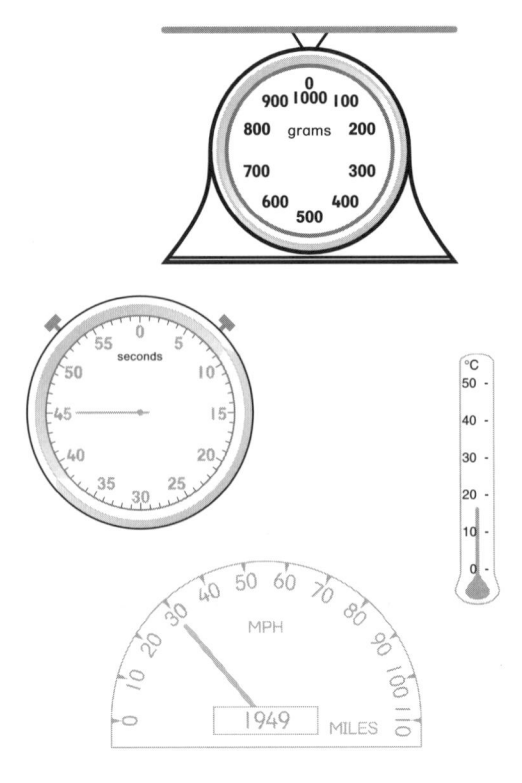

L3:6 Going home

The materials

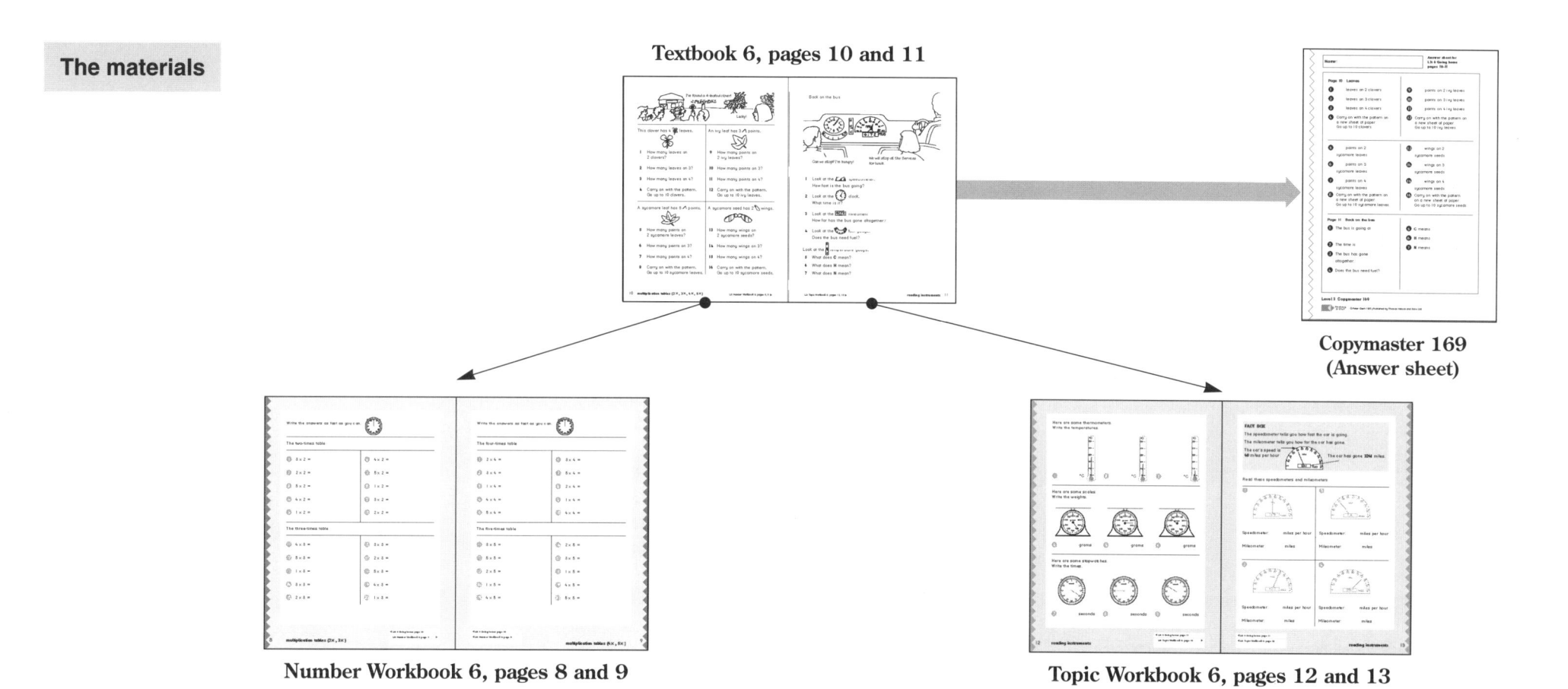

Textbook 6, pages 10 and 11

Copymaster 169 (Answer sheet)

Number Workbook 6, pages 8 and 9

Topic Workbook 6, pages 12 and 13

L3:6 Going home 113

PAGES 12 AND 13

Lunch at the service station

SKILLS, CONCEPTS AND KNOWLEDGE

- Rounding to the nearest £1
- Change from £10

PRE-ASSESSMENT

Can the child:
- round a sum of money to the nearest £1?
- add money up to £10?
- subtract money from £10?

The story

The characters stop at the motorway service station for lunch. There is plenty of choice on the menu. Ask the children whether they like to eat out, and what their favourite restaurants and foods are. There may be a wide variety of examples from different cultures such as kebabs, curries and Chinese meals. Discuss the relative cost of eating out and eating at home. A useful exercise is to compare the price of chips bought in a fast food outlet with the cost of a single potato and the number of chips you can make from it. Ask children to suggest where the profit goes!

Copymaster 170 provides a format for children to record their answers to questions in the textbook.

Maths content and resources

Pages 12 and 13 of the textbook are both about money, in the context of buying lunch. Once again, children will benefit from being able to handle plastic coins, work co-operatively and act out the transactions. They could paint the meals in the questions on paper plates and attach price labels, and then 'buy' the various items. A 'waiter' could take the order and make a list of the foods and the prices. This becomes the 'bill'. The 'diners' then give him a £10 note and wait for their change, checking it carefully against the bill.

Pages 10 and 11 of Number Workbook 6 introduce the very useful skill of rounding sums of money to estimate total cost. Amounts such as £4.99 are used because they are commonly seen in shops. Rounding is explained through a money number line, and children could make their own number lines to help with rounding. Pages 12 and 13 provide a parallel set of exercises to those in the textbook, based on the prices in a fast food outlet.

There is more practice in rounding money on Copymasters 185 and 186. Copymaster 187 is another worksheet about prices of fast foods.

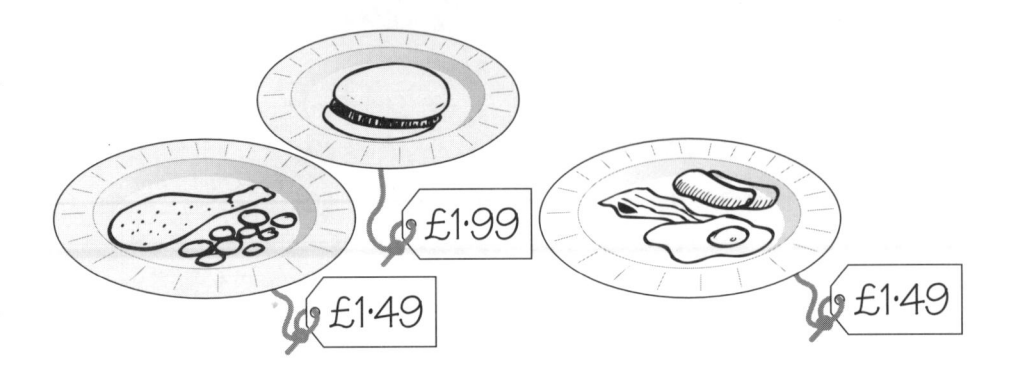

---

114 L3:6 Going home

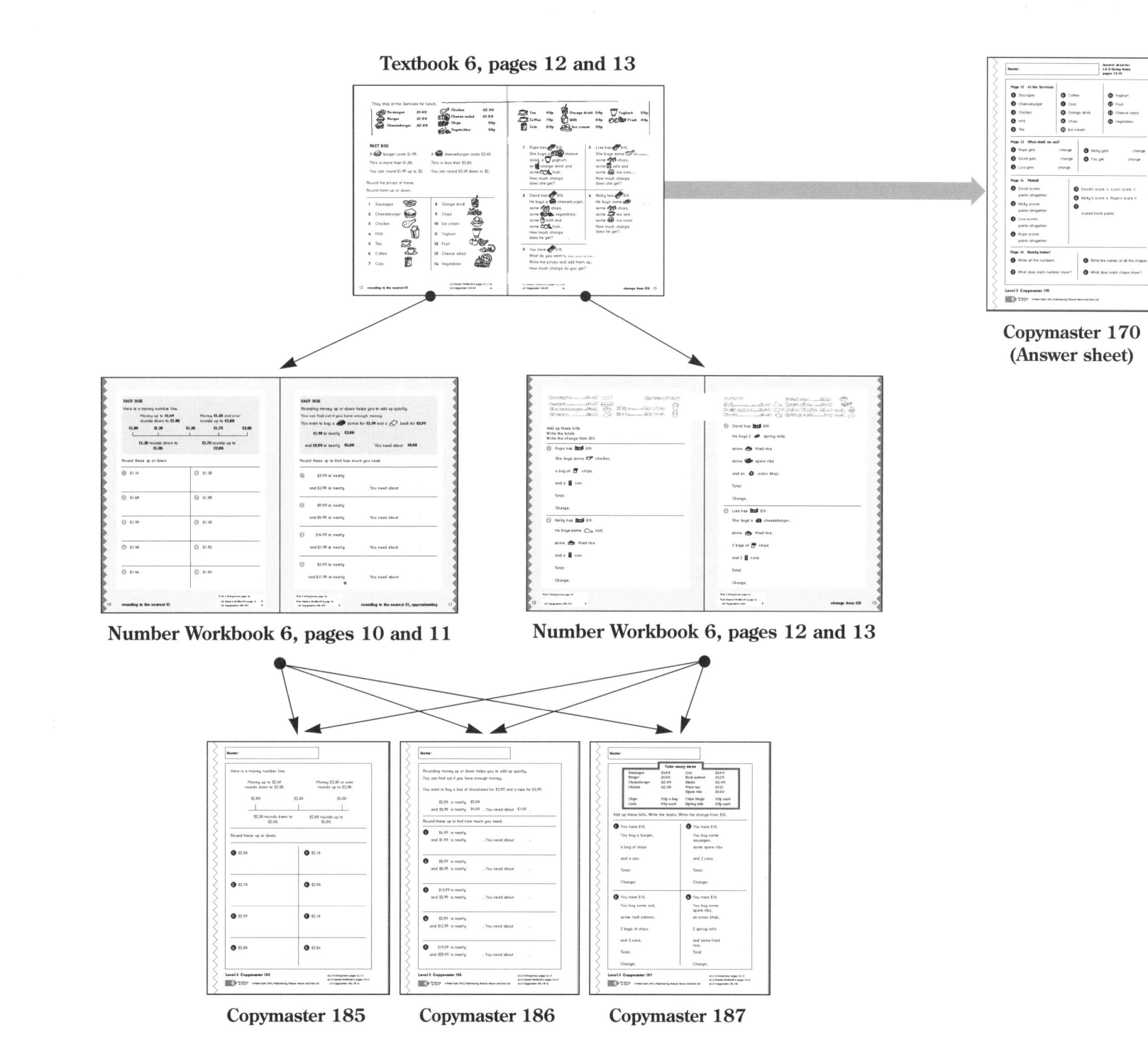

The materials

Textbook 6, pages 12 and 13

Copymaster 170 (Answer sheet)

Number Workbook 6, pages 10 and 11

Number Workbook 6, pages 12 and 13

Copymaster 185

Copymaster 186

Copymaster 187

L3:6 Going home 115

PAGES 14 AND 15
Nearly home

SKILLS, CONCEPTS AND KNOWLEDGE

▶ Thousands, hundreds and tens
▶ Numbers and shapes in the environment

PRE-ASSESSMENT

Can the child:
▶ add four-digit numbers?
▶ recognise the function of numbers in the environment?
▶ recognise different shapes in the environment?

The story

At the motorway service station the characters play on the pinball machine. These machines generate very high scores, and many children who profess to have few mathematical skills can handle these big numbers and discuss them with their friends, particularly when comparing scores. Recording scores could be encouraged in the classroom by developing a 'league table' for any games the children play in school.

The textbook (and Level 3) end by showing the characters driving off into the distance in the minibus. This page is intended as a celebration of some of the mathematics to be found in the environment. Encourage children to look for these features every day.

Copymaster 170 provides a format for children to record their answers to questions in the textbook.

Maths content and resources

Page 14 of the textbook is based on pinball scores. These are usually expressed in thousands, hundreds and tens. Children have to follow the route of the ball and add up the total scores. This could be done using a chart with columns headed *'Thousands'*, *'Hundreds'*, *'Tens'* and *'Ones'*. Some children may be able to do the additions mentally, while others may need a calculator. Encourage them to try two or three different ways of adding for each question to check their answers.

There is more work on pinball scores in Number Workbook 6. Page 14 provides some similar problems to those in the textbook, and page 15 provides pairs of scores in thousands to add and subtract.

There is another worksheet on this on Copymaster 188.

Page 15 of the textbook is intended to encourage children to continue to look for numbers and shapes in the environment. They could follow this up by collecting pictures from catalogues and magazines based on a theme, perhaps 'Numbers on keypads' or 'Shapes used in fabrics'.

Pages 14 and 15 of Topic Workbook 6 may suggest some more ideas as they feature keypads, door numbers, radio dials and tiling patterns. Page 14 provides a missing numbers activity, and page 15 is about continuing patterns.

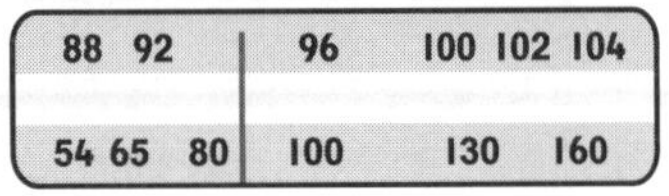

116 L3:6 Going home

The materials

Textbook 6, pages 14 and 15

Number Workbook 6, pages 14 and 15

Topic Workbook 6, pages 14 and 15

Copymaster 170 (Answer sheet)

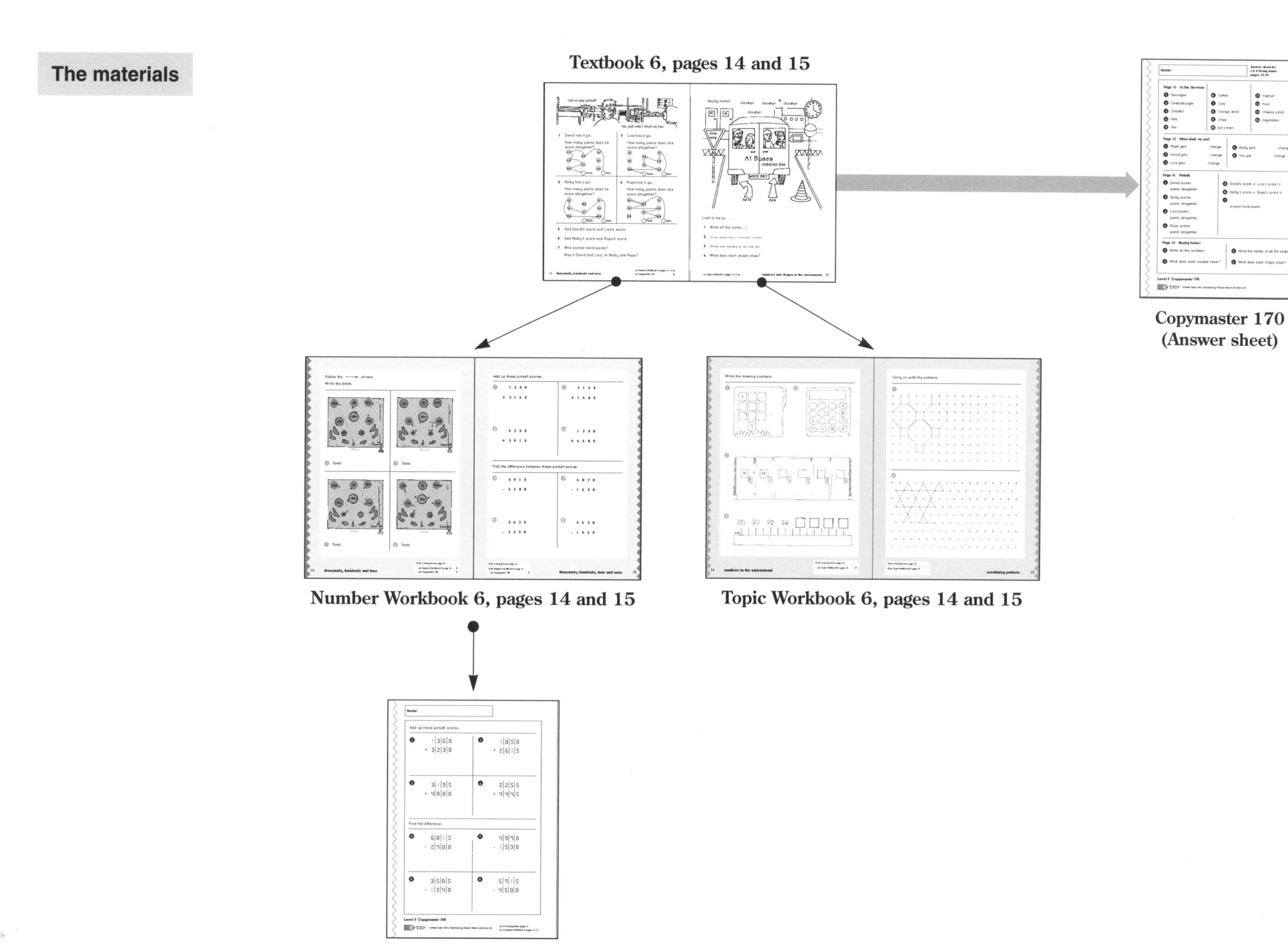

Copymaster 188

L3:6 Going home 117

Answers

Textbook 1

PAGE 2

1. 8
2. 12
3. 4
4. 1
5. 12
6. 13
7. 20
8. 5
9. 25

PAGE 3

1. £14
2. £11
3. £17
4. £19

PAGE 4

1. 3 (pairs)
   2 (pairs)
   5
   5
   4
   1
   5
2. 3, 2, 5, 5, 4, 1, 5 blocks

PAGE 5

1. 5
2. 3
3. 2
4. 4
5. 2

PAGE 6

1. 3
2. $3 \times 2 = 6$
3. 4
4. $4 \times 2 = 8$
5. 5
6. $5 \times 2 = 10$
7. $6 \times 2 = 12$
   $7 \times 2 = 14$
   $8 \times 2 = 16$
   $9 \times 2 = 18$
   $10 \times 2 = 20$

PAGE 7

1. 2
2. 16
3. 20
4. 22
5. 1
6. 8
7. 10
8. 11

PAGE 8

1. £6.75
2. £8
3. £7.50
4. £7.25
5. £7
6. £7.75
7. £14.75

PAGE 9

1. 50 miles
2. 40 miles
3. 25 miles
4. 10 miles
5. 2 o'clock
6. 3 o'clock
7. quarter to 3
8. 15 minutes

PAGE 10

1. the school
2. the shops
3. the church
4. the police station
5. C3
6. D2
7. C4
8. D3

PAGE 11

1. 28
2. 6
3. 4
4. Children should draw the house.

PAGE 12

1. 4
2. 4
3. 16
4. 4
5. 2
6. 3

PAGE 13

1. Sunday
2. James, Sam, Sara and Kim
3. clean the bathroom
4. clean the dayroom
5. James, Sam, Sara and Kim
6. Rikki, Usha, Emma and Helen

PAGE 14

1. 6
   $$\begin{array}{r} 12 \\ -6 \\ \hline 6 \end{array}$$
2. 8
   $$\begin{array}{r} 20 \\ -12 \\ \hline 8 \end{array}$$
3. 11
4. 13
5. 8

PAGE 15

1. 12
2. 14
3. 11
4. 10
5. 9
6. 13

118 Answers

Number Workbook 1

PAGE 2
1. 10 + 5 = 15
2. 12 + 4 = 16
3. 14
4. 17
5. 12
6. 16

PAGE 3
1. 14 − 3 = 11
2. 18 − 6 = 12
3. 13
4. 10
5. 14
6. 10
7. 12
4. 11

PAGE 4
1. 37
2. 47
3. 29
4. 48
5. 41
6. 36

PAGE 5
1. 11
2. 18
3. 23
4. 2
5. 17
6. 16

PAGE 6
1. 1 × 2 = 2
2. 2 × 2 = 4
3. 3 × 2 = 6
4. 4 × 2 = 8
5. 5 × 2 = 10
6. 6 × 2 = 12
7. 7 × 2 = 14
8. 8 × 2 = 16
9. 9 × 2 = 18
10. 10 × 2 = 20

Children should draw the corresponding pattern of twos.

PAGE 7
1. 2, 4, 6, 8, 10, 12, 14, 16, 18, 20
2. 6, 8, 10, 12, 14, 16, 18, 20
   8, 10, 12, 14, 16, 18, 20
   8, 10, 12, 14, 16, 18, 20

PAGE 8
Children should bisect each shape along the line of symmetry.

PAGE 9
1. Children should draw 6 boxes on each cart.
2. 3
3. 4
4. 10
5. 8

PAGE 10
1. £3.25
2. £5.12
3. £10.90
4. £6.10
5. £2.60
6. £4.70
7. £4.30
8. £10.80

PAGE 11
1. 3.70
2. 5.75
3. 5.95
4. 8.40
5. 6.50
6. 5.00
7. Children should draw the appropriate coins.
8. Children should draw the appropriate coins.

PAGE 12
1. 6
2. 9
3. 8
4. 7
5. 6
6. 5
7. 9
8. 8
9. 8
10. 6

PAGE 13
1. 12
2. 17
3. 11
4. 11
5. 14
6. 13
7. 11
8. 14
9. 16
10. 16

PAGE 14
11
4
3
9
10
0

5
4
9, 3
10, 2
11, 1
12, 0

5
4
10, 3
11, 2
12, 1
13, 0

6
5
10, 4
11, 3
12, 2
13, 1
14, 0

PAGE 15
6
7
8
2
1
0

7
8
4, 9
3, 10
2, 11
1, 12
0, 13

7
8
3, 9
2, 10
1, 11
0, 12

8
9
4, 10
3, 11
2, 12
1, 13
0, 14

PAGE 16
I can ...
... add the numbers.
11, 14, 36, 39
... subtract the numbers.
13, 11, 14, 13
... find half of a number.
7, 8
... write money using a decimal point.
£2.70, £5.15

Topic Workbook 1

PAGE 2

𝍷𝍷𝍷𝍷𝍷	6
||||	4
𝍷𝍷𝍷𝍷𝍷	5 (pairs)
|||	3
||||	4 (pairs)
𝍷𝍷𝍷𝍷𝍷	5 (pairs)

PAGE 3

6, 5, 3, 4, 5, 4 blocks

PAGE 4

prism   pyramid
cube   cylinder
         cone
sphere   cuboid

PAGE 5

1 Children should draw lines to map each shape to its name.
2 3
  2
  4
  2
  3
  4
  3

PAGE 6

1 25 miles
2 30 miles
3 40 miles
4 41 miles
5 52 miles
6 50 miles

PAGE 7

1 4 o'clock
  Children should draw hands to show 5 o'clock.
2 3 o'clock
  Children should draw hands to show half-past 3.
3 10 o'clock
  Children should draw hands to show quarter past 10.
4 2 o'clock
  Children should draw hands to show quarter to 3.

PAGE 8

1 A3
2 A4
3 C1
4 D1
5 B2
6 C3
7 B3
8 D2

PAGE 9

1–3 △ □ △
    □ ○ △
    ○ △ □
    △ □ ○

4 Children should colour the shapes to demonstrate the pattern.
5 Children should make a new pattern.

PAGE 10

hexagon   square   triangle
rectangle circle   pentagon
hexagon   pentagon triangle

PAGE 11

1–6 Children should follow the instructions for drawing the shapes.

PAGE 12

1–2 Children should follow the instructions for drawing the shapes.

PAGE 13

1 $1 \times 4 = 4$
2 $2 \times 4 = 8$
3 $3 \times 4 = 12$
4 $4 \times 4 = 16$
5 $5 \times 4 = 20$
6 $6 \times 4 = 24$
(Children should draw 6 squares.)

PAGE 14

1 morning   4 afternoon
2 afternoon   5 Rupa and Lisa
3 morning   6 David and Nicky

PAGE 15

Nicky   Rupa
David   Lisa

Rupa   Nicky
Lisa   David

Nicky   Rupa
David   Lisa

Rupa   Nicky
Lisa   David

PAGE 16

I can ...
... write the names of the shapes.
circle pentagon hexagon
prism   cube   pyramid
... carry on with a pattern of fours.

⁞ ⁞⁞ ⁞⁞⁞ ⁞⁞⁞⁞ ⁞⁞⁞⁞⁞

4   8   12   16   20

Copymasters for Textbook 1

COPYMASTER 5
1 $8 + 2 = 10$
2 $8 + 7 = 15$
3 11
4 13
5 14
6 16
7 15
8 16
9 17
10 15

COPYMASTER 6
1 $11 - 9 = 2$
2 $13 - 4 = 9$
3 10
4 2
5 9
6 10
7 4
8 2
9 9
10 7

COPYMASTER 7
1 37
2 55
3 46
4 49
5 41
6 40
7 55
8 31
9 33
10 34

COPYMASTER 8
1 14
2 22
3 4
4 12
5 15
6 12
7 9
8 21
9 12
10 9

COPYMASTER 9
⃀⃀⃀⃀⃀	6
				3
|||	3 (pairs)
||||	4 (pairs)
||	2 (pairs)
|||	3 (pairs)

COPYMASTER 10
6, 3, 4, 2, 3, 3 blocks

COPYMASTER 16
$1 \times 2 = 2$
$2 \times 2 = 4$
$3 \times 2 = 6$
$4 \times 2 = 8$
$5 \times 2 = 10$
$6 \times 2 = 12$
$7 \times 2 = 14$
$8 \times 2 = 16$
$9 \times 2 = 18$
$10 \times 2 = 20$

COPYMASTER 17
Children should bisect each shape along the line of symmetry and colour half.

COPYMASTER 18
1 6, 3
2 10, 5
3 18, 9
4 16, 8
5 12, 6
6 8, 4
7 14, 7

COPYMASTER 19
1 £2.53
2 £4.18
3 £3.74
4 £1.25
5 £2.35
6 £5.87

COPYMASTER 20
1–8 Children should draw the appropriate coins.

COPYMASTER 21
1 half-past 3
2 quarter to 12
3 quarter past 4
Children should draw the appropriate hands on the clocks.

COPYMASTER 22
1 10 o'clock
2 quarter to 2
3 quarter past 7
Children should draw the appropriate hands on the clocks.

COPYMASTER 23
1 A4, D3, C2, B1
2 B4, A3, D2, C1
3 C4, B3, A2, D1
4 D4, C3, B2, A1

COPYMASTER 24
Children should colour the appropriate squares.

COPYMASTER 26
1–6 Children should follow the instructions for drawing the shapes.

COPYMASTER 27
1 2, 8
2 3, 12
3 4, 16
4 5, 20
5 6, 24

COPYMASTER 28
$1 \times 4 = 4$
$2 \times 4 = 8$
$3 \times 4 = 12$
$4 \times 4 = 16$
$5 \times 4 = 20$
$6 \times 4 = 24$
$7 \times 4 = 28$
$8 \times 4 = 32$
$9 \times 4 = 36$
$10 \times 4 = 40$

COPYMASTER 29
1 2
2 3
3 4
4 5
5 6
6 1

COPYMASTER 30
4 3
4 1
5 4
2 2

COPYMASTER 31
1 9
10
11
12
13
14
15
16
17

2 8
7
6
5
4
3
2
1
0

COPYMASTER 32
1 10
11
12
13
14
15
16
17
18

2 9
8
7
6
5
4
3
2
1
0

Answers 121

Textbook 2

PAGE 2
1 13
2 19
3 6
4 2

PAGE 3
1 12
2 8
3 Children should give the dimensions of the cube/cuboid they have made.

PAGE 4
1 8 7
   4 1
2 4
3 7
4 1
5 8
6 5

PAGE 5
1 2
2 6
3 10
4 4
5 12
6 8
7 2 4 6 8 10 12
8 14
9 16
10 18
11 20

PAGE 6
1 the swimming area
2 E5
3 the dock
4 C1
5 4
6 the boat house
7 C3
8 the sailing area
9 A1
10 3

PAGE 7
1 23 34 42 56 68
2 57
3 76
4 91
5 110
6 124

PAGE 8
1 68 56 42 34 23
2 45
3 8
4 12
5 19
6 26

PAGE 9
1 3
2 6
3 9
4 12
5 15
6 18 21 24 27 30

PAGE 10
1 26
2 8
3 16
4 9
5 24

PAGE 11
1 4
2 5
3 6
4 3
5 Rupa
6 Nicky

PAGE 12
1 2
2 3
3 7
4 3
5 a pentagon
6 2
7 a hexagon
8 Children should draw a sail featuring the shapes.

PAGE 13
1 5 (including the ones the boys are working on!)
2 50
3 84
4 76
5 92
6 87
7 68
8 105

PAGE 14
1 3
2 2
3 320
4 213
5 534
6 265
7 624
8 152
9 421

PAGE 15
1 14
2 James and Sam
3 4
4 Tom and Sanjay
5 12
6 Katy and Nina
7 Lisa and Rupa
8 James and Sam

Answers

Number Workbook 2

PAGE 2
1. $8 + 3 = 11$
2. $7 + 7 = 14$
3. 11
4. 12
5. 14
6. 16

PAGE 3
1. $12 - 3 = 9$
2. $11 - 5 = 6$
3. 4
4. 7
5. 3
6. 3

PAGE 4
1. 2
2. 4
3. 6
4. 8
5. 10
6. 12
7. $7 \times 2 = 14$
8. $8 \times 2 = 16$
9. $9 \times 2 = 18$
10. $10 \times 2 = 20$

PAGE 5
1. 8, 10, 12, 14, 16, 18, 20
2. 8, 10, 12, 14, 16, 18, 20
3. 4
4. 12
5. 20
6. 10
7. 6
8. 18
9. 8
10. 16
11. 14

PAGE 6
1. 61
2. 74
3. 80
4. 75
5. 53
6. 81

PAGE 7
1. 28, 33, 45, 57, 62
2. 62, 57, 45, 33, 28
3. 95
4. 107
5. 61
6. 102
7. 78
8. 73
9. 85
10. 119

PAGE 8
1. 13
2. 18
3. 15
4. 17
5. 17
6. 29

PAGE 9
1. 23, 31, 46, 54, 67
2. 67, 54, 46, 31, 23
3. 36
4. 8
5. 21
6. 8
7. 15
8. 13
9. 23
10. 31

PAGE 10
1. $13 \times 2 = 26$
2. $15 \times 2 = 30$
3. $10 \times 2 = 20$
4. $16 \times 2 = 32$
5. $11 \times 2 = 22$
6. $14 \times 2 = 28$
7. $18 \times 2 = 36$
8. $20 \times 2 = 40$

PAGE 11
1. $12 \div 2 = 6$
2. $8 \div 2 = 4$
3. $20 \div 2 = 10$
4. $16 \div 2 = 8$
5. $14 \div 2 = 7$
6. $18 \div 2 = 9$

PAGE 12
1. 43
2. 16
3. 61
4. 85
5. 27
6. 74
7. 92
8. 38

PAGE 13
1. 125
2. 152
3. 110

PAGE 14
1. 126
2. 244
3. 150
4. 315

PAGE 15

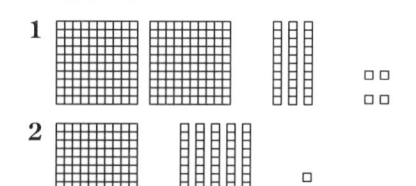

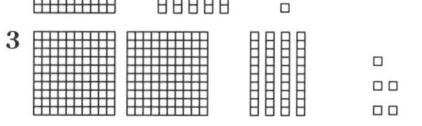

PAGE 16
I can ...
... add numbers.
13, 15, 41, 41
... subtract numbers.
9, 4, 6, 6
... multiply a number by 2.
22, 28
... divide a number by 2.
8
... write hundreds, tens and ones.
251

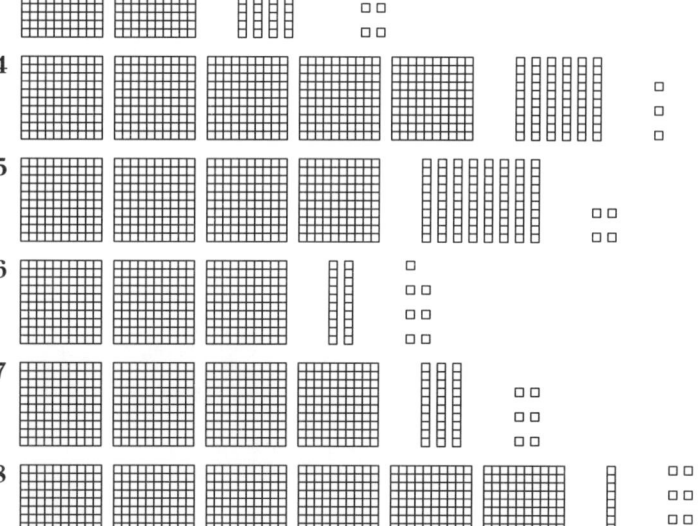

Answers

Topic Workbook 2

PAGE 2
1 2, 2, 2, 8
2 3, 3, 3, 27
3 4, 4, 4, 64

PAGE 3
1 3, 2, 2, 12
2 3, 3, 2, 18
3 4, 3, 3, 36

PAGE 4
1 4
2 3
3 7
4 6
5 3
6 3

PAGE 5
1 Children should draw the shapes in the appropriate places on the chart.

PAGE 6
1 A5
2 E1
3 A2
4 E4
5 the boat house
6 the dock
7 ducks

PAGE 7
1–6 Children should draw the objects in the appropriate squares.
7 Children should colour the plan.
8 Children should make a new plan on Copymaster 25.

PAGE 8
1 $1 \times 3 = 3$
2 $2 \times 3 = 6$
3 $3 \times 3 = 9$
4 $4 \times 3 = 12$
5 $5 \times 3 = 15$
6 $6 \times 3 = 18$
Children should draw 6 triangles.

PAGE 9

	8	9		8	9	10
10	11	12	11	12	13	14	15
13	14	15				

12	13	14	15	16	17	18
19	20	21	22	23	24	
25	26	27				

PAGE 10
1 5
2 8
3 10
4 3

PAGE 11
1 7
2 8
3 13
4 Children should draw a canoe which is 15 cm long.

PAGE 12
Children should colour the shapes in the appropriate colours.

PAGE 13
Children should draw a pattern featuring the shapes.

PAGE 14
1 6
2 8
3 10
4 canoeing
5 sailing

PAGE 15
* * *
* *
* * * *
* * * * *
* * * * * *
*

PAGE 16
I can ...
... read a chart.
6, 8, 4, 10
... carry on with a pattern of threes.

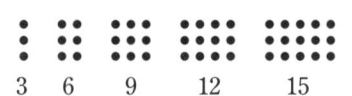

3   6   9   12   15

124 **Answers**

Copymasters for Textbook 2

COPYMASTER 37

1	11	11	14
2	11	12	14
3	12	13	15
4	12	14	13
5	13	15	16
6	8	16	10
7	10	17	13
8	12	18	13
9	12	19	15
10	11	20	10

COPYMASTER 38

1	7	11	1
2	5	12	5
3	7	13	5
4	11	14	3
5	1	15	7
6	12	16	12
7	7	17	10
8	10	18	8
9	8	19	6
10	9	20	1

COPYMASTER 39

1 4, 2, 1, 8
2 5, 2, 1, 10
3 12
4 Children should show the cuboids on a chart.

COPYMASTER 40

1 4, 2, 2, 16
2 5, 2, 2, 20
3 24
4 Children should show the cuboids on a chart.

COPYMASTER 41

1 Children should draw 3 people.
2 Children should draw 2 people.
3 Children should draw 4 people.
4 Children should draw 5 people.

COPYMASTER 42

1–4

COPYMASTER 43

1 $3 \times 2 = 6$
2 $7 \times 2 = 14$
3 $5 \times 2 = 10$
4 $8 \times 2 = 16$
5 $2 \times 2 = 4$
6 $6 \times 2 = 12$
7 $1 \times 2 = 2$
8 $10 \times 2 = 20$
9 $9 \times 2 = 18$
10 $4 \times 2 = 8$

Children should draw the pairs of socks.

COPYMASTER 44

1	6	11	12
2	4	12	8
3	12	13	18
4	18	14	16
5	4	15	2
6	8	16	4
7	10	17	14
8	20	18	6
9	16	19	20
10	14	20	10

COPYMASTER 45

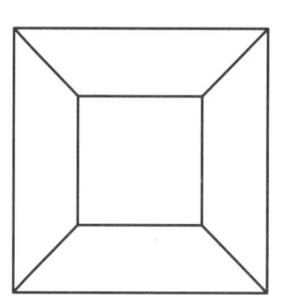

COPYMASTER 46

1–5

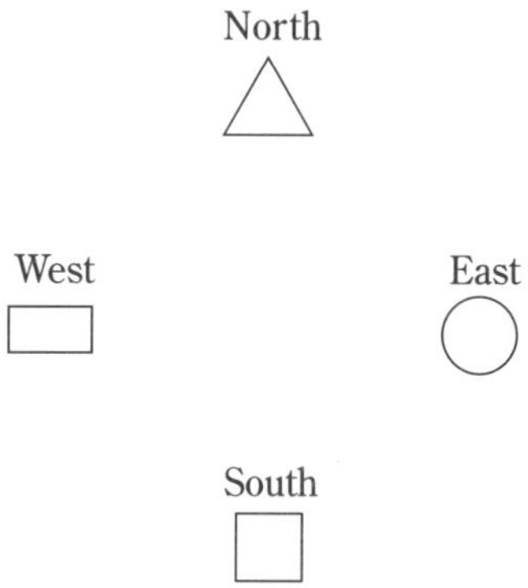

North
West   East
South

COPYMASTER 47

1
$$\begin{array}{r} 26 \\ +46 \\ \hline 72 \end{array}$$

2
$$\begin{array}{r} 37 \\ +35 \\ \hline 72 \end{array}$$

3
$$\begin{array}{r} 46 \\ +37 \\ \hline 83 \end{array}$$

4
$$\begin{array}{r} 25 \\ +38 \\ \hline 63 \end{array}$$

5
$$\begin{array}{r} 47 \\ +28 \\ \hline 75 \end{array}$$

6
$$\begin{array}{r} 24 \\ +29 \\ \hline 53 \end{array}$$

Answers 125

COPYMASTER 48

1. 89
2. 81
3. 59
4. 102
5. 67
6. 73
7. 84
8. 110

COPYMASTER 49

1. 46
   − 28
   ────
    18

2. 38
   − 29
   ────
    9

3. 45
   − 27
   ────
    18

4. 47
   − 28
   ────
    19

5. 43
   − 26
   ────
    17

6. 34
   − 19
   ────
    15

COPYMASTER 50

1. 41
2. 34
3. 28
4. 6
5. 18
6. 33
7. 17
8. 19

COPYMASTER 51

1. $1 \times 3 = 3$
2. $2 \times 3 = 6$
3. $3 \times 3 = 9$
4. $4 \times 3 = 12$
5. $5 \times 3 = 15$
6. $6 \times 3 = 18$
7. $7 \times 3 = 21$
8. $8 \times 3 = 24$
9. $9 \times 3 = 27$
10. $10 \times 3 = 30$

COPYMASTER 52

1. $3 \times 3 = 9$
2. $7 \times 3 = 21$
3. $5 \times 3 = 15$
4. $8 \times 3 = 24$
5. $2 \times 3 = 6$
6. $6 \times 3 = 18$
7. $1 \times 3 = 3$
8. $10 \times 3 = 30$
9. $9 \times 3 = 27$
10. $4 \times 3 = 12$

Children should draw the tripods.

COPYMASTER 53

1. 14
   × 2
   ────
    28

2. 13
   × 2
   ────
    26

3. 20
   × 2
   ────
    40

4. 17
   × 2
   ────
    34

5. 10
   × 2
   ────
    20

6. 12
   × 2
   ────
    24

7. 15
   × 2
   ────
    30

8. 19
   × 2
   ────
    38

COPYMASTER 54

1. $26 \div 2 = 13$
2. $28 \div 2 = 14$
3. $20 \div 2 = 10$
4. $22 \div 2 = 11$
5. $16 \div 2 = 8$
6. $14 \div 2 = 7$

COPYMASTER 55

1. 6
2. 10
3. 16
4. 29
5. 18
6. 14

COPYMASTER 56

1. 10
2. 5
3. 12
4. 7
5. Children should draw a surfboard which is 15 cm long.

COPYMASTER 57

Children should colour the shapes in the appropriate colours.

COPYMASTER 58

1–5 Children should draw the appropriate shapes.

COPYMASTER 59

1. 29
2. 72
3. 47
4. 54
5. 65
6. 81

COPYMASTER 60

1–8 Children should shade the appropriate numbers of squares.

COPYMASTER 61

1–3 Children should shade the appropriate numbers of squares.

COPYMASTER 62

1. 139
2. 211
3. 199
4. 288
5. 149
6. 257

COPYMASTER 63

1. 10
2. 6
3. Nicky and Lisa
4. 12
5. Tom and Rupa
6. David
7. Katy

COPYMASTER 64

Textbook 3

PAGE 2
1. triangle
   square
   rectangle
2. Triangle 5
   Square 6
   Rectangle 23
3. Children should draw another building and make a chart to show the shapes.

PAGE 3
1. C3
2. the grain store
3. the main gate
4. E3
5. fruit trees
6. the fruit store
7. the servants' house
8. A5

PAGE 4
1. 22
2. 38
3. 27
4. 13
5. 60
6. 65
7. 40
8. 51

PAGE 5
1. 4
2. 5
3. 20
4. Children should carry on with the pattern on squared paper.
5. 4
6. 5
7. 20
8. Children should carry on with the pattern on squared paper.
9. Children should devise some pentominoes on squared paper.

PAGES 6 AND 7
1. AD 43
2. AD 400
3. 357 years
4–6. Children should draw the time line and mark the years AD 300 and AD 150.
7. 1985
8. 5
9. 1987
10. 7
11. The answer will vary according to the year.
12. Children should draw time lines to reflect their own lives.

PAGE 8
1. 31
2. 28
3. 135
4. III
5. XXV
6. XIII
7. CXXII
8. CCXXXVII

PAGE 9
1. 4
2. 12
3. 20
4. 40
5. Children should complete the four-times table.

PAGE 10
1. 8
2. 12
3. 16
4. 10
5. 14
6. 18
7–10. There are several correct answers.
11–12. Children should draw some numbers and make up some questions.

PAGE 11

	Hundreds	Tens	Units
1	1	5	8
2	2	4	8
3		6	3
4			9

5. 275
6. 380
7. 438
8. 452
9. Children should make up some more additions.

PAGE 12

	Hundreds	Tens	Units
1	1	6	5
2	2	1	0
3		2	7
4		4	9

5. 21
6. 124
7. 112
8. 166
9. Children should make up some more subtractions.

PAGE 13
1. Chicken 10
   Duck 8
   Pig 4
   Goose 4
2. 10, 8, 4, 4, blocks

PAGE 14
1. 3
2. 9
3. 15
4. 30
5. Children should complete the three-times table.

PAGE 15
1. 8
2. 6
3. 4
4. 5

Number Workbook 3

PAGE 2

1   52
       + 47
  52 + 47 = 99

2 57
3 77
4 97
5 59

PAGE 3

1   56
      − 33
  56 − 33 = 23

2 24
3 22
4 31
5 36

PAGES 4 AND 5

1 1985
2 1985
3 1985
4 1985
5 9
6 10
7 1990
8 6
9 8
10 4
11 9
12 1991
13 1989
14 The answer will vary according to the year.

PAGE 6

1 11, 11
2 6, 6
3 15, 15
4 2, 2
5 16, 16

PAGE 7

1 12, 12
2 8, 8
3 16, 16
4 14, 14

PAGE 8

1 $1 \times 4 = 4$
2 $2 \times 4 = 8$
3 $3 \times 4 = 12$
4 $4 \times 4 = 16$
5 $5 \times 4 = 20$
6 $6 \times 4 = 24$
7 $7 \times 4 = 28$
8 $8 \times 4 = 32$
9 $9 \times 4 = 36$
10 $10 \times 4 = 40$

PAGE 9

1 Children should colour 16, 20, 24, 28, 32, 36, 40
2 Children should colour 16, 20, 24, 28, 32, 36, 40

PAGE 10

1 16
2 18
3 17
4 14
5 16
6 12
7 19
8 13
9 15
10 16
11–16 There are several correct answers.

PAGE 11

1 8
2 9
3 7
4 14
5 7
6 12
7 3
8 11
9 16
10 10
11–16 There are several correct answers.

PAGE 12

1–9 Children should colour the appropriate numbers of squares.

PAGE 13

1 53
2 70
3 53
4 51
5 41
6 62

PAGE 14

1–9 Children should colour the appropriate numbers of squares.

PAGE 15

1 18
2 29
3 15
4 14
5 39
6 9

PAGE 16

I can ...
... add up.
13, 17, 12
... subtract.
7, 7, 6
... multiply.
20, 12, 24
... show numbers as tens and ones.
Children should colour the appropriate numbers of squares.

Answers

Topic Workbook 3

PAGE 2
Children should draw the other half of the building as a mirror image.

PAGE 3
Hexagon 1
Circle 5
Rectangle 5
Triangle 3
Square 8

1, 5, 5, 3, 8 blocks

PAGE 4
1–8 Children should draw the features in the appropriate squares.
9 Children should colour the plan.
10 Children should make a plan, using Copymaster 25.

PAGE 5
1 the woods
2 the town
3 the hill
4 the river
5–6 Children should draw the features in the appropriate positions.

PAGE 6
1 $1 \times 5 = 5$
2 $2 \times 5 = 10$
3 $3 \times 5 = 15$
4 $4 \times 5 = 20$
5 $5 \times 5 = 25$
6 $6 \times 5 = 30$

PAGE 7
1–2 Children should carry on with the patterns to show the five-times table.
3 Children should make another chart on squared paper.

PAGE 8
1 V
2 XIV
3 XVI
4 XII
5 XVII
6 XX
7 3
8 17
9 19
10 8
11 9
12 11

PAGE 9
1
I	II	III	IV	V
VI	VII	VIII	IX	X
XI	XII	XIII	XIV	XV
XVI	XVII	XVIII	XIX	XX

2
XXI	XXII	XXIII	XXIV	XXV
XXVI	XXVII	XXVIII	XXIX	XXX
XXXI	XXXII	XXXIII	XXXIV	XXXV
XXXVI	XXXVII	XXXVIII	XXXIX	XXXX
XXXXI	XXXXII	XXXXIII	XXXXIV	XXXXV
XXXXVI	XXXXVII	XXXXVIII	XXXXIX	L

PAGE 10
Number of sides	Number of shapes
3	7
4	8
5	5
6	6

$3\frac{1}{2}$, 4, $2\frac{1}{2}$, 3 blocks

PAGE 11
1 11
2 5
3 8
4 4
5 2
6 Children should draw $1\frac{1}{2}$ blocks.

PAGE 12
1 2, 4, 6, 8, 10, 12
2 3, 6, 9, 12, 15, 18
3 4, 8, 12, 16, 20, 24
4 5, 10, 15, 20, 25, 30

PAGE 13
1 2, 4, 6, 8, 10, 12, 14, 16, 18, 20
2 3, 6, 9, 12, 15, 18, 21, 24, 27, 30
3 4, 8, 12, 16, 20, 24, 28, 32, 36, 40
4 5, 10, 15, 20, 25, 30, 35, 40, 45, 50
5 15, 15
6 12, 12
7 8, 8
8 20, 20

PAGE 14
1 4
2 4
3 6
4 6

PAGE 15
1 2
2 $1\frac{1}{2}$
3 3
4 $2\frac{1}{2}$
5 4

PAGE 16
1 I can ...
... read Roman numerals.
7, 14
... write Roman numerals.
IX, XII
... draw a pentagon.

... carry on with a pattern of fives.
5, 10, 15, 20, 25

Copymasters for Textbook 3

COPYMASTER 69

1–3 Children should draw the other halves of the patterns as mirror images.

COPYMASTER 70

1–2 Children should draw symmetrical patterns.

COPYMASTER 71

Children should draw 6 rectangles, 4 circles, 3 squares and 5 triangles.

COPYMASTER 72

1 Children should join the dots indicated.
2 a sailing boat

COPYMASTER 73

1. 23
   + 39

    62

2. 34
   + 26

    60

3. 34
   + 39

    73

4. 40
   + 31

    71

5. 36
   + 18

    54

6. 33
   + 49

    82

COPYMASTER 74

1. 34
   − 16

    18

2. 36
   − 27

     9

3. 42
   − 24

    18

4. 43
   − 18

    25

5. 55
   − 26

    29

6. 38
   − 29

     9

COPYMASTER 75

1 $1 \times 5 = 5$
2 $2 \times 5 = 10$
3 $3 \times 5 = 15$
4 $4 \times 5 = 20$
5 $5 \times 5 = 25$
6 $6 \times 5 = 30$
7 $7 \times 5 = 35$
8 $8 \times 5 = 40$
9 $9 \times 5 = 45$
10 $10 \times 5 = 50$

COPYMASTER 76

1 $1 \times 5 = 5$
2 $2 \times 5 = 10$
3 $3 \times 5 = 15$
4 $7 \times 5 = 35$
5 $5 \times 5 = 25$
6 $9 \times 5 = 45$
7 $4 \times 5 = 20$
8 $6 \times 5 = 30$
9 $8 \times 5 = 40$
10 $10 \times 5 = 50$

COPYMASTER 77

1 12, 12
2 15, 15
3 16, 16
4 15, 15
5 12, 12

COPYMASTER 78

1 6, 6
2 9, 9
3 4, 4
4 9, 9
5 7, 7

COPYMASTER 79

1 2, 4, 6, 8, 10, 12, 14, 16
2 3, 6, 9, 12, 15
3 4, 8, 12, 16
4 5, 10, 15

COPYMASTER 81

1, 2, 3, 4, 5, 6, 7, 8, 9, 10, 11, 12, 13, 14, 15, 16, 17, 18, 19, 20

COPYMASTER 82

1 3
2 14
3 6
4 20
5 4
6 17
7 ··
8 ···
9 ·
10 ··
11 ····
12 ···

COPYMASTER 83

1 $1 \times 4 = 4$
2 $2 \times 4 = 8$
3 $3 \times 4 = 12$
4 $4 \times 4 = 16$
5 $5 \times 4 = 20$
6 $6 \times 4 = 24$
7 $7 \times 4 = 28$
8 $8 \times 4 = 32$
9 $9 \times 4 = 36$
10 $10 \times 4 = 40$

Answers

COPYMASTER 84

1. $1 \times 4 = 4$
2. $2 \times 4 = 8$
3. $3 \times 4 = 12$
4. $7 \times 4 = 28$
5. $5 \times 4 = 20$
6. $9 \times 4 = 36$
7. $4 \times 4 = 16$
8. $6 \times 4 = 24$
9. $8 \times 4 = 32$
10. $10 \times 4 = 40$

COPYMASTER 85

1. 20
2. 19
3. 18
4. 15
5. 17
6. 15
7. 18
8. 11
9. 15
10. 20
11–16 There are several correct answers.

COPYMASTER 86

1. 11
2. 8
3. 8
4. 12
5. 8
6. 13
7. 4
8. 12
9. 14
10. 9
11–16 There are several correct answers.

COPYMASTER 87

	Hundreds	Tens	Ones
1	1	9	2
2	4	1	3
3	3	5	3
4	1	7	9
5	5	2	4
6	2	6	5
7	5	3	6
8	2	4	7
9	6	8	8
10	4	9	1

COPYMASTER 88

1. 43
2. 50
3. 65
4. 100
5. 54
6. 61
7. 54
8. 72
9. 35
10. 90
11. 53
12. 64
13. 62
14. 91
15. 61

COPYMASTER 89

	Hundreds	Tens	Ones
1	1	8	3
2	3	0	4
3	2	4	2
4	2	6	8
5	4	1	3
6	3	7	6
7	4	2	5
8	1	3	6
9	5	7	9
10	3	8	0

COPYMASTER 90

1. 16
2. 18
3. 27
4. 45
5. 19
6. 15
7. 24
8. 30
9. 14
10. 9
11. 9
12. 9
13. 9
14. 25
15. 18

COPYMASTER 91

Square	5
Triangle	8
Rectangle	6
Hexagon	7

$2\frac{1}{2}$, 4, 3, $3\frac{1}{2}$ blocks

COPYMASTER 92

1. 5
2. 2
3. 7
4. 6
5. 13
6. Children should colour 6 blocks.

COPYMASTER 93

1. 2   3. 4
   4   8
   6   12
   8   16
   10   20

2. 3   4. 5
   6   10
   9   15
   12   20
   15   25

COPYMASTER 94

1. 3   12. 12
2. 6   13. 2
3. 25   14. 3
4. 4   15. 20
5. 8   16. 20
6. 15   17. 6
7. 6   18. 10
8. 5   19. 9
9. 2   20. 4
10. 16   21. 4
11. 1   22. 25

COPYMASTER 95

1–6 Children should colour the cylinders up to the appropriate levels.

COPYMASTER 97

1. 2 kilograms
2. $2\frac{1}{2}$ kilograms
3. $4\frac{1}{2}$ kilograms
4. 1 kilogram
5. $3\frac{1}{2}$ kilograms
6. $\frac{1}{2}$ kilogram

7–9 Children should draw the hands in the appropriate places.

Answers 131

Textbook 4

PAGE 2
1 43
2 38
3 67
4 the hexagon
5 the rectangle

PAGE 3
1 20
2 4
3 10
4 2
5 15
6 3
7 25
8 5

PAGE 4
1 67
2 79
3 122
4 105
5 43
6 12
7 29
8 5

PAGE 5
1 E6
2 A6
3 B4
4 the tower
5 the horsechestnut tree
6 the bridge
7 the tree house

PAGE 6
1 150 metres
2 225 metres
3 300 metres
4 200 metres
5 oak tree
  tree house
  pond
  bridge
  horsechestnut tree
  tower
  850 metres

PAGE 7
1 twenty to 7
2 10 minutes
3 6:55
4 25 minutes
5 quarter past 7
6 45 minutes
7 7:20
8 50 minutes
9 quarter to 8
10 1 hour 15 minutes
11 8:00
12 1 hour 30 minutes

PAGE 8
1 15
2 17
3 8
4 Helen's group
5 Emma's group
6 Sam's group
7 Rupa's group

PAGE 9
1 Children should make a bar chart.
2 conkers
3 pine cones
4 52

PAGE 10
1 9
2 9
3 13
4 17
5 20
6 10
7 12
8 14
9 14
10 20

PAGE 11
1 25
2 25
3 27
4 23
5 20
6 30
7 26
8 24
9 David
10 Lisa

PAGE 12
1 £478
2 £547
3 £325
4 £451
5 Rupa
6 David
7 £1025
8 £776

PAGE 13

	Thousands	Hundreds	Tens	Ones
1	1	5	2	4
2	3	2	1	9
3	5	1	5	5
4	2	9	2	6
5	3	3	9	8

PAGE 14
1 20   5 6
2 22   6 10
3 28   7 9
4 26   8 7

PAGE 15
1 8
2 20
3 12

132 Answers

Number Workbook 4

PAGE 2
1. Children should colour 2 sectors.
2. Children should colour 1 triangle.
3. Children should colour 1 square.
4. Children should colour 4 squares.
5. Children should colour 4 squares.

PAGE 3
1. 15, 3
2. 5, 1
3. 25, 5
4. 20, 4
5. 30, 6

PAGE 4
1. 54
2. 68
3. 53
4. 69
5. 84
6. 64
7. 59
8. 68
9. 71
10. 84

PAGE 5
1. 10
2. 23
3. 11
4. 17
5. 24
6. 31
7. 11
8. 23
9. 20
10. 22

PAGE 6
1. 17
2. 17
3. 20
4. 16
5. 19
6. 20
7. 14
8. 15
9. 17
10. 19
11. There are several correct answers.

PAGE 7
1. 12
2. 12
3. 2
4. 10
5. 4
6. 13
7. 4
8. 12
9. 15
10. 8
11. There are several correct answers.

PAGE 8
1. 25
2. 21
3. 26
4. 27

PAGE 9
1. Children should link
   0, 10
   1, 9
   2, 8
   3, 7
   4, 6
   5, 5
2. 23
3. 22
4. 29

PAGE 10
1. £256
2. £333
3. £415
4. £142
5. David
6. Nicky

PAGE 11
1. 389
2. 478
3. 569
4. 496
5. 369
6. 499

PAGE 12
1–6 Children should draw the appropriate toy money.

PAGE 13

Thousands	Hundreds	Tens	Ones
2	4	2	3
1	4	3	5
3	2	5	1
2	6	4	7
1	3	3	6

PAGE 14
1. 22
2. 42
3. 50
4. 28
5. 32
6. 44

PAGE 15
1. 12
2. 24
3. 15
4. 10
5. 9
6. 17

PAGE 16
I can ...
... add.
29, 57, 40
... subtract.
8, 14, 16
... multiply.
24, 26, 30
... divide.
11, 14, 15

Answers 133

Topic Workbook 4

PAGE 2

1 the tower
2 the pond
3 the oak tree
4 the horsechestnut tree
5 There are several correct answers.

PAGE 3

Across	Down
1 triangle	*1* circle
2 square	*2* rectangle
3 pentagon	
4 hexagon	

PAGE 4

1 the pond
2 the tree house
3 east
4 east
5 west

PAGE 5

1–6 Children should draw the features in the appropriate squares.
7 B6
8 A1
9 D3

PAGE 6

1 10 centimetres
2 2 centimetres
3 4 centimetres
4 12 centimetres
5 6 centimetres
6 the leaf
7 the acorn

PAGE 7

1–5 Children should draw items of the appropriate lengths.

PAGE 8

1 04:35
2 10:40
3 03:00
4 11:50
5 08:15
6 12:35

PAGE 9

1 10 past 5
2 quarter past 11
3 10 to 9
4 5 to 3
5 20 past 4
Children should draw the appropriate hands on the clocks.

PAGE 10

1 20
2 12
3 7
4 17
5 14
6 conkers
7 white stones
8 Children should draw a bar to show 10 twigs.

PAGE 11

1 Children should draw a bar chart to show the conkers.
2 Helen's group
3 Emma's group

PAGE 12

1 Children should draw a bar chart to show the trees.
2 fir trees
3 oak trees
4 elm trees

PAGE 13

1 ||||| ||
2 8
3 7
4 5
5 10
6 12

PAGE 14

1 2
2 1
3 $1\frac{1}{2}$
4 6
5 10
6 9

PAGE 15

1 400
2 200
3 500
4–6 Children should colour the cylinders up to the appropriate levels.

PAGE 16

I can ...
... read a tally chart.
13
10
16
8
11
... show the time.
Children should draw the appropriate hands on the clock.
... write the time.
20 past 10
04:40

Answers

Copymasters for Textbook 4

COPYMASTER 103
1–2 Children should carry on with the patterns.

COPYMASTER 104
1–6 Children should draw the appropriate shapes.

COPYMASTER 105
1 10
   10, 2
2 20
   20, 4
3 15
   15, 3
4 25
   25, 5

COPYMASTER 106
1 3   **4** 4
2 4   **5** 6
3 2   **6** 8

COPYMASTER 107
1 59   **6** 56
2 56   **7** 59
3 67   **8** 68
4 41   **9** 62
5 69   **10** 60

COPYMASTER 108
1 13   **6** 11
2 12   **7** 23
3 22   **8** 22
4 21   **9** 12
5 24   **10** 10

COPYMASTER 110
1 the tree house   **5** E3
2 the horsechestnut tree   **6** A6
3 the oak tree   **7** C2
4 the pond   **8** E6

COPYMASTER 111
1 11
2 13
3 4
4 17

COPYMASTER 112
1–4 Children should draw items of the appropriate dimensions.

COPYMASTER 114
1 07:45   **4** 11:40
2 10:55   **5** 08:00
3 03:50   **6** 05:30

COPYMASTER 116
1 20 to 2
2 10 o'clock
3 5 to 5
4 quarter past 10
Children should draw the appropriate hands on the clocks.

COPYMASTER 118
1 19   **5** 11
2 8   **6** pine
3 16   **7** ash
4 5

COPYMASTER 119
Children should draw a bar chart to show the animals.

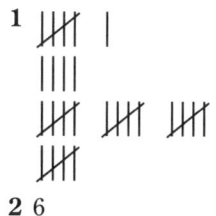

COPYMASTER 120
1 |||| | |||| |||| |||| |||| ||||
2 6
3 4
4 15
5 5

COPYMASTER 121
1 19   **6** 11
2 5   **7** 13
3 18   **8** 9
4 7   **9** 13
5 20   **10** 11
11–12 There are several correct answers.

COPYMASTER 122
1–2 Children should link
   0, 10
   1, 9
   2, 8
   3, 7
   4, 6
   5, 5

COPYMASTER 123

	Hundreds	Tens	Units
1	4	3	6
2	3	5	3
3	1	8	7
4	2	1	9

5 436
6 187

COPYMASTER 124
1 396   **4** 476
2 448   **5** 476
3 399   **6** 396

COPYMASTER 125

	Thousands	Hundreds	Tens	Ones
1	4	5	5	1
2	3	6	1	7
3	1	7	4	7
4	5	2	8	0

5 5280
6 1747

COPYMASTER 126
1–6 Children should draw the appropriate amounts of toy money.
7 5317
8 1536

COPYMASTER 127
1 26   **4** 48
2 40   **5** 46
3 30   **6** 34

COPYMASTER 128
1 11   **5** 12
2 14   **6** 10
3 22   **7** 21
4 8   **8** 16

COPYMASTER 129
1–6 Children should colour the cylinders up to the appropriate levels.

COPYMASTER 130
1 100   **4** 500
2 400   **5** 300
3 200   **6** 250

Textbook 5

PAGE 2

1 a sphere
2 a cuboid
3 a prism
4 a cylinder

PAGE 3

1 2
2 17
3 400
4 13

PAGE 4

1 27
2 24
3 31
4 30

PAGE 5

1 235
2 327
3 258
4 235
5 365
6 526

PAGE 6

1 9
2 3
3 2
4 6
5 15
6 5
7 4
8 12

PAGE 7

1 |||| ||

2 Children should make a bar chart to show the feathers.

PAGE 8

1 10
2 14
3 6
4 16
5 7
6 9
7 Nicky
8 24
9 22
10 16

PAGE 9

1 3
2 3
3 9
4 $3 \times 3 = 9$
5 3
6 4
7 12
8 $3 \times 4 = 12$
9 2
10 4
11 8
12 $2 \times 4 = 8$

PAGE 10

1 8
2 21
3 14 (simple ones)
4 6
5 12

PAGE 11

1 C3
2 E2
3 A4
4 F5
5 E4
6 B3
7 F4
8 C4

PAGE 12

1 45
2 55
3 40
4 35
5 Rupa
6 Nicky

PAGE 13

1 David
2 Nicky
3 5 seconds
4 20 seconds
5 25 seconds
6 5 seconds

PAGE 14

1 60
2 64
3 63
4 62
5 Lisa
6 David
7 249

PAGE 15

1 2500
2 1500
3 1500
4 1750
5 3750
6 2750

Number Workbook 5

PAGE 2
1 36
2 38
3 25
4 37
5 37
6 40

PAGE 3
1–6 There are several correct answers.

PAGE 4

	Hundreds	Tens	Ones	
1	4	6	8	468
2	2	7	5	275
3	3	9	1	391

PAGE 5

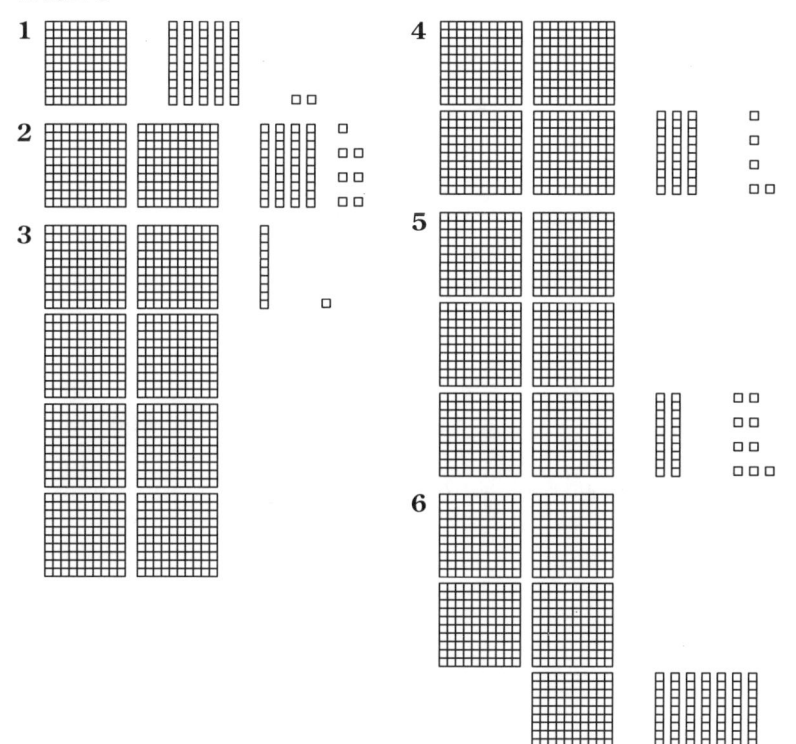

PAGE 6
1 $1 \times 3 = 3$
2 $2 \times 3 = 6$
3 $3 \times 3 = 9$
4 $4 \times 3 = 12$
5 $5 \times 3 = 15$
6 $6 \times 3 = 18$
7 $7 \times 3 = 21$
8 $8 \times 3 = 24$
9 $9 \times 3 = 27$
10 $10 \times 3 = 30$

PAGE 7
1 Children should colour 12, 15, 18, 21, 24, 27, 30, 33, 36, 39 and carry on with the pattern.
2 0, 3, 6, 9, 12, 15, 18, 21
3 9
4 3
5 6
6 15
7 12
8 0

PAGE 8
1 3, 2, 6
2 2, 5, 10
3 4, 3, 12

PAGE 9
1 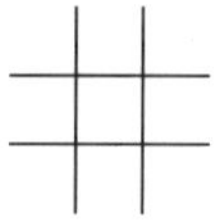
3
4 $2 \times 2 = 4$
9 $3 \times 3 = 9$
2
4
15 $3 \times 5 = 15$
15 $5 \times 3 = 15$

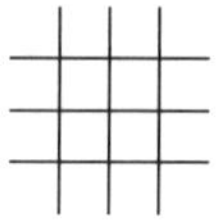

PAGE 10
1 343
2 141
3 122
4 353

PAGE 11
1 389
2 694
3 779
4 489

PAGE 12
1 81
2 62
3 82
4 73
5 43
6 90
7 65
8 80
9 60
10 82
11 74
12 71

PAGE 13
1 518
2 764
3 325
4 618
5 449
6 715
7 518
8 718
9 701

PAGE 14

	Thousands	Hundreds	Tens	Ones
1	1	2	4	6
2	2	3	2	4
3	3	1	5	7

PAGE 15
1 2376
2 2628
3 1457
4 2365

PAGE 16
I can ...
... add.
61, 85
... subtract.
14, 18
... write hundreds, tens and ones.
947
... write thousands, hundreds, tens and ones.
3458

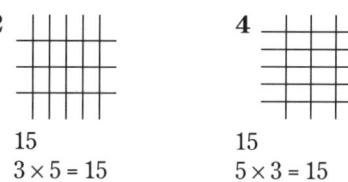

Answers 137

Topic Workbook 5

PAGE 2
1. a cuboid
2. a (hexagonal) prism
3. a sphere
4. a cylinder
5. a (triangular) prism
6. a cube

PAGE 3
2 cuboids
4 spheres
3 cylinders
3 hexagonal prisms
3 triangular prisms
4 cones
2 cubes

PAGE 4
1. 0, 400
2. 0, 600
3. 0, 800
4. 1, 0
5. 1, 200

PAGE 5
1. 200 grams
2. 450 grams
3. 500 grams
4. 50 grams
5. 800 grams
6. 650 grams
7–9 Children should draw the hands in the appropriate places.

PAGE 6
1. ||||
2. 4
3. 9
4. 6
5. 8

PAGE 7
Children should draw a bar chart to show the arrows.
1. 8
2. 10
3. 6
4. 8

PAGE 8
1. 10
2. 19
3. 15
4. 12
5. 8
6. 15
7. David
8. 25
9. 27
10. 27

PAGE 9
Children should draw a bar chart to show the scores.
David, Lisa, Tom, Nicky, Rupa, Emma

PAGE 10
1–6 Children should finish the patterns and colour the shapes in the appropriate colours.

PAGE 11
1–2 Children should draw the appropriate shapes.

PAGE 12
1. B3
2. B5
3. E4
4. C4
5. C5
6. C4
7. D2
8. F2

PAGE 13
1–3 Children should draw the characters and lines to show their new positions.
4. 4

PAGE 14
1. 10 seconds
2. 5 seconds
3. 50 seconds
4. 30 seconds
5. 25 seconds
6. 15 seconds
7–9 Children should draw the appropriate hands on the stopwatches.

PAGE 15
1. 1 minute 25 seconds
2. 1 minute 55 seconds
3. 3 minutes 35 seconds
4. 2 minutes 10 seconds
5. 2 minutes 15 seconds
6. 1 minute 40 seconds

PAGE 16
I can ...
... draw a hexagon.

... draw a pentagon.

... write the time in seconds.
20 seconds
... write the time in minutes and seconds.
2 minutes 50 seconds

Answers

Copymasters for Textbook 5

COPYMASTER 135
Children should colour the shapes in the appropriate colours.

COPYMASTER 136
1–2 Children should map the shapes to their names.

COPYMASTER 138
1. 100 grams
2. 250 grams
3. 600 grams
4. 750 grams
5. 900 grams
6. 450 grams

7–9 Children should draw the appropriate hands on the scales.

COPYMASTER 141
1. 38
2. 38
3. 34
4. 30
5. 45
6. 35

COPYMASTER 142
1–6 There are several correct answers.

COPYMASTER 143

	Hundreds	Tens	Ones	
1	3	7	9	379
2	1	6	4	164
3	4	0	2	402
4	6	3	5	635
5	7	2	8	728

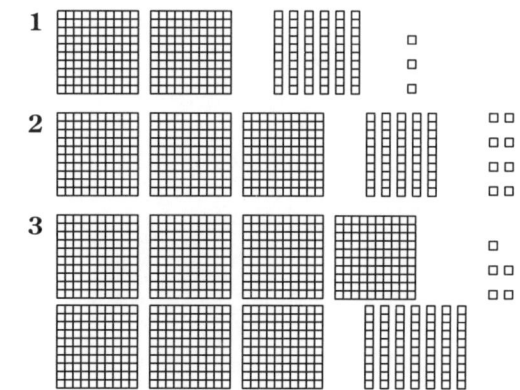

COPYMASTER 144

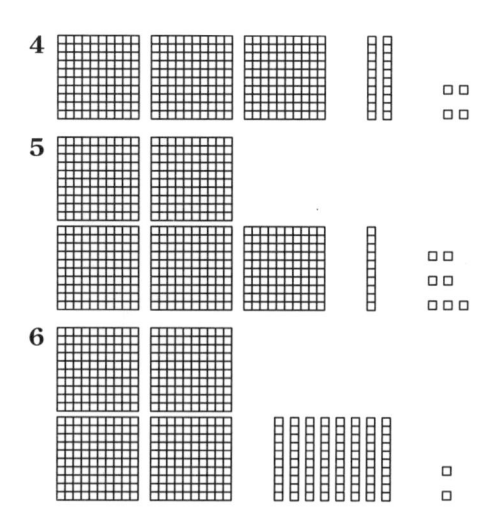

COPYMASTER 148
1. (tally)
2. 6
3. 12
4. 18
5. 7
6. Children should draw a bar chart to show the scores, using Copymaster 117.

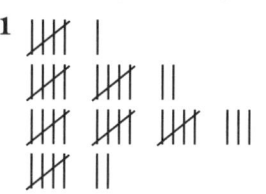

COPYMASTER 149
1. 17
2. 11
3. 18
4. 9
5. 7
6. 8
7. Rupa
8. 26
9. 24
10. 20

COPYMASTER 150
1. 2, 3, 6
2. 3, 4, 12
3. 2, 5, 10
4. 3, 5, 15

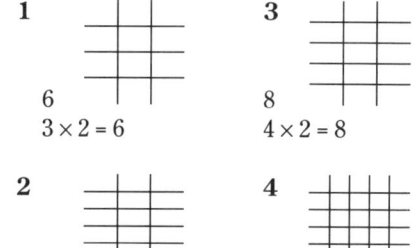

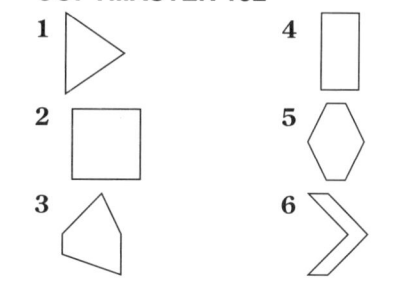

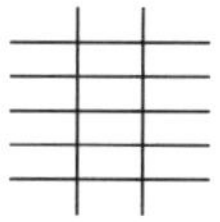

COPYMASTER 151
1. $3 \times 2 = 6$
2. $5 \times 2 = 10$
3. $4 \times 2 = 8$
4. $5 \times 4 = 20$

COPYMASTER 152
1. triangle
2. square
3. pentagon
4. rectangle
5. hexagon
6. arrow

COPYMASTER 153
1. B3
2. B5
3. E2
4. C2
5. D5
6. D3
7. A6
8. C6

COPYMASTER 154
Children should join the appropriate dots.
1. hexagon
2. square
3. triangle
4. rectangle

COPYMASTER 155
Children should plot some shapes and write the co-ordinates.

COPYMASTER 156
1. 20 seconds
2. 45 seconds
3. 55 seconds
4. 10 seconds
5. 35 seconds
6. 40 seconds
7. Children should draw the appropriate hands on the scales.

COPYMASTER 158
1. 1 minute 15 seconds
2. 1 minute 10 seconds
3. 3 minutes 40 seconds
4. 2 minutes 25 seconds
5. 2 minutes 55 seconds
6. 1 minute 5 seconds

COPYMASTER 161
1. 141
2. 21
3. 142
4. 451
5. 240

COPYMASTER 162
1. 598
2. 694
3. 779
4. 700
5. 589

COPYMASTER 163
1. 94
2. 75
3. 84
4. 79
5. 79
6. 43
7. 80
8. 56
9. 78
10. 38
11. 82
12. 62
13. 62
14. 84
15. 58

COPYMASTER 164
1. 539
2. 787
3. 682
4. 742
5. 1070
6. 629
7. 738
8. 931
9. 594
10. 821
11. 618
12. 816
13. 654
14. 783
15. 900

COPYMASTER 165

	Thousands	Hundreds	Tens	Ones
1	2	1	5	8
2	1	2	1	3
3	2	3	4	6
4	3	4	7	4
5	2	6	8	1

COPYMASTER 166
1. 2351
2. 1264
3. 2375
4. 3549
5. 3687
6. 1798

Answers

Textbook 6

PAGE 2

1. |||| |||| |

2. Children should make a bar chart to show the objects.

PAGE 3

1. 20
2. 10
3. 8
4. 16
5. 10
6. 5
7. 4
8. 8

PAGE 4

1. 12 squares
2. 15 squares
3. 8 squares
4. 9 squares
5. 10 squares

Children should draw the nets.

PAGE 5

1. 8 miles
2. 12 miles
3. 34 miles
4. 61 miles
5. 27 miles
6. 32 miles
7. 86 miles

PAGE 6

1. 1865
2. 1809
3. 1732
4. 63 years
5. 53 years
6. 75 years
7. Sarah Bell
8. Elizabeth Wilkins
9. Elizabeth Wilkins'

PAGE 7

1. a rectangle
2. 6
3. a pentagon
4. Children should draw a hexagon.
5. 2
6. a rectangle

PAGES 8 AND 9

1. £3.50
2. 50p
3. £3.95
4. 55p
5. £4.90
6. 60p
7. £2.95
8. 5p

PAGE 10

1. 8
2. 12
3. 16
4. 20, 24, 28, 32, 36, 40
5. 10
6. 15
7. 20
8. 25, 30, 35, 40, 45, 50
9. 6
10. 9
11. 12
12. 15, 18, 21, 24, 27, 30
13. 4
14. 6
15. 8
16. 10, 12, 14, 16, 18, 20

PAGE 11

1. 50 miles per hour
2. 5 past 1
3. 4172 miles
4. no
5. cold
6. hot
7. neutral

PAGE 12

1. £1
2. £2
3. £3
4. £0
5. £0
6. £1
7. £1
8. £1
9. £1
10. £1
11. £1
12. £0
13. £2
14. £1

PAGE 13

1. £6.34
2. £4.55
3. £4.34
4. £6.04
5. Children should price items of their choice and deduct the total from £10.

PAGE 14

1. 900
2. 650
3. 1100
4. 1500
5. 2000
6. 2150
7. Nicky and Rupa

PAGE 15

1. 10, 12   0181 293 614   M123 BKY
   A272, A24   1,2,3,4,5,6,7,8,9,10,11,12
2. door numbers   a telephone number
   a numberplate   main roads   a clock
3. squares   spheres
   rectangles   cones
   triangles   cuboids
   circles   prisms
4. windows   a Belisha beacon
   doors   a road cone
   road signs, fences a church
   a clock

140 **Answers**

Number Workbook 6

PAGE 2
1 15	6 13
2 11	7 12
3 11	8 14
4 11	9 15
5 11	10 8
11 9	16 7
12 3	17 6
13 9	18 7
14 7	19 9
15 15	20 8

PAGE 3
1 59	3 69	5 89
2 80	4 73	6 87
7 23	10 25	13 40
8 19	11 16	14 16
9 25	12 26	15 59

PAGE 4
1 £2.15	7 £3.46
2 £4.05	8 £1.99
3 £5.75	9 £2.50
4 £3.09	10 £0.85
5 £0.50	11 £0.06
6 £4.44	12 £3.08

PAGE 5
1–8 Children should draw the appropriate coins. There are several correct answers.

PAGE 6
1 £2.95	4 £3.20
2 £2.80	5 £3.60
3 £4	6 £3.35

PAGE 7
1 £1.05
2 £1.15
3 65p
4 35p

PAGE 8
1 6	6 8
2 4	7 10
3 10	8 2
4 8	9 6
5 2	10 4
11 12	16 9
12 15	17 6
13 3	18 15
14 9	19 12
15 6	20 3

PAGE 9
1 8	6 12
2 12	7 20
3 4	8 8
4 16	9 4
5 20	10 16
11 15	16 10
12 25	17 15
13 10	18 5
14 5	19 20
15 20	20 25

PAGE 10
1 £1	6 £1
2 £2	7 £2
3 £2	8 £1
4 £1	9 £2
5 £1	10 £2

PAGE 11
1 £4, £3, £7
2 £10, £5, £15
3 £15, £2, £17
4 £3, £12, £15

PAGES 12 AND 13
1 £2.99	3 £1.98
£0.99	£1.10
£0.49	£1.99
£4.47	£1.99
£5.53	£7.06
	£2.94
2 £1.49	3 £2.49
£1.10	£1.10
£0.49	£1.98
£3.08	£0.98
£6.92	£6.55
	£3.45

PAGE 14
1 1050	3 950
2 1200	4 1650

PAGE 15
1 4395	3 3650
2 8170	4 5735
5 1615	7 3220
6 1235	8 3865

PAGE 16
I can ...
... add up fast.
14, 12, 12
14, 12, 10
... remember tables.
12, 10, 15
20, 6, 8
... round money up and down.
£4
£1
... give change.
£3.15

Answers 141

Topic Workbook 6

PAGE 2

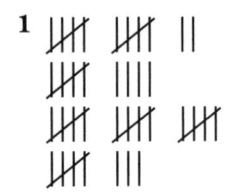

1. |||| |||| ||

2. 12
3. 9
4. 15
5. 8

PAGE 3

1. Children should draw a bar chart to show the objects.
2. 27
3. 17
4. 23
5. 21

PAGE 4

1. 20, 10
2. 28, 14
3. 16, 8
4. 32, 16
5. 36, 18

Children should draw the lines.

PAGE 5

1. 24, 6
2. 32, 8
3. 28, 7
4. 40, 10
5. 36, 9

Children should draw the lines.

PAGE 6

1. 15
2. 12
3. 13

PAGE 7

1. 4, 3, 12
2. 7, 3, 21
3. 4, 4, 16

PAGE 8

1–4 Children should draw the appropriate amounts of toy money.

PAGE 9

1. 1880
2. 1723
3. 1814
4. 46 years
5. 56 years
6. 70 years
7. Jane Elliott
8. Grace Williams
9. Jane Elliot's

PAGE 10

1. 6
2. 3
3. 1
4. 2
5. 1 (or 2)
6. Children should draw a right-angled triangle.

PAGE 11

1–2 Children should draw the appropriate shapes.

PAGE 12

1. 25
2. 15
3. 5
4. 400
5. 250
6. 850
7. 20
8. 45
9. 50

PAGE 13

1. 55, 2430
2. 70, 4012
3. 30, 1949
4. 85, 6945

PAGE 14

1. 23
   456
   789
2. 789
   456
   23
3. 45 47 49 51
4. 96 98 100 102

PAGE 15

1–2 Children should carry on with the patterns.

PAGE 16

I can ...
... find half.
18, 9
12, 6
... find quarters.
8, 2
12, 3
... find the area of a shape in square centimetres.
4, 2, 8
... read a speedometer and a mileometer.
45, 4215

Answers

Copymasters for Textbook 6

COPYMASTER 171
1. 2, 1
2. 8, 4
3. 4, 2
4. 14, 7
5. 10, 5
6. 6, 3
7. 12, 6
Children should draw the lines.

COPYMASTER 172
1. 4, 1
2. 8, 2
3. 20, 5
4. 12, 3
5. 24, 6
6. 16, 4
7. 28, 7
Children should draw the lines.

COPYMASTER 173
1. 3, 1
2. 9, 3
3. 12, 4
4. 18, 6
5. 21, 7
6. 6, 2
7. 15, 5
Children should draw the lines.

COPYMASTER 174
1. 5, 1
2. 25, 5
3. 30, 6
4. 20, 4
5. 35, 7
6. 10, 2
7. 15, 3
Children should draw the lines.

COPYMASTER 175
1. 10, 1
2. 60, 6
3. 20, 2
4. 30, 3
5. 40, 4
6. 50, 5

COPYMASTER 176
1. 12
2. 11
3. 7
4. 19
5. 15
6. 10

COPYMASTER 177
1. 8, 2, 16
2. 7, 3, 21
3. 6, 4, 24

COPYMASTER 178
1. 15
2. 11
3. 15
4. 11
5. 15
6. 18
7. 14
8. 12
9. 8
10. 2
11. 8
12. 6
13. 8
14. 7
15. 8
16. 10

COPYMASTER 179
1. 79
2. 62
3. 89
4. 93
5. 70
6. 94
7. 23
8. 18
9. 22
10. 14
11. 40
12. 6

COPYMASTER 180
1. 5548
2. 3789
3. 5899
4. 7500

COPYMASTER 181
1. 3141
2. 2043
3. 1212
4. 2461

COPYMASTER 182
1. £1.25
2. £3.75
3. £7.90
4. £2.08
5. £0.30
6. £4.40
7. £2.99
8. £5.35
9. £0.65
10. £0.09

COPYMASTER 183
1–8 Children should draw the appropriate coins. There are several correct answers.

COPYMASTER 184
1. £1.35
2. £2.15
3. £2.60
4. £2.10
5. £1.70
6. £1.80

COPYMASTER 185
1. £2
2. £3
3. £3
4. £2
5. £2
6. £3
7. £2
8. £3

COPYMASTER 186
1. £5, £2, £7
2. £9, £6, £15
3. £14, £4, £18
4. £3, £13, £16
5. £20, £30, £50

COPYMASTER 187
1. £1.99, £0.99, £0.49, £3.47, £6.53
2. £1.49, £1.29, £1.98, £1.47, £6.23, £3.77
3. £1.49, £1.99, £0.98, £4.46, £5.54
4. £1.99, £0.99, £1.98, £1.10, £6.06, £3.94

COPYMASTER 188
1. 4590
2. 7995
3. 3665
4. 6700
5. 4115
6. 2245
7. 3440
8. 1215

Key vocabulary

These lists provide a summary of new vocabulary used in the Level 3 textbooks.

LEVEL 3 – VOCABULARY OF MATHEMATICS (NEW)

Number
- total
- tally
- in the right order
- counting
- decimal point
- fifth
- twice
- multiplication(s)
- subtract
- subtraction(s)
- addition(s)
- divide
- find the difference between
- twos
- threes
- three-times table
- four-times table
- thousand(s)
- ten(s)
- hundred(s)
- unit(s)
- how far
- how long
- how {much/many} more

Shape and space
- diagonal
- squared
- pentagon
- cube(s)
- plan
- sides
- area

Measures
- fastest
- slowest
- wide
- small
- pound
- millilitres
- grams
- milligrams
- second(s)

Position/direction
- high
- north
- south
- east
- west

Handling data
- bar chart

LEVEL 3 – GENERAL VOCABULARY (NEW)

a
about, acorns, activity weekend, afternoon, against, animals, apart, archery, area, arrows

b
badger, barn, bars, bathroom, beans, beds, behind, bet, bin, black, born, bottles, bowls, box, boxes

breakfast, brilliant, bring, Britain, building, bullets, buoys, butter

c
canoes, cases, cereal, cheat, choc pops, churchyard, classroom, cleans, climb, climbing, clover(s), coats, coloured, coming, conkers, cooks, course, cracked, cups, cute

d
dark, dayroom, dead, deodorant, didn't, different, dinner, dock, doing, drawers

e
each, Elizabeth Wilkins, Emma, every, everything

f
fair, fall, Farbury, farmyard, feather(s), fire station, floor, forget, found, fox, Friday, fuel

g
gate, gauge, geese, getting, glad, goes, going, grain, gravestone(s)

h
had, hair gel, hands, happened, heading, hedgehog, Helen, helps, her, his, holds, hope, horsechestnut

i
I'll, Iron Age island, isn't, ivy

j
James, jeans, job, Junction

k
Katy, Kim, kitchen, knots, know-all

l
lake, last, Laura, 4-leafed leave(s), Lee, legs, letters, life jacket, list, lived, Longmoor, Longmoor Guide Book, losing, lots, love, lucky

m
main, making, Mark, mark, maths, Middleton, mileometer(s), Miss, Monday, money, morning, motorway, museum

n
names, nearly, net, night, Nina

o
oak, oars, obstacle course, oldest, old-fashioned, otter, our, ours, one, own

p
packing, paid, peel, pellets, pick, pig(s), pigsty, pinball, pine cones, place, plates, points, pond, pool, postcards, Post Office, potato(es)

q
questions, quickly, quite

r
race, ready, rest, Rikki, Robin Hood, Romans, rooms, ropes, rotten, round, rowing

s
safe, sail(s), sailing, salad, Sam, Sam's, Samuel Thompson, Sanjay, Sara, Sarah Bell, Saturday, saucers, sausages, Saxons, score(s), seeds, servants, services, sewing, shooting, shots, show-off, since, sister, sitting, skittles, sleep, slices, snack, so, soap, some, special, speedometer, sports, started, stay, staying, stones, stool(s), stop, stopwatch, store, stuff, Sue, Sunday, sure, surprise, swimming, sycamore

t
taken, takes, taking, tapes, tea, temperature, their, they've, think, thirsty, Thursday, timed, times, tin(s), tired, today, Tom, Tom's, tomorrow, toothpaste, top, tops, trainers, treasure hunt, tree(s), try, Tuesday

u
until, us, Usha

v
vegetables, Victorian villa

w
wafers, wait, Warren Study Centre, was, wash(es), washing, water, Wednesday, we're, wet suit, while, white, who's, whose, windsurfer(s), windsurfing, winning, won, would

x
–

y
year, yoghurt, you've

z
–

144 Key vocabulary